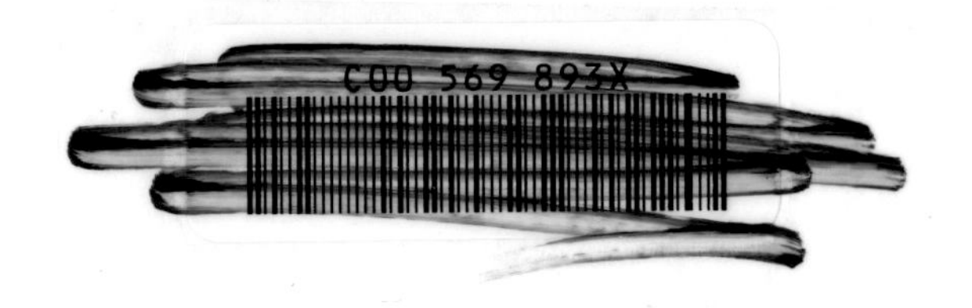

Pension Reform

Pension Reform

A Short Guide

Nicholas Barr and Peter Diamond

2010

Oxford University Press, Inc., publishes works that further
Oxford University's objective of excellence
in research, scholarship, and education.

Oxford New York
Auckland Cape Town Dar es Salaam Hong Kong Karachi
Kuala Lumpur Madrid Melbourne Mexico City Nairobi
New Delhi Shanghai Taipei Toronto

With offices in
Argentina Austria Brazil Chile Czech Republic France Greece
Guatemala Hungary Italy Japan Poland Portugal Singapore
South Korea Switzerland Thailand Turkey Ukraine Vietnam

Published by Oxford University Press, Inc.
198 Madison Avenue, New York, New York 10016

www.oup.com

Library of Congress Cataloging-in-Publication Data
Barr, N. A.
Pension reform : a short guide / Nicholas Barr and Peter Diamond.
p. cm.
An abridgment of the authors': Reforming pensions : principles and policy choices.
Includes bibliographical references and index.
ISBN 978-0-19-538772-8 (pbk.)
1. Pensions. 2. Pension trusts. 3. Pensions—Chile. 4. Pensions—China.
I. Diamond, Peter A. II. Barr, N. A. Reforming pensions. III. Title.
HD7091.B249 2010
331.25'22—dc22 2008055924

9 8 7 6 5 4 3 2 1
Printed in the United States of America
on acid-free paper

For Thomas and James, Matt and Andy

Foreword

A key test of a decent society is the living standards of its older people, particularly the poorer among them. This includes their ability to participate in their community and thus their relative income and access to health care and other services. The financing of their consumption in old age depends on the accumulation of past resources, by themselves and by the state, and its reflection in overall current income flows. Any sensible set of policies must take into account both the effects on such accumulation and the uncertainties surrounding life expectations, abilities, and disabilities. Thus policy analysis must examine issues of efficiency, distribution within and across generations and over individual lifetimes, as well as substantial uncertainties in individual circumstances.

Any approach to the formulation of policies toward pensions that tries to oversimplify by focusing on just one element, such as efficiency, risks grave policy errors, which can have a profound effect on the welfare of many individuals. It is a special strength of this book that it refuses to oversimplify in this way, while at the same time offering clear and analytically sound principles for the formulation of policy. It shows not only where these principles lead but also the mistakes that can be made when simplistic or formulaic policies are followed.

Policy toward pensions, and particularly policy reform, must depend on the broad economic, social, and demographic situation in a country, on the starting point for pension and related policies, and on where the economy and society are likely to go. Although many of the examples in the book draw on experience in the United Kingdom and the United States, reflecting the location of the authors, there is considerable discussion of other developed and developing countries, notably Chile and China, where they have worked. The analytical principles they set out so clearly and rigorously can and should guide the formation of pension policy across a very broad range of country circumstances, tailoring, of course, to those circumstances.

It is not possible to summarize the richness of Barr and Diamond's analysis in a few sentences or paragraphs, but one or two examples may be helpful. First, the authors stress that it is not correct to design pension policy as if the sole purpose were consumption smoothing. That would involve only an efficiency perspective on market failure. Even if efficiency were to be in some sense achieved, the potential would remain for substantial (first-order) distributional gains from introducing an element of transfers into the policy, with only a small (second-order) loss in efficiency.

A second, and related, example is that a system that attempts to focus only on efficiency issues in relation to intertemporal allocation or smoothing will lose an opportunity to provide insurance against adverse outcomes during working life and in old age. This insurance element is a key and worthy purpose of most pension systems and cannot straightforwardly be allocated to another arm of policy in a world where markets for risk operate, for theoretical and practical reasons, in a very imperfect way.

Barr and Diamond go beyond these basic conceptual starting points and analytical perspectives and show explicitly how policy choices should be analyzed. For example, in the context of changing demography and increased life expectancy, they examine the choice among higher contribution rates, lower monthly benefits, later retirement, and policies such as increased saving, designed to increase output. Further, they consider carefully the problems of administration, which loom large in systems covering very large numbers of people over a long period. They not only show how analysis should be done, but also identify very instructive examples of serious mistakes that can arise and have arisen in practice by failure to apply a clear framework, which is sufficiently comprehensive to embrace efficiency, distribution, uncertainty, and administration. This includes a number of important cases from the World Bank (see, for example, box 11.1).

In both its long and short versions, this is a most important book, which should be compulsory reading for all those involved in making, discussing, and studying policies on pensions. The subject matter is of great significance in a world whose demography and economic and social structures are changing so rapidly. We are extremely fortunate to have before us such a clear, comprehensive, and thoughtful analysis of the issues. Barr and Diamond, as outstanding theorists, have thought these issues through very carefully; they have also been very closely involved with the practicalities of administration and reform. Theirs is a splendid piece of work.

Nicholas Stern

Preface

This book contains a summary of the analysis in our longer book, *Reforming Pensions: Principles and Policy Choices* (2008). When selecting the material for this version, we could not resist making alterations when we found something we wanted to say differently, so the books do contain a few differences. The full table of contents of that book appears at the end of this one. As a summary, this book no longer cites the sources for much of our cited evidence and analyses. The book project is the result of two pieces of luck. The first came about when we were asked to participate in a group invited to advise the government of China on pension reform; the group presented its core recommendations to Premier Wen Jiabao in November 2004. The second was the opportunity that one of us had to participate in reforms of the pension system in Chile, including discussions with the Presidential Advisory Council in May 2006.

Although those experiences are reflected throughout, the book is also an attempt to step back from those activities and from the continuing and at times heated debate about pension reform. It sets out the relevant economic theory and international experience, its central aim being to arm readers with the analytics to enable them to form their own views about pensions policy. Thus the book's intent is educational; it is neither a polemic nor a training manual. In some ways the book should be set alongside Barr 2004, which sets pensions within the broader context of the welfare state, and, at a more technical level, Diamond 2003, which places the analysis of pensions in an optimal taxation framework.

In the longer book, the chapters in part I set out the analytics that should shape discussion of pension reform. There is minimal use of algebra and diagrams, and the results are always explained verbally so that any technical material can be skipped by readers prepared to take the conclusions on trust. Part II considers experience in different countries. The core of the longer book is summarized in chapters 1, 10, 11, and 16, which became the basis for much of this book, with some material pulled from other chapters.

In the academic world this book, like the longer version, will be of interest to economists because of their roots in economic theory and to colleagues in departments of social policy because of their subject matter. The book should be of interest also in such related areas as political economy and public policy and to colleagues studying the postcommunist transition and economic development. The book is written to be relevant to readers in a wide range of countries, developed, former communist, and developing; to officials in ministries of finance and of social security; and to readers in international organizations, such as the International Monetary Fund, the World Bank, and the International Labour Organization.

Our first—and considerable—debt is to the other members of the group that advised the government of China: Mukul Asher, Edwin Lim, and James Mirrlees. We are grateful also to colleagues who advised us during that process—Axel Börsch-Supan, Stanley Fischer, Nicholas Stern, and Salvador Valdés-Prieto—and to colleagues in China who provided us with background papers and other assistance, including Yonghong Cheng, Bihong Huang, Shi Ming Jiang, Shaoguang Li, Wei Zhang, and Bingwen Zheng.

The chapter on Chile owes a great debt to Ana Wheelock, who provided tireless advice on factual matters and contributed ideas. We are grateful also for helpful comments from Mario Marcel, Andrea Repetto, and Salvador Valdés-Prieto.

András Simonovits and two anonymous referees read the longer book in draft and provided cogent and helpful comments. A special issue of the *Oxford Review of Economic Policy* in the spring of 2006 (vol. 22, no. 1) gave us the opportunity to refine some of the analytical arguments: we are grateful to colleagues at an editorial seminar in Oxford in November 2005 for comments and guidance, including Christopher Allsopp, Christopher Bliss, Andrew Glyn, Dieter Helm, David Hendry, Stephen Nickell, and Margaret Stevens.

Many other people helped, by commenting on draft chapters of the longer book, by providing information, and by asking pertinent questions. They included Mukul Asher, Martin Neil Baily, Fabio Bertranou, Lans Bovenberg, Axel Börsch-Supan, Agnieszka Chlon-Dominczak, Elaine Fultz,

Gunnvald Grønvik, Robert Hancké, Bill Hsaio, Maureen Lewis, Frances Lund, Truman Packard, Debora Price, Susan St John, Annika Sundén, Lawrence H. Thompson, Peter Whiteford, and Adrian Wood. Aaron Grech and Johannes Spinnewijn read the entire text for coherence and readability and gave very helpful comments. Catarina Reis, Johannes Spinnewijn, and especially Maisy Wong provided valuable research assistance, supported by the National Science Foundation under grants SES-0239380 and SES-0648741.

We owe a particular debt to Michael Treadway for his customary skill, care, efficiency, and enthusiasm in editing the longer book, greatly improving its readability.

None of those mentioned should be implicated in the result, which is very much our joint responsibility: through discussions and primarily e-mail, exploiting our different time zones and complementary experiences and perspectives, the text has gone through repeated revisions to the point where virtually every sentence bears the marks of both of our pens.

Finally, and most important, our thanks to our wives, Gill and Kate, for their unfailing support and continuing forbearance, even after the longer book was finished, over our forays to various countries and over truncated weekends.

Nicholas Barr and Peter Diamond
London, England, and Cambridge, Massachusetts

Contents

List of Boxes, Tables, and Figures

Boxes

Figures

Tables

Pension Reform

Chapter 1

The Backdrop

1.1 The context

The "aging crisis"—an amalgam of "pensions crisis" and "health care crisis"—is not a sudden surprise, nor wholly bad news, nor insoluble. The problem, projected large increases in spending on pensions and medical care, is largely the result of long-term trends that are good news: longer lives, lower birth rates, earlier retirement, and more and better medical care. Why does ongoing good news amount to a crisis? The answer lies less in the underlying economic and demographic realities than in the political difficulty of adapting pension and health care systems to those realities.

This book—a shorter version of Barr and Diamond 2008—brings together the analytics of pensions with discussion of some country experiences to explain how to design pensions so as to limit the negative side effects of what in reality is a valuable opportunity: comfortable retirements for millions more people. Our goal is to equip readers to understand and evaluate the debates about pension reform now taking place in many countries. We do not discuss the organization or finance of health care.

The starting point is a series of long-run and well-known trends.

DECLINING MORTALITY. People are living longer in most countries, often considerably longer, and are expected to live even longer in the future. Figure 1.1 shows a very long-run trend improvement in mortality—a trend that, as

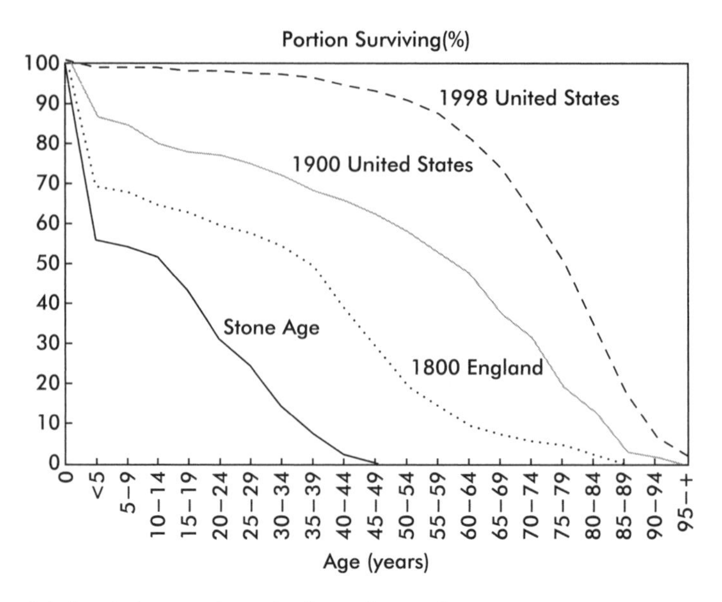

Figure 1.1 Survival curves from the Stone Age to the present
Source: Based on data from the Foundation for Infinite Survival, Inc., Berkeley, California.

figure 1.2 shows, is projected to continue. But to call this an "aging problem" is a grotesque misnomer—it is neither a "problem" nor entirely a phenomenon of the elderly. Much of the improved life expectancy at birth has come through large declines in child mortality. Although wonderful, this decline has little direct connection with pensions, which focus on people's earning and retirement years. Remaining life expectancy at the ages when most people start work, such as 16, 18, or 21, also has grown steadily; the fraction of those starting work who survive to an age where they can collect a pension has increased considerably; and, among those reaching pensionable age, life expectancy in retirement also has grown considerably, as figure 1.3 illustrates. (Sadly, these improvements have been reversed in the countries worst ravaged by HIV/AIDS.) Among men currently retiring in the United Kingdom, for example, many more have lived to retirement age than their grandfathers did, their average age of retirement is 64 rather than 67, and in retirement they can expect to live, on average, for twenty years rather than eleven. These trends are not a catastrophe, but rather great good news. Longer healthy lives are in many ways the great triumph of the nineteenth and twentieth centuries, and looking ahead, there is every expectation of continuing improvements in mortality and morbidity.

DECLINING FERTILITY. Alongside declining mortality, a second long-term trend, illustrated in figure 1.4, is a decline in the number of children that the average

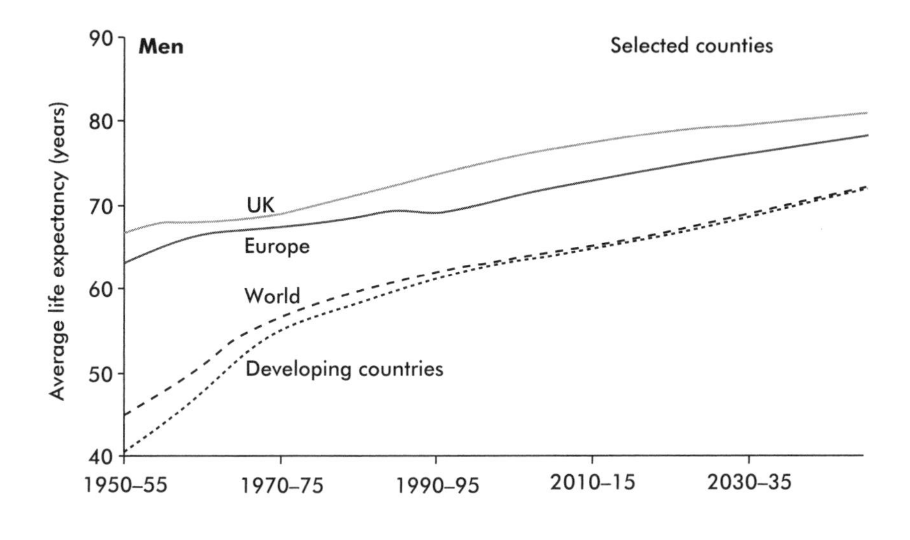

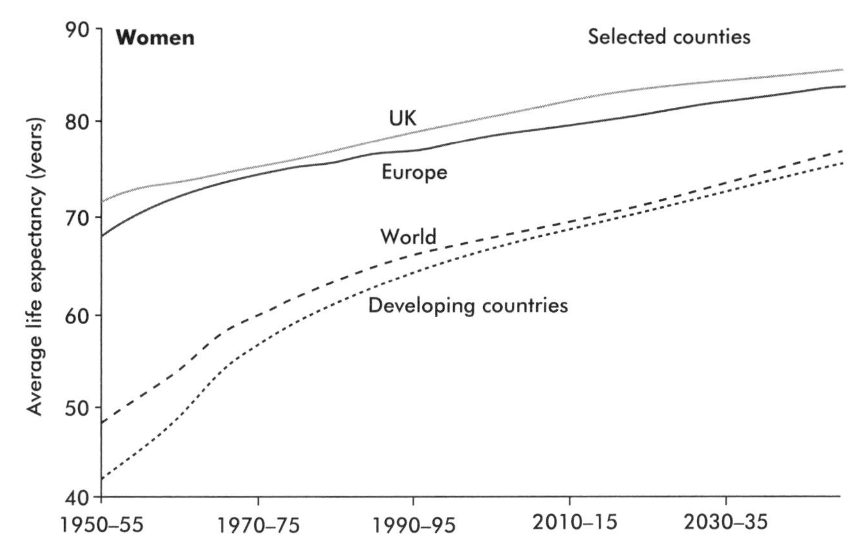

Figure 1.2 Life expectancy at birth for men and women, various countries, 1950–55 to 2030–35
Source: United Nations Population Division.

woman has during her lifetime. On the whole, declining fertility is arguably good news to the extent that as infant mortality declines people are choosing to have smaller families. This means that people are implicitly concentrating on the quality rather than the quantity of life. Other potential advantages include decreased environmental pressures due to slower growing populations. The transition to smaller families is most marked in the developed world but is occurring in many developing countries as well.

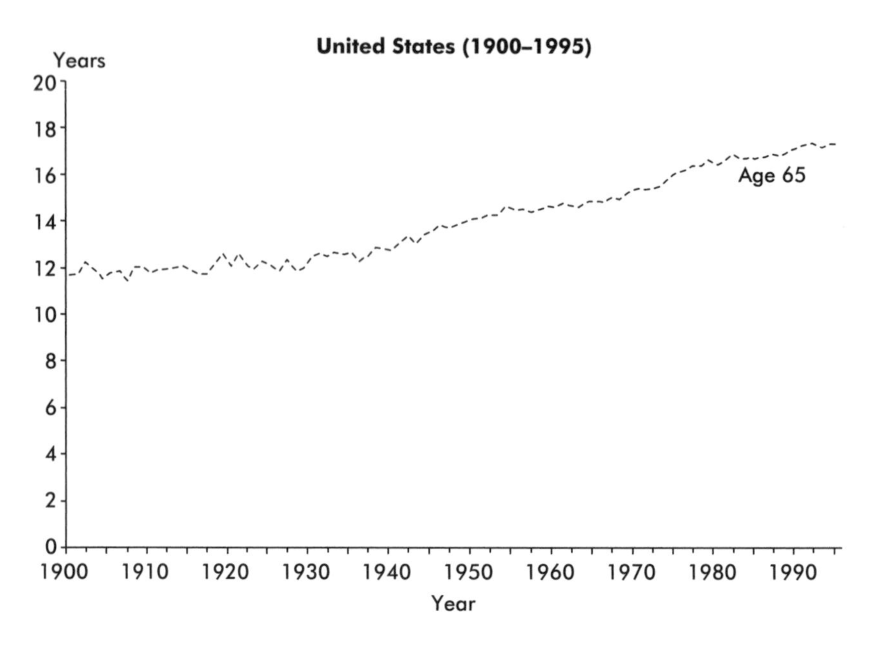

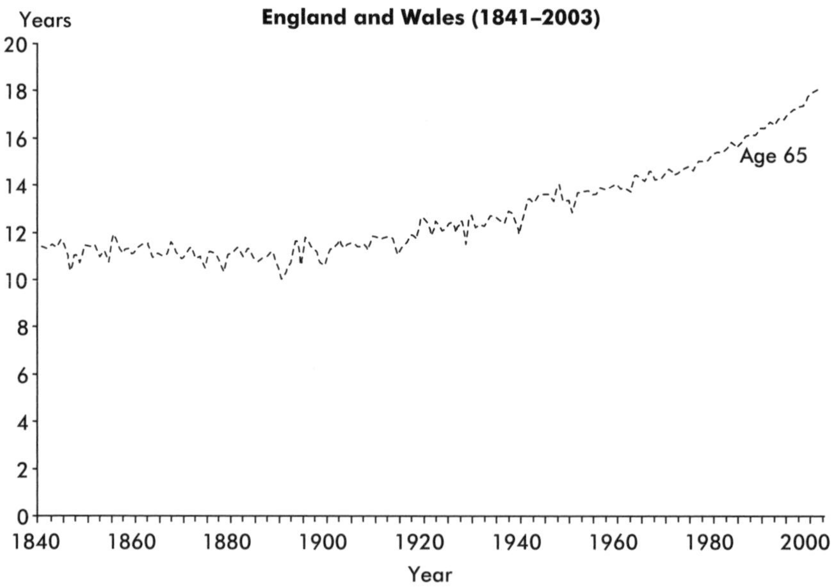

Figure 1.3 Life expectancy at age 65, United States, England and Wales, and Sweden
Period life expectancies using age-specific mortality rates for a given period, with no allowance for any later actual or projected changes in mortality. Life expectancies are calculated using the total (not just the civilian) population and thus include mortality due to war. *Sources*: Berkeley Mortality Database, demog.berkeley.edu/~bmd, and Human Mortality Database, www.mortality.org/.

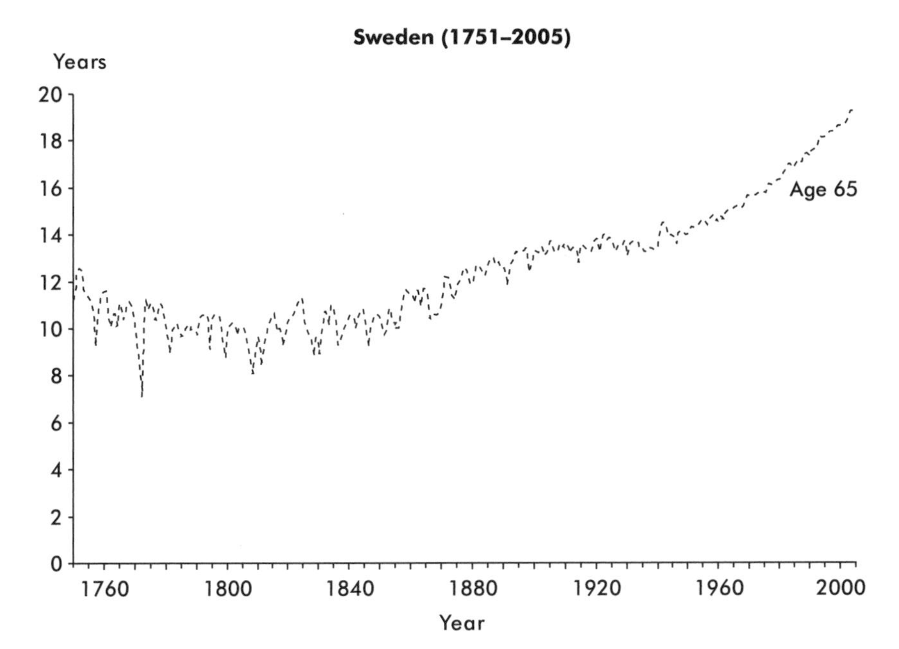

Figure 1.3 (Continued)

These trends toward longer life and lower fertility result in a steady change in the population-age pyramid, illustrated by figure 1.5 for China, India, and the United States for the 100 years after 1950. The result has been trend growth in most countries in the old-age dependency ratio—the number of older people relative to the number of people of working age—as illustrated in figure 1.6 for China, India, and the United States. With many pension systems relying on payroll tax revenue to finance current benefits, this trend is part of the reason many countries face rising pension spending relative to the gross domestic product (GDP).

DECLINING LABOR FORCE PARTICIPATION OF OLDER MEN. Figures 1.1 through 1.6 show how the number of older people has increased, in both absolute and relative terms. A separate question is how the number of pensioners has increased. Here another long-term trend is relevant, namely, a decline in the labor force participation of older male workers, as shown in figure 1.7 for Britain, France, Germany, and the United States. Just as the workday has shortened in many countries, and the workweek and the work year, so has the working lifetime. Indeed, male labor force participation rates have declined at all ages in many countries, as figure 1.8 shows for the United States. To the extent that this withdrawal from work is a voluntary response to sensible incentives, it is further good news that reflects the enormous growth in earnings that has accompanied (and contributed to) increasing life

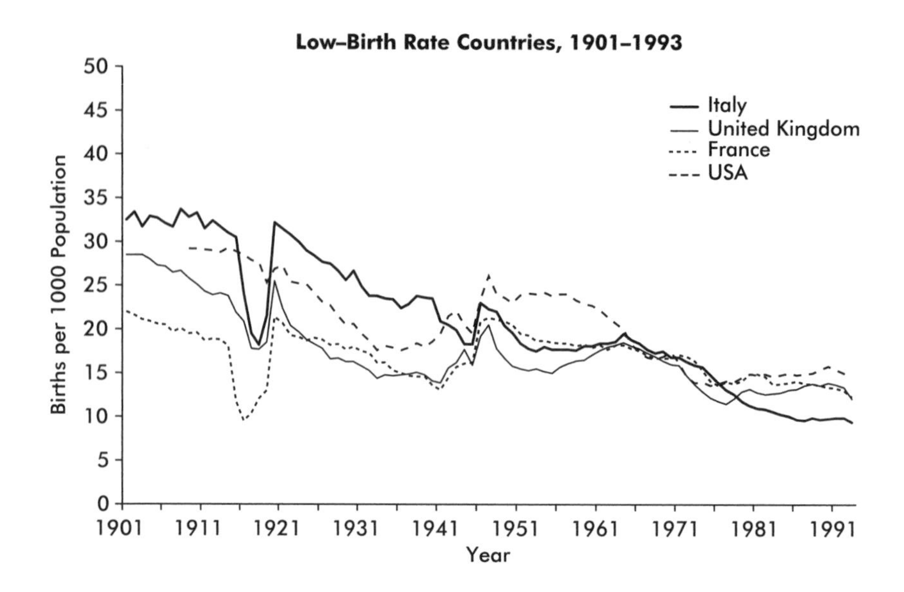

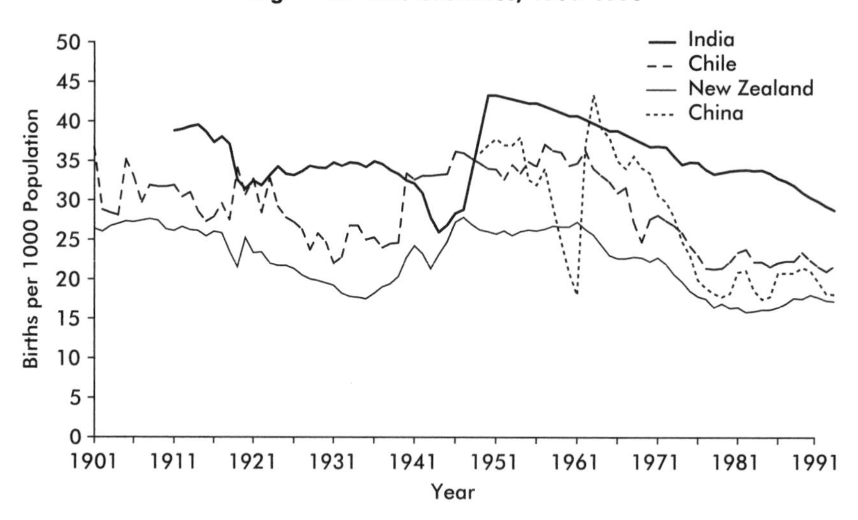

Figure 1.4 Crude birth rates for selected low– and high–birth rate countries, 1901–93
For India, rates before 1949 are for British India; rates between 1949 and 1969 are at five-year intervals, with rates within each five-year period interpolated using a second-order moving average; all other years for India are annual rates. *Sources*: Mitchell 1998*a*, 1998*b*, 1998*c* for all countries except India between 1949 and 1969, data for which are from the United Nations Population Database.

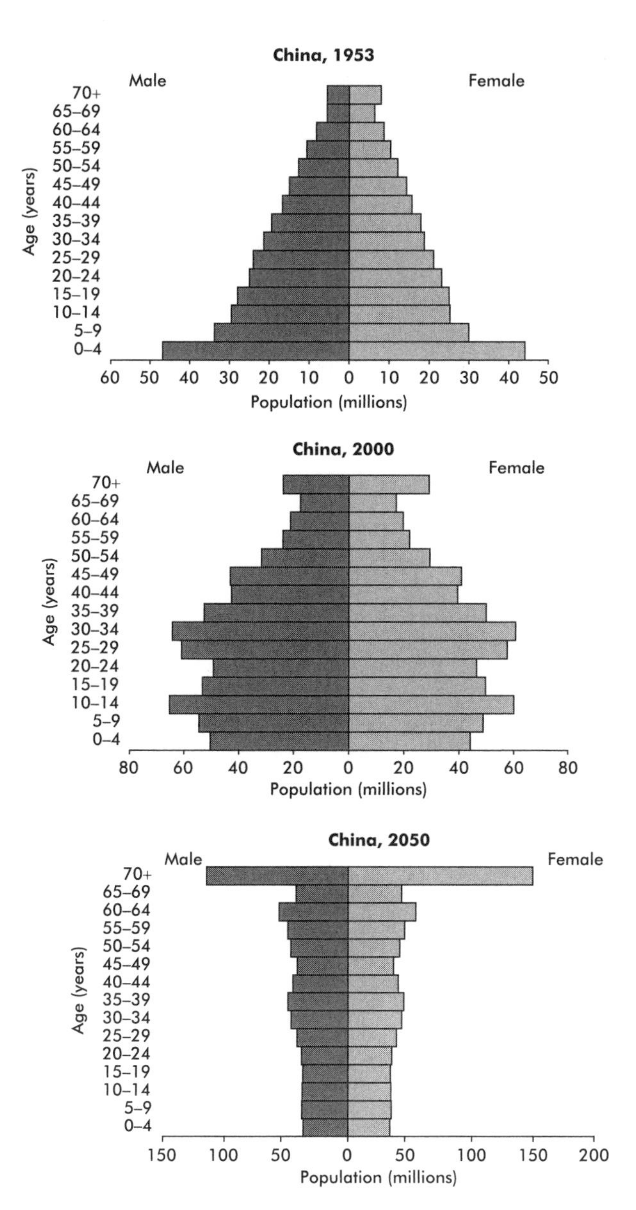

Figure 1.5 Age pyramids, China, India, and the United States, 1950, 2000, and projected 2050

All data for India exclude Burma. Pakistan was separate by 1951. Goa is included from 1961 and Sikkim from 1971. *Sources*: Mitchell 1998*a*, 1998*b*; U.S. Census Bureau, International Data Base.

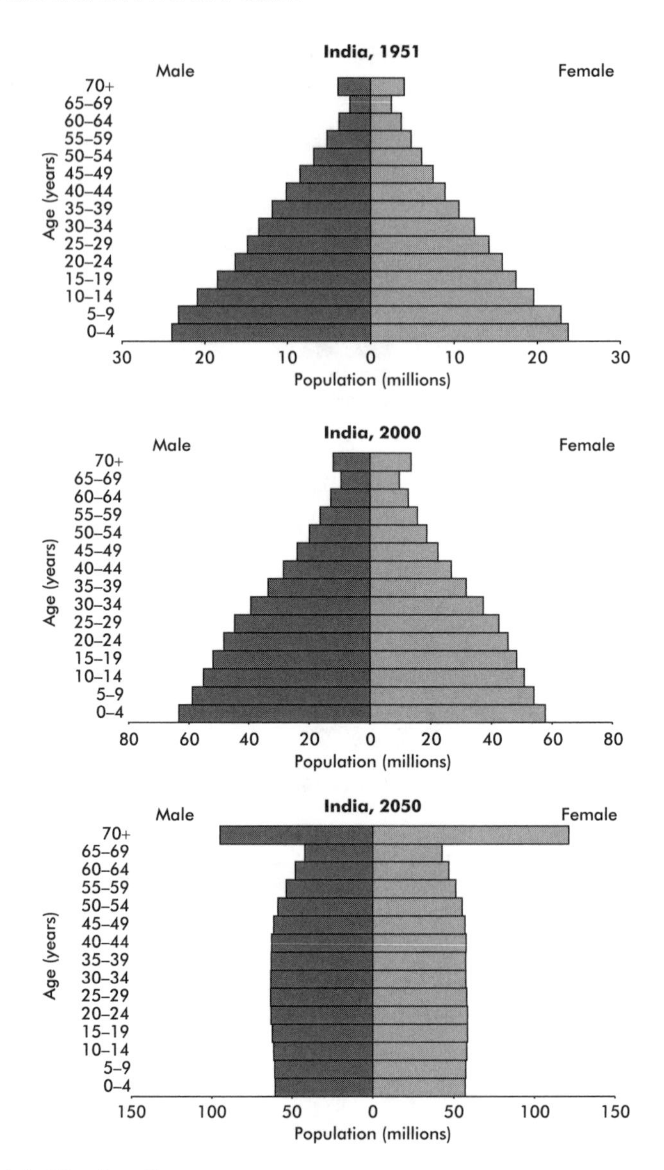

Figure 1.5 (Continued)

expectancies. And it has been helped by improved access to savings instruments for ordinary savers. In addition, older people are healthier now than in previous decades, and in many countries poverty among the elderly has declined over the long term.

Women, meanwhile, have become increasingly active in the labor market and are pursuing careers longer than previously. This pattern among working-age women, which historically has differed from that of men, has its

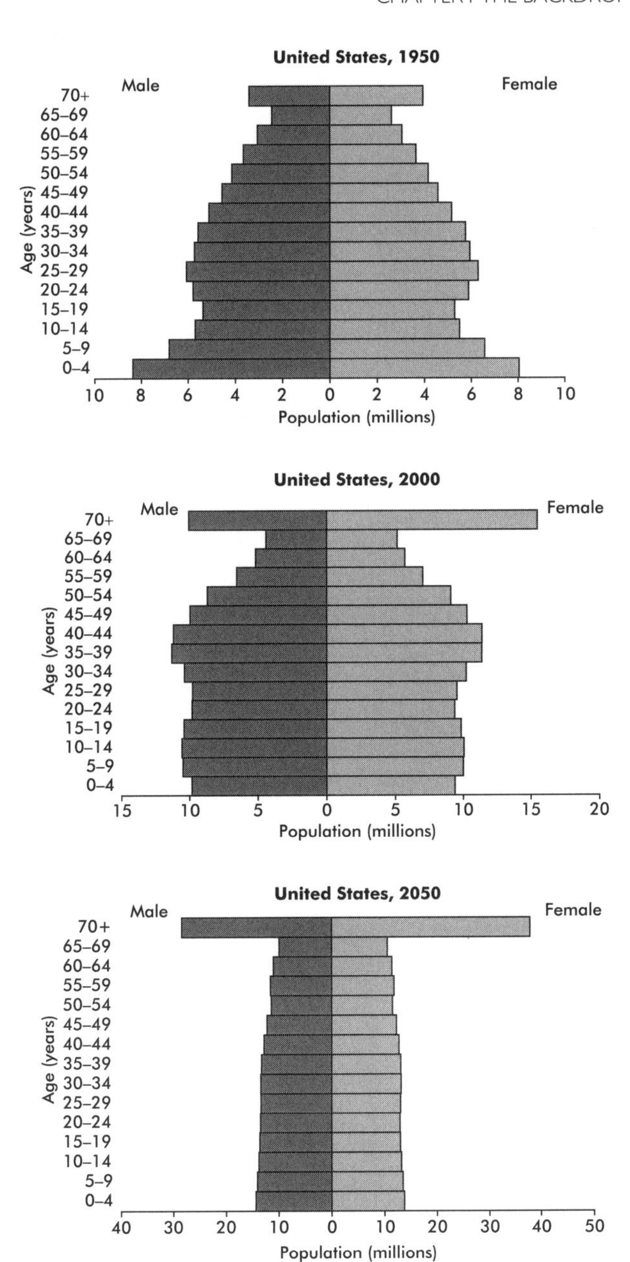

Figure 1.5 (Continued)

own implications for retirement, along with the general effects of increased earnings and wealth and growing pension systems. We return to this issue below.

THE RESULT: RISING PENSION COSTS. Obviously, as people live longer it becomes more expensive to provide a monthly pension of a given size from a given

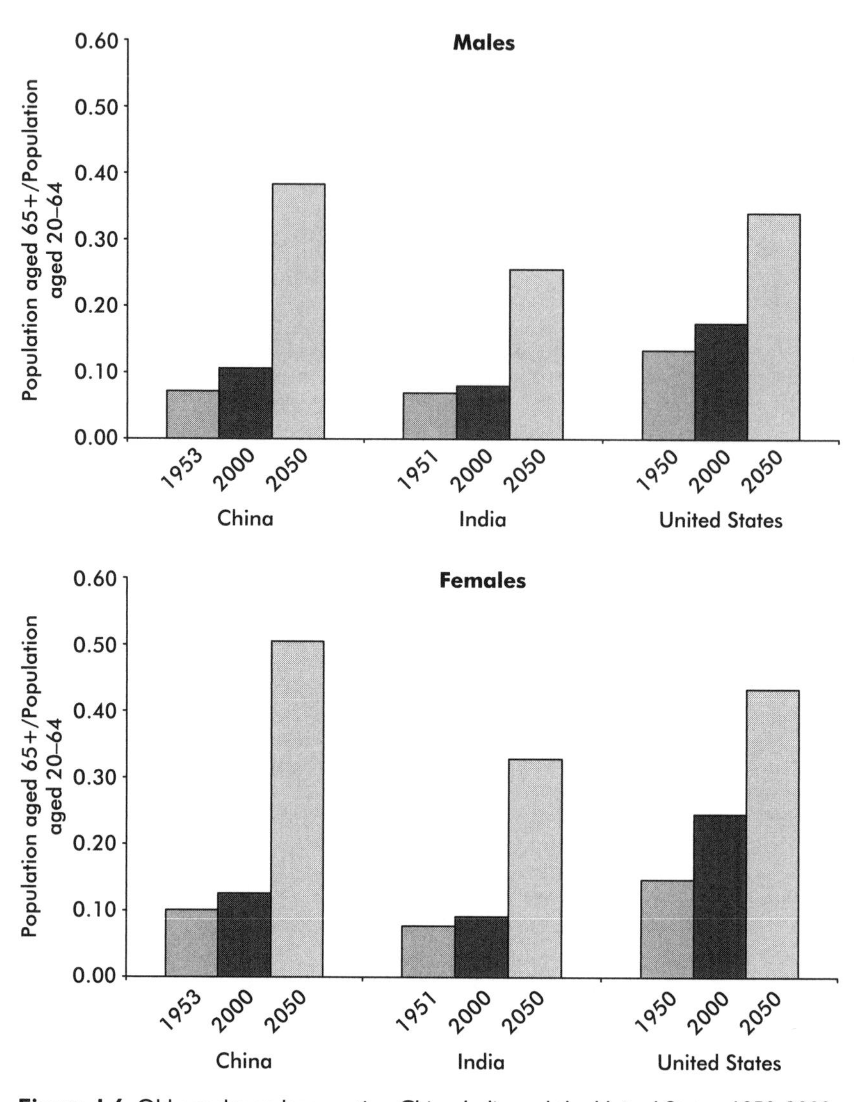

Figure 1.6 Old-age dependency ratios, China, India, and the United States, 1950, 2000, and projected 2050

Ratio of population aged 65 and over to the total working-age population.

Sources: Mitchell 1998*a*; U.S. Census Bureau, International Data Base.

age. The issue is compounded when people start to work later and retire earlier and is augmented by falling fertility rates. This increase in costs can be seen in rising ratios of pension spending to total output. In 2001 average pension spending in the (mostly developed) countries of the Organization for Economic Cooperation and Development (OECD) was 7.4 percent of GDP. But spending in some rapidly aging countries was already significantly higher: 10.4 percent in France, 10.8 percent in Germany, and 12.6 percent

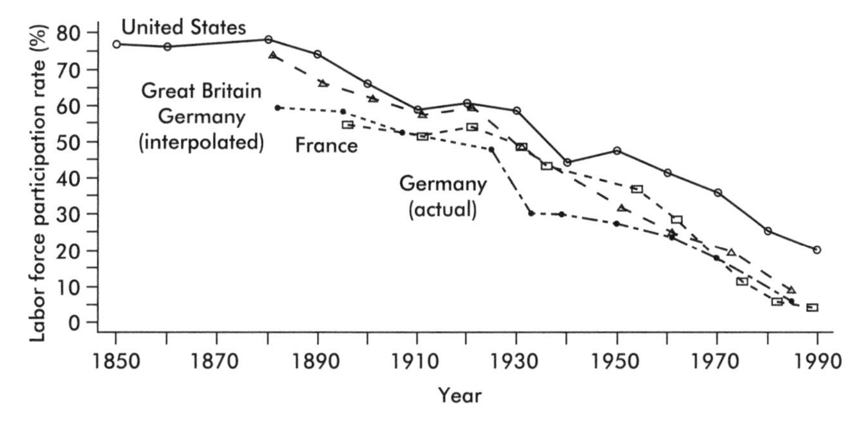

Figure 1.7 Labor force participation rates of men aged 65 and over, Britain, France, Germany, and United States, 1850–1990
Source: Costa 1998, p. 12.

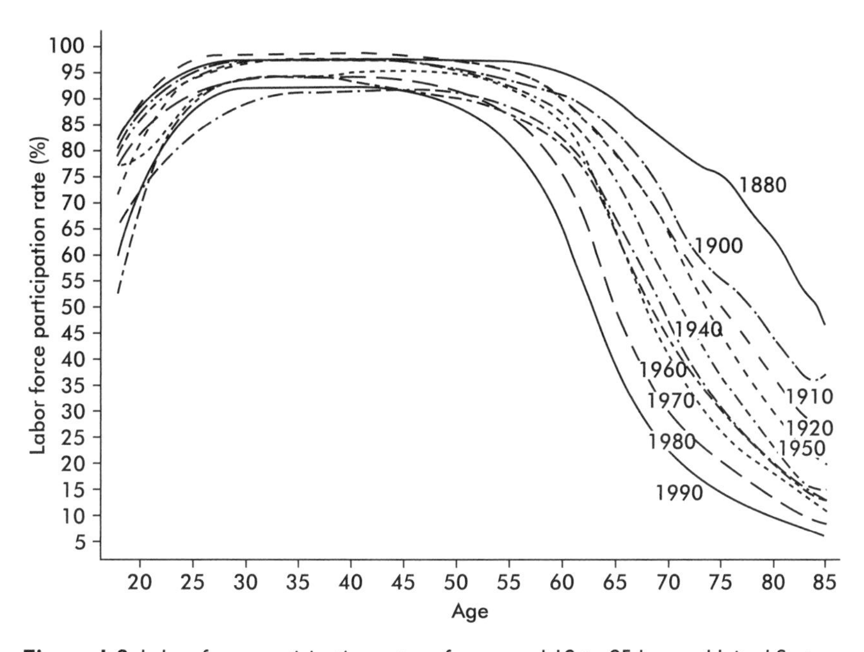

Figure 1.8 Labor force participation rates of men aged 18 to 85 by age, United States, 1880–1990
Source: Costa 1998, p. 12.

in Greece. If pension formulas remain unchanged, projected trends in longevity, fertility, and economic growth suggest that pension spending relative to GDP will increase substantially: in Greece, for example, spending is projected to double to nearly 25 percent of GDP in 2050 if no action is taken

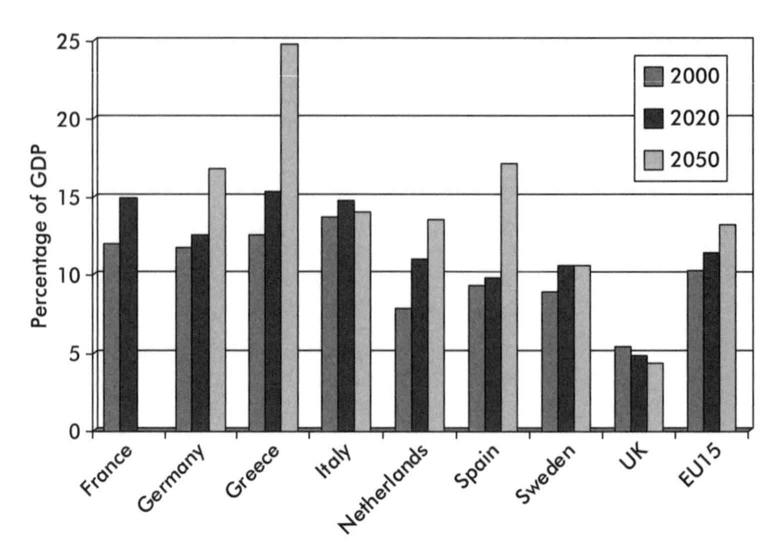

Figure 1.9 Public pension spending as share of GDP, EU15, 2000–2050
The EU15 are Austria, Belgium, Denmark, Finland, France, Germany, Greece, Ireland, Italy, Luxembourg, the Netherlands, Portugal, Spain, Sweden, and the United Kingdom. *Source*: Economy Policy Committee of the European Union (2001).

(figure 1.9).[1] These projected expenditure trends, though important, should not obscure the fact that problems of pension finance are, in part, a side effect of longer lives and, moreover, a side effect that can be contained.

INCREASING RIGHTS FOR WOMEN. A fourth long-term trend, increasing political and economic rights for women, though not influencing the cost of pension systems, has a considerable and continuing impact on the way pensions are designed. In particular, this trend has led to gender-neutral rules for pensions in many countries and, along with the increase in female labor force participation, to greater consideration of how the design of pension systems affects two-earner couples.

Table 1.1 shows one measure of the spread of women's political rights, namely, the extension of voting rights to women. The first quarter of the twentieth century saw a flurry of activity, with steady progress thereafter. In many countries, however, the date when women were first able to vote is not the date of full suffrage, which includes the right to stand for election.[2]

1. For wide-ranging projections of spending on pensions, health care, long-term care, and other services in the EU25 until 2050, see Economic Policy Committee of the European Union (2006).

2. Curiously, women in the United States were able to stand for election in 1788 but not to vote until 1920.

Table 1.1 Year when women were first able to vote, selected countries[a]

Year	Countries
1893	New Zealand
1902	Australia
1906	Finland
1913	Norway
1915	Denmark, Iceland
1918	Austria, Canada, Germany, Ireland, Poland, United Kingdom
1919	Belgium, Hungary, Netherlands, Sweden
1920	United States
1930	South Africa[b]
1931	Chile, Portugal, Spain
1944	France
1945	Japan
1946	Italy
1947	Argentina, Mexico, Singapore
1971	Switzerland

Source: Inter-Parliamentary Union, "Women in Politics," www.ipu.org/wmn-e/suffrage.htm.

a. These dates do not necessarily represent the date of full suffrage: in some countries women faced additional restrictions, such as a voting age later than that of men, and the right to vote did not always include the right to stand for election.

b. For whites; the right to vote was extended to blacks of both sexes only in 1994.

No single variable similarly encapsulates the trend toward more equal economic rights, and so the following examples only indicate the trend. Sweden was in many respects a leader: In 1884 the Married Women's Property Act was passed. In 1921 majority at age 21 was extended to married women, equalizing it with that of men, along with other rights, including equal division of property upon divorce. In 1939 it became illegal for employers to dismiss women for marriage or pregnancy.

In the United Kingdom, historically, a woman's property was absorbed by her husband upon marriage. The Married Women's Property Act of 1882 gave married women the same rights as unmarried women to buy, sell, and own property. Although this was an important step toward equality, a major gap remained: "only in 1935...did Parliament secure a married woman's right to assume personal liability for her contracts" (Shanley 1986, p. 74). Until the mid-1970s a woman could not normally obtain a mortgage without the countersignature of her father, husband, or similarly related man, and until 1990 a married woman's income was normally taxed in the hands of her husband.

In the United States the law relating to women and property was primarily a matter for the states rather than the federal government. As a former British colony, the United States started from a point similar to that in the United Kingdom. The 1848 Married Women's Property Act in New York, amended to include more rights in 1860, played a key role by giving women the right to hold property. Ironically, although the Social Security Act was gender-neutral from 1961 onward, control of property in some states was not.[3]

In France, women were given extensive property rights in 1907, with further extension to the rights of married women in 1938.

Although the gender neutrality of rules has become standard in developed countries, concern remains about gender-neutral rules affecting men and women differently, since, on average, women have lower annual earnings, shorter careers, and longer lives.

POSTWAR TRENDS. The long-term trends outlined above are the main drivers of change in the demographics of pensions. Superimposed on these trends are a number of more recent phenomena. First is the growth since World War II of pension systems in terms of both benefits and coverage, which has contributed to the much larger share of GDP devoted to pensions, making the effects of population aging more important than when systems were small. In 2007 pension benefits in mandatory systems in the OECD countries averaged 59 percent of a worker's previous earnings (more precisely, the replacement rate for a worker with average earnings, averaged over all the OECD countries, was 59 percent). For such workers, benefits were lowest in the United Kingdom, Ireland, and Japan, averaging 32.6 percent, and tended to be highest in Southern Europe (Greece, Italy, Portugal, Spain, and Turkey), averaging 74.3 percent.[4] The average replacement rate for lower earners (those earning less than half the average) was 73 percent.

A second element in the postwar story is the speed of population aging coming from the population bulge representing the baby boom generation and the decline in fertility that followed. This factor aggravates the problem of pension finance, but the problem would exist even in its absence. The projected age pyramids for 2050 in figure 1.5 are not strikingly different for the United States, which experienced a baby boom (figure 1.10), than for India, which did not, and for China, whose one-child policy has led to rapid

3. In Florida, for example, until the 1970s a woman had to petition the state for legal recognition that she was competent to control her property—a frequent occurrence for widows who had to be declared competent to manage their inheritance.

4. In Greece the replacement rate for a worker with average earnings was 95.7 percent of previous earnings.

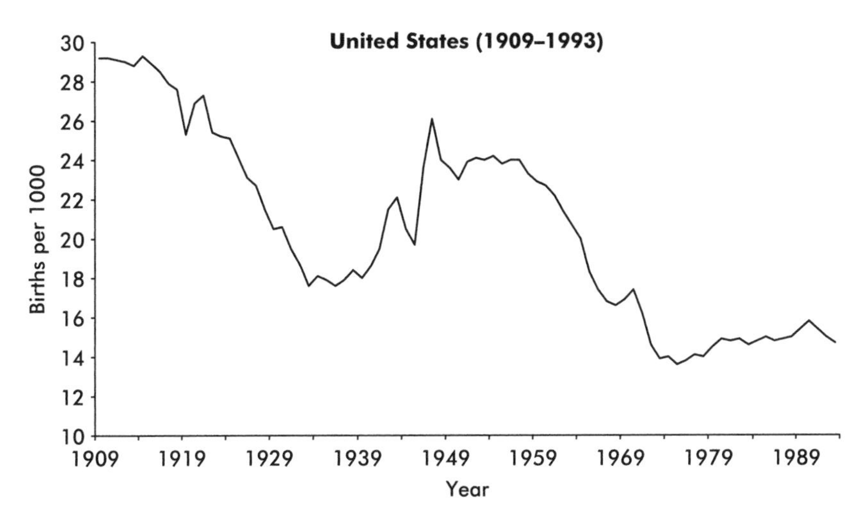

Figure 1.10 Crude birth rate, United States, 1909–93
Source: Mitchell (1998*b*).

population aging. Thus the analysis in this book is not limited to countries that experienced a baby boom.

A third element, already mentioned, has been the strong trend growth in labor force participation by women, which partly derives from and further reinforces women's expanding economic rights. In addition, the trend has partly offset declining participation by older men and is thus important for the finances of pensions.

Table 1.2 shows female employment rates in 1960, 1980, and 2000 and the rates for men in 2000 for a range of OECD countries. The average participation rate for females rose from 36.5 percent in 1960 to 58.6 percent in 2000, still well below the male participation rate of 75.2 percent in 2000. There is considerable cross-country diversity around the average. In terms of rate of change, the increase was smallest in Finland (where participation was already high in 1960), France, and Italy and largest in Norway and Sweden. In terms of level, female participation was lowest in 2000 in Greece, Italy, and Spain, at about 40 percent, and highest in Denmark, Norway, and Sweden, all over 70 percent; in Sweden the female participation rate was only slightly lower than men's.

Other countries have different patterns. Women's labor force participation was very high under communism and declined in some former communist countries after 1990. Other countries had, and continue to have, low rates of participation, particularly of married women. Thus not all countries have experienced significant growth in participation.

THE INTERNATIONAL CONTEXT. These trends play out against a backdrop of changes in the international economic environment. Since 1970, international

Table 1.2 Female employment rates, 1960–2000, selected OECD countries (Percentage of all persons aged 15 to 64)

Country	Females 1960	Females 1980	Females 2000	Males 2000	Females in 2000 as percentage of males in 2000
Austria	n.a.[a]	52.4	59.3	78.1	75.9
Belgium	29.6	35.0	51.1	69.8	73.2
Canada	n.a.	52.3	65.1	75.2	86.6
Denmark	42.7	66.2	71.2	80.4	88.6
Finland	54.9	65.0	64.3	69.7	92.3
France	42.9	50.0	53.1	68.1	78.0
Germany	35.0	34.8	58.1	73.5	79.0
Greece	n.a.	30.7	40.4	70.2	57.5
Ireland	n.a.	32.2	52.2	74.0	70.5
Italy	28.1	33.2	39.7	68.5	58.0
Netherlands	n.a.	35.7	62.1	81.1	76.6
Norway	26.1	58.4	73.4	88.1	83.3
Portugal	n.a.	47.1	60.1	75.9	79.2
Spain	21.0	28.4	40.3	70.3	57.3
Sweden	38.1	67.6	72.1	76.2	94.6
United Kingdom	43.1	54.5	65.2	79.3	82.2
United States	39.5	53.9	68.0	80.4	84.6
Average	36.5	46.9	58.6	75.2	77.5

Source: Garibaldi et al. 2005, table 2.1.

a. Not available.

trade has become increasingly open. A rising fraction of trade is electronic (software, music and video downloads, and the like), and though the size of the phenomenon should not be exaggerated, the result is to make national boundaries more porous. In addition, restrictions on capital mobility have been considerably reduced in many countries. International labor mobility also has increased since 1980, including greater opportunity for movement within the European Union (EU). Through all its dimensions—trade, finance, and labor mobility—globalization reduces, but does not eliminate, the ability of a country to act independently in designing its institutions; it also enhances the benefits of international coordination.

That said, the role of labor mobility should not be exaggerated. Immigration has many effects on an economy and society. It is beyond our scope to consider immigration policy, but we note that although immigration can ease somewhat the problems of an aging population, plausible levels of politically acceptable immigration are not sufficient to reverse the concerns discussed in this book.

1.2 Policy responses

Policymakers have responded to these trends in various ways. As far as public pensions are concerned, they have

- increased contributions (many countries), either by raising the percentage rate of contribution or by widening the range of income on which contributions are payable;
- reduced benefits, by changing the parameters of existing systems, as in the United Kingdom and the United States, or by retaining and significantly altering the basic structure, as in Germany, or as part of a process of systemwide change, as in Chile and Sweden;
- reduced benefits by raising the age for full benefits (a few countries, including the United States), announced a future increase (the United Kingdom), or discussed doing so (many countries);
- increased the earliest age for claiming retirement benefits (nearly two-thirds of the OECD countries in the years 1993 to 2004) after periods with frequent decreases;
- shared risks differently, by moving from a defined-benefit formula to a notional defined-contribution arrangement (as in Sweden) to a funded defined-contribution arrangement (as is part of the arrangement in Sweden and happened in Chile and many Latin American countries) (see definitions in box 1.1) or by indexing pensions less generously to changes in wages and prices (as in Finland);
- put in place policies, such as incentives to increase saving, intended to increase retirement saving and national output;
- adopted a mix of these policies; or
- buried their heads in the sand, hoping to get by with minor adjustments, leaving painful strategic reform to the next government.

Policymakers have also been increasingly concerned with private pensions. Some countries have encouraged funded private pensions (the United Kingdom), and others have mandated them (Chile and, more recently, some of the former communist countries). And regulation and insurance of private pensions have been strengthened.

The question of when building up a pension fund (as opposed to paying for pensions out of current contributions and taxes) contributes to good

Box 1.1 Terminology

The glossary defines many of the terms we use in this book, but a number require immediate discussion, especially those where different writers use them with different meanings.

Actuarial benefits. If a person's pension is fully actuarial, the expected present value of all of his or her future monthly pension benefits is equal to his or her pension accumulation at the time the pension starts. The price of an annuity that satisfies this condition is referred to as an *actuarially fair price*. Higher prices are said to reflect a *load factor*, which would reflect administrative costs and profits. For a given accumulation, the size of an actuarially fair pension therefore depends on the person's remaining life expectancy and on the rate of return on assets available to the provider of the annuity over the person's remaining expected life span. Similarly, actuarial adjustment of benefits for a delayed or an early start in benefits means that monthly benefits are raised or lowered to maintain equality in present value, reflecting both the above factors. A pension system that follows this approach in broad outline, but without precise use of projected life expectancy and market interest rates, is referred to as quasi-actuarial.

Annuity. An arrangement that pays benefits (for example, annual or monthly) as long as a person is alive. A *single-life* annuity pays an income for the life of one person. A *joint-life* annuity (also called a joint-and-survivor annuity) pays a regular income to two people until both have died. The size of the monthly payment typically depends on whether one or both are still alive and could depend also on which of the two is still alive. The payments can be from a defined-benefit system, a defined-contribution system when an individual exchanges his or her pension accumulation for an annual or monthly benefit, or from a purchase using some other lump sum. This allows the individual to insure against the risk of outliving his or her pension savings. With an immediate annuity, payments begin immediately; with a deferred annuity, payments are delayed until some point after the date of purchase. Different forms of annuities adjust payments over time on different bases.

Compliance. Noncompliance arises where a person does not make contributions that are legally required.

Consumption smoothing. Behavior that allows a household to maintain its desired level of consumption over time despite variations in income. Pensions assist consumption smoothing by allowing individuals to redistribute their resources over their lifetime by saving in their earning years so as to consume more in retirement.

(continued)

Box 1.1 (Continued)

Coverage. Coverage can be incomplete because of noncompliance or because a person is currently working at a job that is not covered by the pension system and does not make voluntary contributions (if that option is available). The most commonly used measure of coverage is the share of the economically active population contributing to the pension system at any time.

Defined-benefit pensions. In this arrangement a person's pension benefit is based on his or her wage history and commonly also on length of service and does not depend on the value of assets accumulated in the person's name. Thus a fully funded, pure defined-benefit plan adjusts funds to meet anticipated obligations, and so the risk of varying rates of return to pension assets falls on the sponsor, that is, the employer or the government. A defined-benefit plan need not be fully funded.

Defined-contribution pensions. In this case a person's pension benefit is determined by the value of assets accumulated toward his or her pension. Thus, a pure defined-contribution plan adjusts obligations to match available funds, and so the individual faces the risk that the portfolio might perform poorly. The accumulated funds can be used to purchase an annuity, to finance a series of withdrawals or taken as a single lump sum.

Funded pensions. Funded pensions are paid from an accumulated fund built up over a period of years out of contributions by or on behalf of its members.

Notional defined-contribution (NDC) pensions. NDC pensions are financed on a pay-as-you-go (PAYG) basis (or with partial funding) through social insurance contributions. As with a funded defined-contribution pension, an individual has an account that grows from contributions and from returns credited to the notional value in the account. The notional rate of return for this crediting is set by legislated rules. Pension benefits are adjusted for a measure of the cohort's life expectancy. Thus a person's pension bears a quasi-actuarial relationship to his or her lifetime pension contributions.

Pay-as-you-go (PAYG) pensions. PAYG pensions are paid out of current revenue (usually by the state from tax revenue) rather than out of an accumulated fund. A pension system may also have some assets and so be partially funded.

Public pension system. We use this term to refer to a government-run pension system (also called a state pension system) that is open to all workers.

Replacement rate. The replacement rate is the ratio of the monthly income a pensioner receives to the income he or she received while working

(continued)

Box 1.1 (Continued)

(both net of taxes and transfers). Thus defined, the replacement rate is a measure of the effectiveness of consumption smoothing.
The term is used also to mean the ratio of the average pension to the average wage, in which case it is a measure of the pension system's ability to relieve poverty among the elderly. A *survivor replacement rate* is the ratio of the benefit going to a widow or widower compared with what was received by the couple when both were alive.

Retirees and pensioners. For some purposes it is necessary to distinguish two separate events: stopping work and receiving a pension. We use the term *retiree* for someone who has stopped work and *pensioner* for someone who is receiving pension benefits. A retiree usually will also be a pensioner but not necessarily: for example, a person may choose to retire early and live off his or her savings until reaching pensionable age. Similarly, a pensioner may have retired or he or she may be receiving a pension while continuing to work.

Social security. We avoid the term because it is used with different meanings. In the United States, social security refers to government retirement and disability benefits only; in the United Kingdom, to all cash benefits provided by the government; in mainland Europe, to all cash benefits and health care. Instead of social security we use the term *pension system* and its component parts.

State pension system. The term *state* has different meanings. It can refer to a national government (for example, the federal government in the United States) or to subnational government (state governments in the United States). We therefore avoid the term where possible. Where it is used, the term describes a national government and refers to a general system, not just one for government employees.

Voluntary pensions. Pensions can be voluntary in two different ways. They can be voluntary for an individual worker or a firm may voluntarily introduce an employer plan, membership of which may be compulsory for its workers.

policy outcomes and when it does not has been and continues to be the subject of a heated debate in which we are both protagonists;[5] The World Bank's "multipillar" model (see glossary) explicitly advocated funded pensions. Given the World Bank's importance in pension policy, subsequent chapters

5. See Barr 2000, Diamond 2004, Diamond and Orszag 2005*a*, 2005*b*, and, for contrasting views, Feldstein 2005 and Holzmann and Hinz 2005. For an attempt to summarize the core of the dispute, see Barr and Rutkowski 2005.

evaluate this view, and section 8.3 and box 11.1 summarize our critique and that of a recent evaluation by the World Bank (2006*a*, 2006*b*) of its own work.

The private sector also has responded to the various trends. Longer life spans increase the cost of providing a pension of a given size, and increasing regulation, for example to protect workers' accumulated pension entitlements, has added further to the cost of employer systems. These factors were brought to a head in many developed countries by stock market turbulence in the years after 2000. Many employers responded by reducing benefits, and many moved from defined-benefit to defined-contribution arrangements for newly hired workers and in some cases also for future contributions by existing workers.

1.3 Organization of the book

To assist the broader debate, chapters 2–6 summarize the analytics of pensions that are central for considering pension reform (these analytics are spelled out in detail in our longer book). Although we are open about expressing our own views, the main purpose of the book is to lay out the analytical process by which we reach our conclusions, to enable readers to form their own views.

Chapter 2 sets out the basic economics of pensions. The next five chapters are the book's analytical core. They look at labor markets (chapter 3), finance and funding (chapter 4), redistribution and risk sharing (chapter 5), and gender and family issues (chapter 6). These chapters establish the primary conclusions we derive from economic theory.

The theoretical arguments have three centers of gravity:

- Pension systems have multiple objectives, including consumption smoothing, insurance, poverty relief, and redistribution, all of which cannot be fully achieved at the same time. Thus policy has to optimize—not minimize or maximize—across a range of objectives. To illustrate, an exclusive focus on consumption smoothing (that is, redistribution to oneself over the life cycle) would suggest a system in which benefits bear a fairly exact relationship to a worker's accumulated contributions; such a system, however, would fail to relieve old-age poverty for low-paid workers and would not offer insurance against adverse labor market outcomes. Thus policy has to seek the best balance among consumption smoothing, poverty relief, and insurance, a balance that will depend in each society on the weights given to those and other objectives.

- The analysis is couched in what economists call "second-best" terms, that is, assuming a world with imperfect information, incomplete markets, and distorting taxation. For example, the goal of minimizing (as opposed to optimizing) labor market distortions is misplaced, not least because a pension system that provides poverty relief inescapably creates distortions; thus minimizing distortions would imply little or no poverty relief: the cure would be worse than the disease. Depending on their design, pension systems can have substantial effects on behavior, including labor supply, saving, and the division of resources within a household. But these effects are not always and everywhere adverse, and even where they are, the system can still raise welfare if the benefits of improved old-age security outweigh the costs of the adverse incentives. In short, policy has to seek the best balance among poverty relief, insurance, and containing distortions, which again will depend on the weights given to these different objectives.
- Many people (particularly noneconomists) think that economics is only or mainly about efficiency. That view is, of course, mistaken: economics is, and always has been, about equity as well as efficiency—indeed, one of the major thrusts of the optimal taxation literature (Diamond and Mirrlees 1971*a*, 1971*b*) has been to integrate the two concerns. Thus readers should not be surprised at the extent of discussion throughout the book of the distributional effects of different pension arrangements. This material is included not only for completeness but also because it reflects our value judgment that distributional effects are important.

Some omissions should be noted. Our focus is on retirement benefits, with little discussion, despite its importance, of disability insurance. Nor, as already mentioned, do we analyze the provision of health care. We do not address the pension systems or reforms, actual or desirable, of all countries or even of all the major countries. Although we discuss the experiences of different countries to illustrate our theoretical discussion, this is not a comparative volume. The examples have a center of gravity in the United States and the United Kingdom, since those are the countries we know best, but are chosen to illustrate points of general relevance.

Chapters 2 through 6 address the question of good pension design, including background matters (chapter 2), pensions and labor markets (chapter 3), finance and funding (chapter 4), redistribution and risk sharing (chapter 5), and gender and family (chapter 6). However, good design is not enough. It is necessary also to implement that design, and that poses the question of what pension designs are feasible in different countries. Chapter 7 discusses implementation, including the financial and technical requirements of different types of pension arrangements, with explicit discussion of what is necessary to run funded individual accounts.

Chapter 8 discusses changes since 1950 and some of the policy responses, including some common policy errors. Chapter 9 illustrates the wide array of pension arrangements in different countries. Chapter 10 looks in more detail at Chile (including major reform in 2008) and China (including directions for reform, drawing on the earlier work of a panel on which we served [Asher et al. 2005]). Chapter 11 draws together the conclusions we derive from economic theory for the design of pension systems, including some important analytical errors, and summarizes the key messages of the book, including discussion of pension systems at different levels of economic development.

Chapter 2

The Basic Economics of Pensions

Chapters 2–6 have twin purposes. They set out the economic analytics of pensions to give readers a systematic way of thinking about the topic. They are intended also as a contribution to a continuing debate, hence some of the discussion rebuts arguments that we regard as false, or equivocal, or true in some circumstances but not necessarily always.

This chapter sets out some background matters: the core purposes of pension systems (section 2.1), their basic features (section 2.2), and the economic framework (section 2.3).

2.1 Core purposes of pension systems

While acknowledging broader aspects of old-age security, this book is about its economic aspects. To that end, this chapter considers two groups of primary objectives of pension systems. Pension systems should

- offer a mechanism for consumption smoothing across one's lifetime (what might be thought of as the "piggybank" function of pensions) and provide insurance against low income and wealth in old age as well as
- relieve poverty and redistribute income and wealth (what might be called the "Robin Hood" function).

These two sets of objectives are discussed in sections 2.1.1 and 2.1.2, respectively.

Addressing these objectives involves interactions, since saving for old age and insuring against the risk of outliving one's assets also help to relieve poverty and affect the distributions of income and wealth. In addressing these objectives it is necessary to consider also the costs of achieving them. As a useful shorthand:

- The primary objective of pensions is economic security in old age, achieved through consumption smoothing, insurance, poverty relief, and redistribution.
- The primary objective of pension *design* is to optimize old-age security, including the cost of providing it.

2.1.1 Individual and household objectives

From the viewpoint of individuals and families, income security in old age requires two sets of instruments: a mechanism for smoothing consumption and a means of insurance. For those who are poor on a lifetime basis, income security additionally includes transfers provided to them in old age.

CONSUMPTION SMOOTHING. People seek to maximize their well-being not at a single point in time, but over time. Most people hope to live long enough to be able to retire. They save to that end, in effect redistributing income from their younger to their older self. Thus a central purpose of retirement pensions—consumption smoothing—is to enable a person to transfer consumption from her earnings in middle years to her retired years, allowing her to choose a better time path of consumption over working and retired life. The extent to which a pension provides such smoothing is reflected in the replacement rate, which measures the size of pension benefits relative to previous earnings.

The objective of consumption smoothing applies to the family, not only to individuals. People are concerned about their children and their partners. Pension systems commonly include life insurance benefits for workers with young children and the option or the requirement of benefits for a surviving elderly spouse, commonly as an annuity.

Studies find that a single survivor of a couple typically needs more than half of the couple's income—commonly 65 to 70 percent—to maintain a broadly constant standard of living. That is, a desirable "survivor replacement rate" is thought to be larger than one-half. Thus, in the absence of survivor benefits, if two spouses have identical pension benefits, the death of one may lower the living standard of the other, depending on the level of other wealth available to the surviving spouse. The issue is more important if the person who dies first is the higher earner of the two. Men typically have higher earnings and so higher benefits than women, are commonly older than their wives, and have higher annual mortality rates than women; thus inadequate survivor benefits is part of the mechanism that results in higher poverty among widows in many countries as well as a significant decline in living standards for many survivors with incomes above the poverty line. Survivor pensions, discussed in chapter 6, are therefore an important element in preserving the living standards of elderly people.

INSURANCE. In a world of certainty, individuals would save during their working life to finance their retirement. However, people do not live in a world of certainty, not least because they do not know how long they are going to live. Thus a pension based on individual saving confronts the individual with a choice: either risk outliving his or her retirement savings or consume very little throughout old age to prevent that from happening. But although any one person does not know how long he or she is going to live, the average life expectancy of a group of people is much more predictable. Pooling of individual risk can be organized through insurance companies or through the government, though there remains the risk that the aggregate life expectancy is somewhat different from what was anticipated.

This is the essence of annuities, whereby an individual exchanges his pension accumulation at retirement for regular payments for the rest of his or her life, however long that may be. Insurance in the form of an annuity increases individual welfare by reducing the need for people to accumulate very large savings to avoid destitution should they live longer than their life expectancy. While some annuitization is part of a sensible plan, uncertainty about future expenditures and bequest motives both imply that not all wealth should be annuitized, even if prices were actuarially fair. As noted, annuities can be used to provide resources to a spouse who outlives a worker.

Alongside the risk of outliving one's savings, which annuities can cover, there are risks also to future earnings during one's working life. The latter risks can be insured in part through unemployment and disability insurance, but they have consequences also for retirement, which pension systems can address at least partly through redistributive elements. In addition, pension systems can insure against disability, and they can protect young children if a working parent dies before retirement.

ARE VOLUNTARY ARRANGEMENTS SUFFICIENT? In the simplest of all worlds a person provides for his pension through voluntary savings during working years to achieve his optimal time path of consumption and by buying an annuity to protect against the longevity risk. Were matters that simple, pensions could be left to voluntary decisions and private insurance, with no need for government involvement. There are two sets of reasons why this approach, on its own, is insufficient. First, the simple model assumes, apart from the recognized uncertainty about the date of death, that individuals are well informed, that there are no other distortions, and that individuals are able to make good decisions. These assumptions are useful to formulate a simple theory but, as discussed in section 2.3.1 and boxes 2.1 and 2.2, bad guides to policy design in areas like pensions. The simple models, in implicitly assuming a first-best world, ignore a range of market failures and thus assume away the very problems that government intervention is designed to address. In contrast, second-best analysis seeks the optimal policy given the presence of such distortions. Moreover, realistic models of actual insurance markets recognize both administration and transactions costs. Public systems can (and frequently do) cost a lot less than private market alternatives.

In the face of these market imperfections, government intervention in a variety of forms can improve the efficiency of consumption smoothing and insurance, thus helping (and, where necessary, forcing) individuals to make better use of the resources they command to benefit themselves and their families.

A second reason for government involvement is that public policy generally has objectives in addition to improving consumption smoothing and insurance, notably poverty relief and redistribution. Reinforcing this argument for intervention, a means-tested program to provide income to the elderly poor creates a disincentive to retirement saving for workers with low earnings (referred to as free riding); compulsory retirement savings can lessen the cost of this disincentive.

2.1.2 Public policy objectives

POVERTY RELIEF. In pursuit of poverty relief, pension systems target resources on people who are poor on a lifetime basis and thus unable to save enough to support themselves in old age. In some respects the design of poverty relief is simpler for older people: potential labor earnings are less of a consideration for people beyond retirement age, so transfers to the elderly are less likely to weaken incentives to work. (Of course, such transfers may influence labor supply and savings among the younger population looking forward to retirement, and this has to be taken into account.) Given this lessened concern about possible impacts on the labor market, it is potentially advantageous to have separate rules for the elderly. Such programs can target all elderly persons or can concentrate on those who have contributed to the pension system. Many countries have both types of programs.

REDISTRIBUTION. Pension systems can redistribute incomes on a lifetime basis, complementing the role of progressive taxes on annual income. Lifetime redistribution can be achieved by paying pensions to low earners that are a higher percentage of their previous earnings (i.e., a higher replacement rate) thus subsidizing the consumption smoothing of people who are less well off but not necessarily poor. Since lifelong earnings are uncertain from the perspective of an individual, such a system can provide some insurance against the consequences for retirement of low earnings during an extended portion of one's career. There can also be redistribution toward families, for example, paying a higher pension to a married couple than to a single person, even though both households have paid the same contributions. Conversely, mandatory pension contributions by workers can reduce the later cost of providing income support to the elderly poor from general revenues.

Pension systems can redistribute across generations as well. For example, a government may reduce the contribution rate or increase the benefits of the present generation. Such a move requires future generations to pay higher contributions or to have lower pensions, thus redistributing from those later generations to the earlier elderly generation. This has been a common feature in the startup of pension systems, as those who worked before the pension system was created would otherwise generally have had relatively low retirement incomes. Also, depending on timing, they may have had adverse economic opportunities, for example, depression or wartime.

2.1.3 Other objectives

Alongside the primary objectives of consumption smoothing, insurance, poverty relief, and redistribution, pension policy may have secondary objectives that are related to but not direct purposes of the system itself. One broad objective is economic development; a more specific objective is economic growth. Even well-designed pensions create some adverse labor market incentives, and badly designed ones can have a large impact. Excessive public pension spending can contribute to high tax rates, putting growth at risk, and may excessively decrease national saving. Conversely, pension arrangements can assist the operation of labor and capital markets and may encourage saving. There is debate about the relative weights accorded to old-age security and to these secondary objectives.

2.1.4 Recognizing costs

It is always important to recognize that providing resources—in this case consumption for retirees—has costs. Not only are the resources themselves costly, but costs arise also from the rules that determine how benefits are provided and how revenue is collected in order to pay for those benefits as well as from administrative costs, which are inevitable in any arrangement for retirement incomes. In considering pension design it is important to recognize that there are other distortions, including those caused by taxation: governments need tax revenue in order to function. Thus a key concern is to avoid implementing a system that costs more than is necessary to accomplish its objectives and to balance the level of achievement of those objectives with the costs of achieving them, a topic to which we return in box 2.3.

2.2 Basic features of pension systems

Pension systems can be considered in different ways, such as according to (a) the degree of funding, (b) the relationship between contributions and benefits, and (c) the way benefits and contributions are adjusted over time.

2.2.1 Fully funded, partially funded, and pay-as-you-go pensions

In a fully funded system, pensions are paid out of a fund built over a period of years from contributions by and/or for members. With pay-as-you-go (PAYG) systems, in contrast, pensions are paid out of current contributions. Pensions can also be partially funded, paying benefits out of a combination of current contributions, returns on assets, and sometimes their sale.

FULLY FUNDED PENSIONS. These pension systems are based on savings: contributions are invested in assets, the return on which is credited to the system's fund. Funding is thus a method of accumulating financial assets, which are exchanged for goods at some later date. While fully funded systems can take many forms, in principle they always have sufficient reserves to pay all outstanding financial liabilities. This can be done by adjusting contributions to match projected liabilities or by having liabilities defined by available funds.

If there is no redistribution across generations, a generation is constrained by its own past savings and a representative individual gets out of a funded system no more than he or she has put in (in present discounted value). If, in addition, there is no direct redistribution across individuals, when an individual retires, the pension fund will be holding his past contributions, together with the interest and dividends earned on them. This accumulation finances the person's consumption in retirement, through an annuity or in some other way.

PAYG PENSIONS. These systems usually are run by the state.[1] They are contractarian in nature, based on the fact that the state can, but does not have to, accumulate assets in anticipation of future pension claims but can tax the

1. There is a sad history of the breakdown of PAYG pensions run by firms and industries.

working population to pay for the pensions of the retired generation. Most state pension systems are primarily PAYG in that funding covers only a small part of annual benefit payments.

From an economic viewpoint, PAYG can be looked at in several ways. As an individual contributor, a worker's claim to a pension is based on legislation that, if he pays contributions now, he will receive a pension in the future. The terms of the legislated benefits are fairly precise, being set out in each country's social security laws (although subject to legislative change). From an aggregate viewpoint, the state is simply taxing one group of individuals and transferring the revenues to another. State-run PAYG systems, from this macroeconomic perspective, are little different from other income transfers, although the determinants of who pays and who receives and thus the incentive structure can be very different from other income transfer systems.

A major implication of a PAYG system (or any less than fully funded system) is that it relaxes the constraint that the benefits received by any generation must be matched by its own contributions. Thus a PAYG system, in sharp contrast with fully funded arrangements, can redistribute across generations (particularly toward retirees and older workers when a system starts or expands) and can share risks across generations.

DEBATES. There is considerable controversy over the relative merits of PAYG and funded systems. There are debates about:

- the right basic economic model, for example, how to model individual behavior;
- empirical magnitudes, for example, labor supply elasticities and life expectancy in 2050;
- the extent of a country's institutional capacity;
- the political economy of reform, for example, whether citizens regard their pension as safer when they are owners of accounts or when the pensions are based on a promise by government;
- ideology, for example, the role of the state or the relative weights given to different objectives, in particular, the relative weights accorded to poverty relief and consumption smoothing; and
- the normative framework to be used.

2.2.2 The relationship between contributions and benefits

Whether pensions are funded or PAYG, a separate question is how closely benefits are related to a worker's previous contributions. Three approaches are common.

DEFINED-CONTRIBUTION PLANS. In a defined-contribution (DC) plan, also called funded individual accounts, each member pays into an account a fixed fraction of his or her earnings. These contributions are used to purchase assets, which are accumulated in the account, as are the returns earned by those assets. When the pension starts, the assets in the account finance post-retirement consumption through an annuity or in some other way. In a pure defined-contribution system (i.e., one with no redistribution across individual accumulations), a person's consumption in retirement, given life expectancy and the rate of interest, is determined by the size of his or her lifetime pension accumulation, preserving the individual character of a person's lifetime budget constraint. A structure with funded individual accounts can have redistribution across workers' accounts or between general revenues and the accounts.

Although annuities protect the individual against the risks associated with longevity, a pure defined-contribution system leaves him or her facing the wide range of risks (discussed below) associated with varying real rates of return to pension assets, the risks of future earnings trajectories, and the future pricing of annuities. The pure case can be modified to share risks somewhat more broadly, for example, via a guaranteed minimum pension or by pooling a part of contributions or by a legislated response to capital market outcomes. Labor market incentives are affected by the details of rules about asset accumulation, redistribution across accounts, and the benefit formula.

DEFINED-BENEFIT PLANS. In a defined-benefit (DB) plan, a worker's pension is based not on his accumulation, but on his or her wage history, possibly including length of service. The sponsor's contribution is conceptually the endogenous variable ensuring the system's financial balance. Beyond that, defined-benefit systems can be structured in a range of different ways.

- A key design feature is the way wages enter the benefit formula. In a final-salary system, pensions are based on a person's wage in his or her final year or final few years. Alternatively, the pension can be based on a person's real or relative wages over an extended period, including an entire career. In either case, a person's annuity can be, in effect, wage-indexed until retirement.
- The rules of the plan specify how the level of benefits changes when a worker delays claiming a pension. Such adjustments may or may not be actuarial.
- The assets of a defined-benefit plan (if any) are in a central pool. An employer or government can have several defined-benefit plans covering different groups of workers.
- Defined-benefit systems can be run by the state or by employers.

NOTIONAL DEFINED-CONTRIBUTION (NDC) PLANS. A recent innovation internationally, pure NDC plans are conceptually similar to pure DC plans in that contributions are notionally "accumulated" to determine a balance which is converted into an annuity at retirement, but NDC plans are different in that that they are not fully funded and may be entirely PAYG. Thus the accumulation in the accounts follows a rule rather than necessarily equaling the actual returns on the assets held.

NDC plans parallel DC plans in that:

- Each worker pays a contribution of $x\%$ of his or her earnings, which is credited to a notional individual account; that is, the state "pretends" that there is an accumulation of financial assets.
- The cumulative contents of the account are credited with a notional interest rate, specified by the government, and chosen to reflect what can be afforded.
- At retirement, the value of the person's notional accumulation is converted into an annuity in a way that mimics actuarial principles, inasmuch as the present value of a person's benefits (given mortality rates based on the worker's birth cohort and age) is equal to the value of the person's notional accumulation, using the notional interest rate as the discount rate.
- The account balance, however, is for record keeping only, because the system does not own matching funds invested in the financial market. This explains the term *notional*.[2]

Thus NDC plans mimic funded DC plans by paying an income stream whose present value over the person's expected remaining lifetime equals his or her accumulation at retirement but with an interest rate set by government rules, not market returns. As with defined-contribution pensions, there are multiple ways of incorporating a redistributional element into the accounts, for instance, by including a minimum pension guarantee or by subsidizing the contributions of people who are out of the labor force because they are bringing up young children or are unemployed.

On the face of it, NDC plans, where benefits depend on a history of contributions, are very different from standard defined-benefit plans, where benefits depend on a history of earnings. But the difference should not be exaggerated. If contribution rates do not change, a plan based on contributions is effectively a plan based on earnings. Indeed, NDC plans are very close to some existing DB plans, particularly those based on a person's lifetime earnings history, differing primarily in the vocabularies used to describe them. The choice of vocabulary can have political implications for the process of pension reform.

2. Preserving the acronym, these have been referred to also as nonfinancial defined-contribution systems.

THE TAX TREATMENT OF PENSIONS. Whether pensions are defined-contribution, defined-benefit, or notionally defined-contribution plans, a separate issue is how contributions, pension accumulations, and pension benefits are treated for tax purposes. Pensions represent both delayed compensation for earlier work and the accumulation of returns on the delayed compensation.

Several patterns of taxation appear in different countries. As noted on an EU website:[3]

> Most current Member States tax occupational pensions according to the EET system (Exempt contributions, Exempt investment income and capital gains of the pension institution, Taxed benefits) or ETT principle (Exempt contributions, Taxed investment income and capital gains of the pension institution, Taxed benefits). This means that:
>
> - the contributions by both employer and employee are tax deductible,
> - the investment results of the pension fund are usually exempt (they are taxed only in Denmark, Italy and Sweden) and
> - the benefits are taxed.
>
> This system of deferred taxation is logical, since contributions to pension funds diminish a person's ability to pay taxes; at the same time it encourages citizens to save for old age. In addition, it will help Member States to deal with the demographic time-bomb, as the State will receive tax revenue by taxing the pensions paid to people when more people will be dependant upon state aid.
>
> However, many Member States do not allow tax deduction for pension contributions paid to a pension fund in another Member State. This effectively seals off their national markets from competition from other Member States, it makes it difficult to create pan-European funds and it constitutes a major obstacle to the free movement of workers within Europe.

There are several complications in choosing between the different approaches: the normative theory of the taxation of capital income is unsettled territory; separately, the current state of research on optimal tax does not include much analysis of the optimal taxation of retirement savings relative to other capital income.[4]

3. Available online at ec.europa.eu/taxation_customs/taxation/personal_tax/pensions/index_en.htm.

4. For fuller discussion, see Banks and Diamond 2009.

2.2.3 Adjusting contributions and benefits over time

THE NEED FOR ADJUSTMENT. Future earnings, future rates of return, future life expectancies, and future growth of the labor force are all uncertain. Thus any system must adapt to actual developments. A *pure* defined-contribution system maintains financial balance by adjusting benefits to available funds; so does a *pure* notional defined-contribution system. In contrast a *pure* defined-benefit system adjusts future contribution rates or injects funds from outside the system to match anticipated obligations. In practice, systems regularly adjust both contributions and benefits (and, in public systems, government transfers) to preserve financial balance.

Thus the relationship between contributions and benefits needs to be considered not only at a point in time, for example, for a given cohort of workers or pensioners, but also over time, for example, in response to rising longevity, falling fertility, or a baby boom. Choosing methods of adjustment poses a range of questions:

- Should some adjustment be built into legislation so that it is automatic, or should it be managed fully through periodic legislative changes?
- Should adjustment take place through changes in contributions, changes in benefits, or a mix?
- What relative weights should be given to the various social purposes of pensions, and how should the achievement of those purposes be weighed against the costs of achieving them?

WHO BEARS THE RISK? Different rules for adjustments have different implications for the pattern of risk bearing. Where a pure defined-contribution state system is financed from contributions, the risk of adverse outcomes falls on current contributors once they retire; where there is a taxpayer subsidy, the risk falls on taxpayers. Where a pure fully funded defined-benefit state system is financed from contributions, the risk of adverse outcomes falls on current workers. A less than fully funded pure defined-benefit system can spread the risk among current and future workers. Thus in a pure defined-benefit system none of the risks fall directly on pensioners. In practice, governments change benefits as well as contributions when revenue and expenditure do not balance, thus sharing some of the risk with pensioners. Such adjustment can be automatic (for example, where benefits are indexed to changes in prices) or the result of specifically legislated change.

In a pure defined-benefit system provided by an employer, the risk of varying rates of return to pension assets falls on the employer and hence on some combination of the industry's current workers (through effects on wage rates), its shareholders and the taxpayer (through effects on profits),

its customers (through effects on prices), and/or its past or future workers, if the company uses surpluses from some periods to boost pensions in others or modifies the benefit formula relative to expectations. In practice, company defined-benefit systems may also adjust current and/or future benefits in light of financial outcomes.[5] A key difference between defined-benefit and defined-contribution pensions is how and how widely risks are shared.

2.3 Economic framework

2.3.1 Simple economics

In thinking about the economics of pensions it assists analysis to have three propositions in mind: national output matters; imperfect information and imperfect decision making are pervasive; and pension systems face large and unpredictable risks. A fourth important point is that pension arrangements have administrative costs that can be significant.

OUTPUT MATTERS. There are two (and only two) ways of seeking security in old age. One is to store current production for future use. But, housing excepted, this approach is inadequate for most consumption needs: it is expensive; it does not address uncertainty (e.g., about how a person's tastes might change); and it cannot be applied to services deriving from human capital, notably medical services.

The alternative is for individuals to exchange current production when younger for a claim on future production when older. There are two broad ways to do so: by saving part of his wages a worker could build up a pile of *assets* that he would exchange for goods produced by younger people after his retirement or he could obtain a *promise*—from his children, his employer, or government—that he would be given goods produced by younger workers after his retirement. The two main ways of organizing pensions broadly parallel these two types of claim. Funded systems are based on accumulations of financial assets; PAYG systems, on promises.

The purpose of pensions is to allow people to continue to consume after they have stopped working. Pensioners are not interested in money, but in consumption—food, clothing, heating, medical services. Consumption comes from goods produced at the time—and therefore by younger workers. To that end, future output is central. PAYG and funding are simply financial

5. Benefits might be the outcome of repeated employer-union negotiations. While current benefits are normally protected from change by law, such protection does not fully extend to the bankruptcy of the sponsoring firm.

mechanisms for organizing claims on that future output (as well as for how current output is divided up). In macroeconomic terms, though there are differences between the two approaches, those differences should not be exaggerated.

The centrality of output remains true in an open economy. Openness means that consumption can include goods made abroad, that pension accumulations can include investments abroad, and that domestic production can use capital owned by foreigners.[6] The increased opportunities from openness enhance the potential for pensions but do not alter the basic logic. Openness will also alter wages and rates of return within a country, which will alter the actual outcomes of pension systems. In considering aging and the future of pensions, it should be noted that aging is not restricted to just a few countries. Countries with aging populations include all of the OECD and many others, China being a notable example.

IMPERFECT CONSUMER INFORMATION AND DECISION MAKING ARE WIDESPREAD. The simple theory of consumer choice is predicated on well-informed, rational consumers who save and borrow optimally over their life cycle in the context of labor markets, savings institutions, and insurance markets that also operate optimally. Though broadly applicable in many areas—so that consumer sovereignty is widely useful—such assumptions are misplaced for complex products like pensions. There are two key sets of problems:

- deviations from first-best markets, summarized in box 2.1, notably imperfect information, missing markets, many dimensions of risk and uncertainty, and distortions, such as progressive taxation; and
- imperfect decision making, discussed in box 2.2: there are serious concerns about the abilities of individuals to make the most of the market opportunities available to them.

Some ignorance—information problems—can be reduced by public education. Some, however, is not readily resolved in that way. Even financial sophisticates cannot necessarily be regarded as well-informed consumers, and in cases where they are so regarded, they nonetheless face many of the problems discussed in box 2.2. Given the high potential cost of mistaken choice, imperfect information and suboptimal choices create an efficiency justification for stringent regulation to protect consumers in an area where they are not well enough informed to protect themselves. Evidence suggests it is difficult and expensive to provide information that succeeds in altering behavior.

Beyond the imperfect acquisition and processing of information are issues of the quality of decision making as it affects both workers and their

6. Openness also involves increased migrations into and out of countries.

Box 2.1 Deviations from first-best

In the simple theory of saving in a first-best world with a well-functioning market for savings, the individual is assumed to make choices about saving and borrowing that maximize his or her lifetime utility. The underlying logic continues to apply in an economically richer environment (one with uncertain variable returns to savings) in the setting of a model where all markets needed for retirement savings exist and function well. In those circumstances, consumer choice and competitive markets maximize welfare. Pensions, however, face a number of serious deviations from such a theoretical world.

Imperfect information. Although complete markets can help people adapt to uncertainties about the future, they require people to understand the uncertainties they face and the options that markets offer in order to make good use of those options. In fact, individuals are imperfectly informed in several ways:

- Some individuals have a poor sense of the risks and uncertainties they face, for example, about their longevity.
- Individuals are unlikely to be well informed about complex products, such as defined-contribution pensions, which are based on an array of financial institutions and financial instruments. Many people do not understand basic concepts in finance: Orszag and Stiglitz (2001, p. 37) quote the chairman of the U.S. Securities and Exchange Commission as stating that over 50 percent of Americans did not know the difference between a stock and a bond (see glossary). The problem is not only one of efficiency but also has distributional implications because the worst-informed people are disproportionately among the least well off; that is, information poverty and financial poverty are highly correlated.
- Defined-benefit plans are complex, and participants may understand them only incompletely. Complexity is a particular problem with corporate plans, where labor mobility and any financial problems the firm faces have implications for pensions that can be hard to see. Complexity may be less of a problem with a public system, though arrangements in some countries—the United Kingdom being an example—are sufficiently complex to be very hard to understand. And public systems are likely to need to be adjusted to changing demographic and economic conditions as well as with political circumstances, thus adding to their complexity.
- For some purposes it is useful to recognize that the problem may not be lack of information but an information-processing problem. An information problem in a given market—say, the market for automobiles—can be resolved by providing the necessary

(continued)

Box 2.1 (Continued)

> information, in this case, the characteristics of different models of automobile. Once informed, the individual can then make his or her own choices. With an information-processing problem, in contrast, the problem is too complex for many agents to make rational choices even when they have the necessary information. Such problems are more likely where the time horizon is long, where the good or service involves complex probabilities, or where information about the features of the product is inherently complex. All of these conditions characterize most pension products.

For these and other reasons, people can be myopic, giving a justification for compulsion. The problem is not trivial and implies that the simple assumption of rational utility maximization may not hold in the market for pensions.

Incomplete markets. Even for a well-informed consumer with good information processing, actual markets may be limited in their ability to provide products tailored to his or her exact needs and wants. In the case of pensions, the market for indexed contracts, for example, is thin. Asymmetric information in the insurance market makes perfect insurance impossible. When insurance is linked to employment, labor market decisions must be distorted if workers are to have insurance—another manifestation of an incomplete market. Indeed, a theorem holds that if there is asymmetric information, the *absence* of labor market distortions is a sign of nonoptimal provision of insurance. This can make it hard to judge whether the design of a particular insurance product is optimal for a particular worker. Insurance firms, meanwhile, must cope with potential consumers with different risks and so different costs of providing coverage. This problem of adverse selection can be eased by making insurance mandatory. Generally marketing insurance products is highly costly, leaving the possibility of government provision of a uniform product at much lower cost.

Progressive taxation is a further deviation from first-best. In comparing defined-contribution and defined-benefit plans, it is not possible to say that one approach dominates the other if labor market distortions are present:

> With a progressive annual income tax and age-earnings profiles that are generally increasing in real terms, the marginal income tax rate is rising with age, on average. Thus, a well-designed DB [defined benefit] system may well have better labor market outcomes since the overall tax burden, income tax plus net tax from social security, will vary less over

(continued)

Box 2.1 (Continued)

> the life-cycle. That is, income taxes are lower on the young and net social security taxes are higher. Therefore, without a detailed calculation, one cannot reach an efficiency conclusion. In any case the difference is likely to be much smaller than the difference between DB systems with long and short averaging periods. (Diamond 2002, p. 57)

All these deviations from first-best call into question the simple model of market choice and competition. The resulting problems with the exercise of consumer choice are taken up in box 2.2.

Box 2.2 Do consumers choose well? Lessons from behavioral economics

Two bodies of literature help to explain why choices about saving and about one's pension provider may be suboptimal: that on the economics of information, discussed in box 2.1, and a recent and growing literature on behavioral economics (see U.K. Pensions Commission 2004*a*, pp. 207–10, Tapia and Yermo 2007, and Thaler and Sunstein 2008).

Many people do not save enough voluntarily to maximize lifetime utility, and few buy annuities voluntarily despite their considerable value. Instead, widespread manifestations of suboptimal behavior are observed.

Failure to choose, or delay doing so:

- Procrastination: People delay saving, do not save, or do not save enough. There is considerable evidence (Choi et al. 2001) that, with retirement saving as elsewhere, people agree they should do more but put off the action itself.
- Avoiding explicit choice: In theory it should make no difference whether individuals face an opt-in or an opt-out provision; in practice, automatic enrollment leads to much higher participation. Participation rates in employer 401(k) plans in the United States differ sharply depending on whether or not enrollment was automatic with an opt-out (Madrian and Shea 2001).
- Immobilization: Complexity and conflicting information can lead to passive behavior. People presented with a larger range of 401(k) options have been found to participate less. A large fraction of new workers in Sweden make no choice at all.

(continued)

Box 2.2 (Continued)

Faulty choice: In addition, when people do choose, their choices may make little sense:

- Short-term gratification: Many people retire at the earliest age permitted, which may be too early for their own good or that of their spouses. In the United States a very large spike in retirements occurs at age 62, even though pensions rise for later retirement on roughly an actuarially fair basis for the average worker.
- Framing: Choices are influenced by how they are presented, even at the simplest level. As Loewenstein and Ubel (2008, p. 1806) note: "people who learn first about the risks of a treatment followed by its benefits make different choices than people who first learn about its benefits and then its risks. Decision aid developers have no choice but to present information in one order or another, but unfortunately the order they choose will almost inevitably affect people's decisions."
- Familiarity: Another poor but common choice is to invest heavily in the stock of one's own employer; if the firm goes bankrupt, employees invested in the firm lose both their wage income and much of their capital accumulation, as happened to many employees of Enron. Such behavior shows a failure to understand the benefits of diversifying risk.
- Herd instinct: People follow fashion, as, for example, in the technology stock boom of the late 1990s. A related phenomenon is excessive trading: many people appear to trade too much, on average worsening their position on the risk-return frontier while also incurring trading costs. Another is trying to time the market, moving between classes of assets in a way that increases risk relative to expected return, and also seems, on average, to lower the expected return.
- Poor use of annuities: Decisions about annuities tend to be flawed, not least because most people do not understand the underlying idea of insurance.

Recent experimental evidence supports a tendency in some circumstances for people to have a high discount rate in the short run (that is, a tendency toward instant gratification) and a lower one in the medium term. The problem is that when the future arrives, it becomes the present; hence short-term gratification continues, resulting in time inconsistency.

Implications for pension design: These findings suggest a number of implications for policy design in both employer and public plans:

- Keep choices simple to avoid immobilization, for example, by offering only a small number of clearly differentiated funds.

(continued)

Box 2.2 (Continued)

- Use automatic enrollment, thus turning inertia to the individual's advantage: once automatically enrolled, most people will stay with the plan.
- Design a good default option: an arrangement based on automatic enrollment plus worker choice of plans requires a default option for workers who do not make a choice. The existence and design of the default option are important (see Beshears et al. 2008 for a fuller discussion).
- In employer plans a further option is to design policy so that people commit now to action in the future, thus making use of procrastination to assist policy. People are happy to promise to save more in the future, as in the "Save More Tomorrow" plan of Thaler and Benartzi (2004). The essence of that arrangement is that people commit to saving a given fraction of their salary but not until the next pay increase; the fraction is initially small, but unless the individual takes explicit action to end the arrangement, it rises with each successive pay increase.

families. If workers' decisions about savings or annuitization do not pay sufficient attention to the future needs of themselves or other family members, then there are bases for state intervention, bases that have been recognized for centuries, for example, through restrictions on estates to protect widows.

PENSION SYSTEMS FACE LARGE RISKS THAT ARE HARD TO PREDICT.

- *Economic risk:* Unforeseen macroeconomic events (both good and bad surprises) can affect output, prices, or both. Since both funding and PAYG are simply different ways of organizing claims on future output, it should not be surprising that output shocks are likely to affect any pension arrangement.
- *Demographic risk:* Developments in fertility, mortality, or other demographic variables also affect all pension arrangements (see section 4.3.3), directly through the rules of the pension system and indirectly by affecting market prices and quantities and, thus, pension revenue and claims.
- *Political risk:* Political uncertainty affects all pension arrangements because all depend critically—albeit in different ways—on effective and stable government.

Alongside these common risks, the presence of funds to be organized and managed results in additional risks:

- *Management risk:* This can arise through incompetence or fraud, which imperfectly informed consumers generally cannot monitor effectively.
- *Investment risk:* Pension accumulations held in the stock market until retirement are vulnerable to market fluctuations. Pension accumulations held in nominal bonds are vulnerable, in addition, to unanticipated inflation.
- *Longevity risk:* Holding assets that are not in the form of an annuity leaves the individual facing the risk of outliving his or her assets.
- *Annuities market risk:* For a given pension accumulation, the value of an annuity depends on a person's remaining life expectancy and on the rate of return the insurance company can expect over those years and thus involves both investment risk and longevity risk.

Private insurance markets can help individuals bear some of the risks inherent in preparing for retirement. But there are limits to private insurance from adverse selection, from selling costs, from the limited ability of consumers to make good decisions, and from incomplete markets for risk sharing, particularly across cohorts. With social insurance, the intention is for risk to be shared more broadly. The costs of adverse outcomes can be borne by the pensioner through lower pensions, by workers through higher contributions, by the taxpayer through tax-funded subsidies to pensions, and/or by future taxpayers and beneficiaries if subsidies are financed by government borrowing. In addressing risks, social insurance plans have limited complexity and thus cannot exactly match what idealized markets would do.

ADMINISTRATIVE COSTS. The previous arguments all apply even in a frictionless world. But analysis must also take into account the fact that any method of arranging for future consumption has administrative costs. These include the costs of record keeping and the costs of transactions insofar as there are accumulations of assets or purchases of benefit streams. Different ways of organizing future consumption have very different costs and thus provide very different levels of future consumption. For example, the individual mutual fund market is far more expensive than the institutional mutual fund market.

2.3.2 But not too simple

The following chapters offer analysis and conclusions relating to five sets of issues.

PENSIONS AND THE LABOR MARKETS. It is not possible to have a modern economy without distorting the labor market. Analysis of pension systems has to recognize the trade-off between narrow efficiency in labor markets, on the one hand, and the contribution to the goals of consumption smoothing, insurance, redistribution and poverty relief, on the other.[7] Thus the real issue is to balance the narrow efficiency goal with other goals, not to pretend that there is a way to accomplish multiple goals without distortions. What is needed, therefore, is second-best analysis, which considers the impact of the entire program for retirement income. It can lead to error to consider one part in isolation. These topics are discussed in chapter 3.

PENSIONS AND NATIONAL SAVINGS. A mandatory system of retirement income affects national savings. An important issue, therefore, is the extent to which a system is funded in a way that increases national savings and so increases future output. Chapter 4 presents a framework for thinking about the extent of funding—recognizing that, depending on savings needs, a good system can have any degree of funding, from none to full.

REDISTRIBUTION AND RISK SHARING. These elements are discussed in chapter 5. While private insurance markets, along with capital markets, are devices for sharing risks, a public pension system can improve risk sharing in ways that are not available to the market. Furthermore, private insurance markets are subject to some significant limitations that public provision can overcome. Chapter 5 also discusses how the design of the pension system affects lifetime income distributions.

GENDER AND FAMILY. These issues are discussed in chapter 6. Many systems have different rules for men and women. Even systems that have gender-neutral rules, however, impact men and women differently because of their differing economic and demographic circumstances. Recognition of the presence of families is important for pension design, particularly survivor pensions.

IMPLEMENTATION AND PENSION COSTS. These issues are important and are discussed in chapter 7.

These elements lead to the core conclusion that there is no single best pension system. The arguments for this viewpoint are summarized in box 2.3.

A number of common analytical errors are discussed as they arise:

- tunnel vision, that is, considering one objective in isolation;
- improper use of first-best analysis, ignoring the problems of information and decision making discussed in boxes 2.1 and 2.2;
- improper use of steady-state analysis, that is, focusing on a pension system in steady state while ignoring or underplaying

7. While the vocabulary of a trade-off between labor market efficiency and other goals is useful, it is worth remembering that with incomplete markets and imperfect decision making there are interventions that can improve labor market efficiency (suitably defined) while also advancing other goals.

Box 2.3 No single best pension system

Pensions have multiple objectives, notably the achievement of consumption smoothing, insurance, poverty relief and redistribution.

The pursuit of these objectives faces a series of constraints:

- Fiscal capacity: other things equal, a larger tax base can finance a given pension with a lower contribution rate and hence result in less potential distortion.
- Institutional capacity: stronger institutional capacity enlarges the formal tax base and makes feasible a wider range of options for pension design. Fiscal and institutional capacity figure prominently in the discussion in chapter 7.
- The empirical value of behavioral parameters, such as the responsiveness of labor supply to the design of the pension system, and the effect of pensions on private saving.
- The shape of the pre-transfer income distribution: a heavier lower tail of the income distribution increases the need for poverty relief.

There is no single best system for several reasons:

- Policymakers in different countries and at different times will attach different relative weights to the objectives, including different views about the importance of poverty relief and about how risks should be shared within and across generations.
- The pattern of constraints, including the value of key parameters, will differ over time and across countries.
- Political processes, which vary across countries, affect what is politically feasible, given the range of alternatives that are economically and administratively feasible.

In sum:

- Different countries have different structures for addressing the multiple goals, as illustrated in chapter 9.
- Albeit no country's system is perfect, we find a number of different structures that work pretty well.

the necessary transition steps to get from one steady state to another;

- incomplete analysis of implicit pension debt, for example, considering only the cost of future pensions while ignoring their benefits;
- incomplete analysis of the effects of funding, for example, an excessive focus on financial flows while ignoring real resource effects;
- ignoring distributional effects that are an inevitable consequence of any choice between PAYG and funded arrangements.

These analytical errors are discussed more fully in box 11.1.

Chapter 3

Pensions and Labor Markets

This chapter discusses the influence of pension design on labor markets during working life (section 3.1) and when considering retirement (section 3.2). Section 3.3 considers the balance between mandatory and voluntary pensions.

3.1 The effects of benefit design during working life

The impact of a pension system on the labor market depends on the design of the system as a whole, not on any part in isolation. Labor mobility is essential for an efficient labor market. Pension design should therefore pay particular attention to limiting impediments to labor supply generally and to labor mobility in particular. Two issues stand out: the problems associated with final salary systems and the extent to which an actuarial relationship between contributions and benefits is or is not an advantage.

3.1.1 Problems with final salary systems

The way earnings in different years affect a person's pension benefit can have a powerful influence on his or her labor market behavior. Particularly salient is whether benefits should depend on a person's entire contributions record or only on a subset of years and, if the latter, how many and which ones.

Corporations use pensions to attract and retain workers. Historically, many systems paid pensions at a standard retirement age, with the benefit dependent on length of service and the worker's wage toward the end of his or her career. Such a structure makes it easy for workers to see the advantages of staying with a firm until retirement.

Systems of this sort can create labor market problems. A young worker recognizes that current earnings do not affect the size of his future pension, weakening the incentive to work extra hours or to take on a harder job at higher pay. There are, of course, offsetting incentives, since the worker might recognize that hard work and accomplishment improve the chances for promotion and, so, a higher wage and, hence, a larger pension later on.

The opposite incentive operates toward the end of a career, when workers might be over eager to work extra hours. An extreme version of this problem arose in Boston, where the subway system bases pensions on the earnings (not the base pay) of workers at the end of their careers. Older workers therefore do a great deal of the overtime, which has caused accidents when, working excessive hours, they fall asleep at the controls of trains. One need not go so far as endangering lives to see that such pension arrangements can have adverse incentives. A similar problem in a large organization is promotion toward the end of a career to raise the pension entitlement of a person favored by the middle managers who control promotions. The shorter the period of earnings used in determining benefits, the stronger the incentive for such manipulative collaboration.

A third problem with corporate final-salary defined-benefit systems is their effect in locking a worker into employment with that corporation. Historically, indeed, that was one of the main purposes of that benefit design. In a modern economy, the efficiency costs of the resulting impediments to labor mobility are likely to be substantial.

A fourth problem relates to the distribution of pension incomes, which favors workers whose earnings rise more rapidly, particularly toward the end of a career. Since highly paid workers tend to have more rapidly rising earnings, the system favors the best off. This can be regarded as unfair.

Although uniform national systems do not face the labor immobility problem, they face the other problems. Within a single corporation, these effects can be lessened by the other controls a corporation has in relation to its workers and by relating pensions to base pay and not actual earnings. In a national system, the government does not have similar controls over the entire economy. Thus, it is important that a national system bases benefits on most or all of a worker's earnings history once the pension administration has the necessary administrative capacity.

For all these reasons, analysts agree that a well-designed plan—corporate or industry or national—should base benefits on a fairly long period of contributions. Within that consensus it is not clear whether the period should include a person's entire career (France, Germany, Sweden) or somewhat less (the United States, the United Kingdom). In important respects the choice is determined by the weights given to the different objectives of pension systems. Systems that include an entire career give relatively greater weight to consumption smoothing; including most, but not all, of a full career allows a worker to exclude years with low or no earnings, thus giving relatively greater weight to insurance and redistribution. In our view, either of these approaches makes sense. In contrast, pension systems—whether employer-based or public—should not place heavy reliance on final wages in determining a person's pension.

3.1.2 Problems with strict adherence to actuarial benefits

It is frequently argued that a strictly actuarial relationship between contributions and benefits is optimal: "Funded defined-contribution systems are the closest to an actuarially fair system, so the labor market distortions should be low" (Holzmann and Hinz 2005, p. 50). There are three sets of arguments: that actuarial benefits minimize distortions to labor supply, that they improve compliance with contribution conditions, and that they encourage later retirement.

In a first-best world, actuarial benefits face each individual with an efficient choice between consumption when younger and consumption when older. In practice, however, policy design must address at least three sets of market imperfections. People can be myopic and/or imperfectly informed, giving a justification for compulsion. The problem is nontrivial and means that the simple assumption of rational utility maximization may not hold, particularly in the face of the major information and decision problems discussed in boxes 2.1 and 2.2. A second problem is missing markets. The market for indexed contracts, for example, is thin. Insurance with asymmetric information requires distorting labor market decisions in order to have insurance. Progressive taxation is a third deviation from first-best. Thus, in the comparison between defined contribution and defined benefit systems, there is no simple dominance of one over the other in the presence of other labor market distortions. Formulating the issue as an optimal taxation problem would make it clear that in a second-best world a system that is strictly actuarial is not, in general, the most efficient.

What, then, of the three specific advantages claimed for actuarial benefits?

LABOR MARKET DISTORTIONS. Actuarial benefits will generally not minimize labor market distortions, given the presence of other distortions. Furthermore, pensions have objectives additional to consumption smoothing, for example, poverty relief, and, as already noted, the policies necessary to achieve those other objectives (e.g., taxation) inescapably involve labor market distortions. And third, the provision of insurance against adverse labor market outcomes, particularly toward the end of a career, calls for deviations from actuarial insurance to provide better protection, given the asymmetry of information on the extent to which low labor market participation is due to choice (preference for more leisure) or constraints (low pay or no work available). In sum, (a) actuarial benefits do not minimize labor market distortions and (b) minimizing labor market distortions is not the right objective: policy has to balance labor market efficiency against the various objectives of pension systems.

COVERAGE AND COMPLIANCE. Pension systems can have low coverage for either of two reasons: because many workers participate in the uncovered sector or because workers or employers in the covered sector fail to comply with their legal obligations. The incentives for compliance in the covered sector depend on the perceived payoff from making additional contributions, the cost of those contributions, and the strength of enforcement. Actuarial benefits eliminate very weak links (and very strong ones) between benefits and contributions in any one year, thus strengthening the incentive to work in the covered sector and to comply with pension rules. That incentive, however, is absent for workers who are guaranteed a minimum income, either as part of the pension system or through a separate program. And improved compliance depends on individuals being well informed and able to afford contributions out of current earnings or through borrowing. In reality, people may be badly informed about the relationship between contributions today and pensions tomorrow; or they may be myopic, with too great a preference for consumption today over consumption tomorrow; or constraints on their current earnings and borrowing capacity may lead them to choose current over future consumption.[1] For all these reasons it is no surprise that the change in Chile in 1981 from a diverse set of defined-benefit plans to a defined-contribution system did not have a significant impact on coverage.

LATER RETIREMENT. Actuarial benefits, it is argued, encourage the appropriate amount of later retirement by offering a person who defers retirement a pension that is sufficiently larger as to involve no implicit tax. Again, this oversimplifies the argument by implicitly assuming a first-best world. Moreover,

1. In some developed countries a significant number of people earning low incomes have more or less permanent credit card debt at interest rates of around 20 percent. In those circumstances it makes no sense to save in a pension plan, which is unlikely to offer an annual rate of return anywhere close to 20 percent.

as discussed in section 3.2.4, a defined-benefit system could adjust benefits for work beyond the earliest pensionable age on an actuarial basis even though the determination of initial benefits at the earliest pensionable age is not actuarial.

In all three cases—minimizing distortions, improving compliance, and encouraging later retirement—the simple argument holds only in a first-best world. That does not mean that the relationship between contributions and benefits is unimportant. Indeed, good policy design should avoid obvious and major distortions in this relationship. But it does mean that a strictly actuarial relationship is generally suboptimal.

3.2 Determining benefits at retirement

An array of design features at the time a person retires can have major effects on labor markets. This section considers in turn the relationship between retirement age and aggregate unemployment; the undesirability of mandatory retirement; the choice of age at which a worker is first entitled to benefit; and adjusting benefits when a person retires later than that age.

3.2.1 Retirement age and unemployment

The common view that early retirement eases unemployment is generally mistaken. From a long historic perspective, developed countries have seen a vast decrease in the average retirement age, yet unemployment has shown no trend decrease. Box 3.1 presents evidence for a number of countries over a 10-year period which shows no pattern whereby countries that encourage

Box 3.1 Pension design and the decision about when to retire

Pension rules have a major impact on decisions about when to retire. In particular, badly designed rules can encourage people to retire earlier than is efficient; in the limit, such incentives can have an effect similar to that of a mandatory retirement age.

Empirical studies that support this conclusion include a collaborative project analyzing pensions and retirement in eleven countries (Gruber and Wise 1999, 2004). The authors of the study calculated for each year the implicit tax on earnings by workers eligible to retire (the decrease in expected lifetime income as a consequence of the pension rules should the worker continue earning for another year). The variable they call the

(continued)

Box 3.1 (Continued)

"tax force" then adds up these implicit taxes from the age at which a male worker becomes eligible to claim a retirement benefit up to age 70. In a crude, aggregate way, this variable measures the extent to which the design of the pension system contains a financial incentive to do less work.

To see how this measure of retirement incentives related to actual retirement decisions, the study used a simple aggregate measure of labor supply. For each age between 55 and 65 the authors calculated the fraction of the male population not in the labor force and added up these fractions over these ages. They called the resulting variable "unused productive capacity." The first figure shows their regression of unused productive capacity on the logarithm of the tax force. A strong correlation is evident (the R^2 is about 0.8), and the coefficient on the tax force variable was sizable and statistically significant: at the mean, the coefficient (which can be interpreted as the elasticity of unused capacity with respect to the tax force) was 0.36. Moreover, time-series evidence and analyses using data on individuals

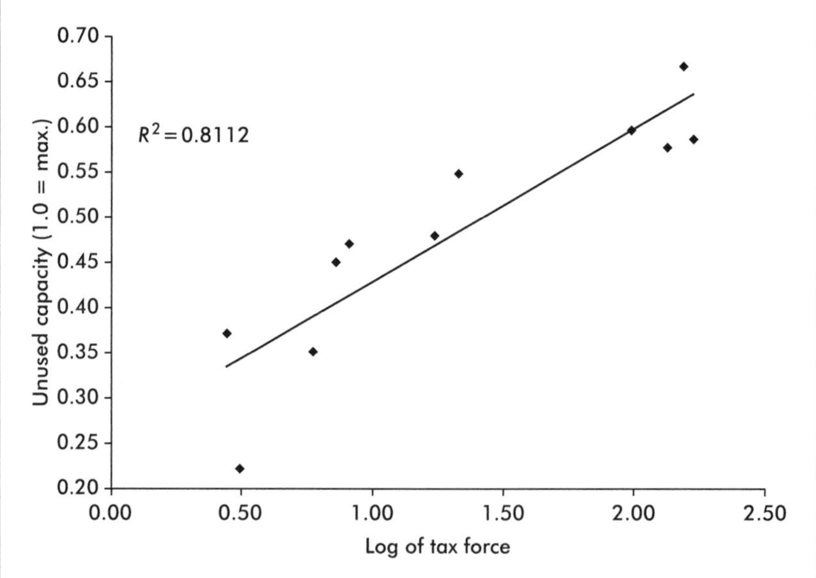

Figure B3.1.1 Unused labor force capacity and the implicit tax on earnings due to pension rules

Unused capacity is among workers aged 55–65. Each observation represents a single OECD country; the countries represented are Belgium, Canada, France, Germany, Italy, Japan, the Netherlands, Spain, Sweden, the United Kingdom, and the United States. The "tax force" variable measures the implicit tax on earnings from working an additional year between the age of earliest eligibility for retirement with a pension and age 70. *Source:* Gruber and Wise (1999).

(continued)

Box 3.1 (Continued)

suggest that at least a large part of the correlation reflects the impact of the implicit tax as an incentive to early retirement.

In contrast, the same tax force variable had no impact on male unemployment rates in the same countries (as measured by a decadelong average unemployment rate), as the second figure shows. The conclusion is the same whether the regression is interpreted in either of two ways: as showing directly that large implicit taxes to encourage early retirement do not lower unemployment rates; or as an instrumental variables regression demonstrating that early retirement does not reduce unemployment (Diamond 2006). The research indicates that discouraging work through high implicit tax rates creates large inefficiencies that do not accomplish social goals and therefore should be avoided.

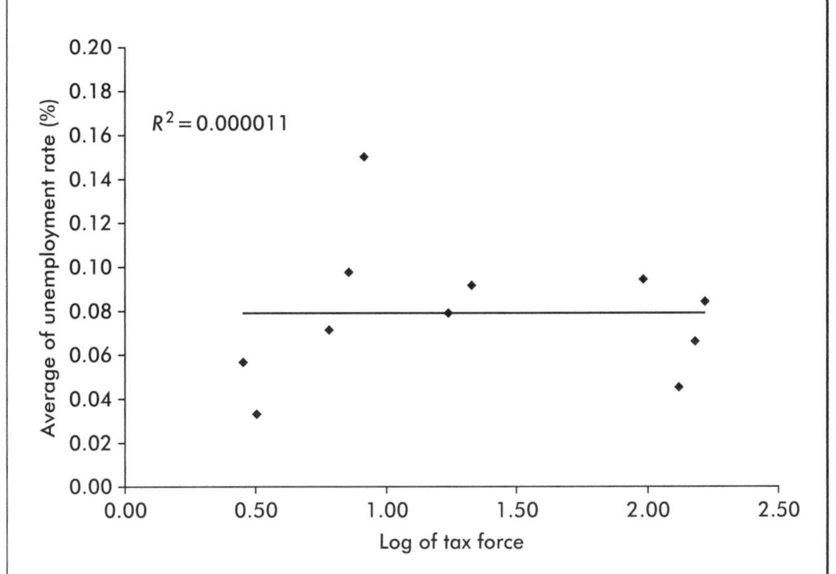

Figure B3.1.2 Male unemployment and the implicit tax on earnings due to pension rules, 1991–2000

Each observation represents a single country. *Source:* Diamond (2006).

early retirement have lower unemployment. Indeed, when comparing two countries, it is possible to observe one with higher unemployment over an extended period, and then the other, even where their retirement systems do not change significantly. Thus there is not a tight relationship between retirement age and the level of unemployment.

It is mistaken for several reasons to think in terms of a fixed number of jobs. First, increased numbers of workers, by exerting downward pressure on wages and by making it easier to find suitable workers, tend to encourage the creation of new jobs. Thus the number of jobs is variable and is influenced by the number of workers. Second, early retirement does not always remove workers from the labor force, since some continue to work while receiving a pension. Third, in a developing economy urban unemployment depends on migration as well as on the availability of jobs. Any attempt to reduce urban unemployment by encouraging early retirement may be dwarfed by migration.

It is therefore mistaken to allow or mandate early retirement (which is long term) as a palliative response to unemployment (which generally is short term). Better to focus on incentives that encourage long-run growth than to distort the labor market in the vain hope that retirement will have a sizable impact on unemployment. Similarly, disability benefits should be awarded on the basis of disability, not as a response to unemployment.

3.2.2 Mandatory retirement

Forcing people to leave the labor force has no sustained benefit for workers seeking jobs. Thus there is no reason to have a mandatory retirement age on a nationwide basis. Older workers differ greatly in their health, interest in work, ability to work, and job opportunities. Employers differ greatly in their potential use of and need for older workers. Flexibility in ending employment relationships is an important part of the efficient long-run use of labor. The United States, with some exceptions, has made mandatory retirement illegal *at the firm level*, and the EU is following suit. But it is not necessary to go as far as this to recognize a role for allowing firms and workers to select retirement ages. Mandatory retirement on a nationwide basis is neither necessary nor desirable.

3.2.3 What "retirement age"?

The concept of retirement is multidimensional. When thinking about "the" retirement age in a pension system, two variables are particularly important. Corporate systems often give a single retirement age a central role, perhaps with a smaller or larger pension for earlier or later retirement, respectively. We refer to the age that plays this central role as the age for full benefits. For a national system, it may be more useful to think in terms of (a) the earliest age at which a worker is allowed to start benefits (earliest pensionable age or earliest eligibility age) and (b) the increase in pension of someone who delays the start of benefits beyond that age. Different countries have different earliest eligibility ages. The United States has both an earliest pensionable age

(62) and an age for full benefits (previously 65, rising to 67). In the United Kingdom, the two ages are the same.

What factors should guide the choice of earliest eligibility age? Raising the earliest eligibility age does not help long-run pension finance if benefits are actuarially adjusted for the increase in the age at which they start. Raising the age at which benefits start lowers costs only if accompanied by a decrease in the level of benefits at each age below what it would have been under the old system.

Increasing the earliest eligibility age helps some workers and hurts others. The age should be chosen to balance these gains and losses at the margin. Increasing the earliest eligibility age from 65 to 66 has varied effects:

- It hurts workers who should sensibly stop working at 65 but do not have enough savings to stop working without access to their pensions.
- It helps workers who ought to wait until 66 but who, given the choice, would retire at 65 on a pension that may be inadequate as the worker, and possibly spouse, age.
- It helps some workers who retire at 65 and can afford to live from savings until benefits start at 66 by providing higher pensions and so more insurance.
- Similarly, if benefits are not conditioned on actual retirement, it helps workers who would have worked until 66 anyway, by providing higher benefits. It also helps those who might have consumed too much, given their cash flow, to save more for later spending.
- If benefits are paid only to workers who retire, it will not affect those who would have worked until 66 anyway.

An optimal earliest eligibility age strikes a balance between helping some workers and hurting others—it should be set in the interior of the range of sensible retirement ages for different workers. Whatever the earliest eligibility age, the system should be designed to allow flexibility in retirement decisions.

3.2.4 Adjusting pensions for earlier and later retirement

VARIATION IN RETIREMENT AGE. Having selected an age for full benefits, a traditional corporate system has a formula that calculates a person's pension at the age for full benefits as a function of (a) years of service and (b) the person's earnings in the years relevant to the benefit formula. However, some firms want some workers to continue beyond the age for full benefits, at least on a part-time basis, and in other cases it may be in the interests of both worker and employer for the worker to retire at a younger age. Actuaries can estimate what reduction for earlier retirement allows a firm broadly to break even from offering an early retirement option.

Actuarially fair adjustments, however, may or may not be in the firm's best interests. A firm might want to give workers more or less encouragement to retire early by setting pensions above or below the level that would break even. Setting pension levels for these alternative options represents an additional control variable for encouraging or discouraging retirement at different ages separate from the rules that determine benefits at the age for full benefits. In addition, a firm can choose at which ages the early retirement option is available and may offer that opportunity only to a subset of its workers or only at some times (when reducing employment is more useful).

If a firm wants to retain some workers beyond the age for full benefits, it can offer a larger pension for delayed retirement. Alternatively, a firm could pay benefits, wholly or in part, while continuing to employ the worker, for example, by hiring the worker as a consultant after he or she has formally retired and started to receive benefits. Cognizant of differences in jobs and in the varying abilities of different workers, firms recognize that they do not want all their workers to retire at exactly the same age.

Similar issues arise in a national system. Whatever the rules for pensions at some normal age, there are good reasons—for the economy and for society—for different workers to retire at different ages. Some workers enjoy their work and want to continue working. Others no longer enjoy their work (if they ever did) and want to stop as soon as they can afford a decent retirement. A good pension system will not excessively discourage the first group from continuing to work at ages at which the second group will already have retired.

BENEFIT ELIGIBILITY AND WORK AT DIFFERENT AGES. Typically, retirement from a firm is a condition for the start of a pension. But that does not necessarily mean the end of all work. Many workers retire from one firm, collect a corporate pension, and then work elsewhere; some firms allow workers who have retired from full-time work to continue part-time, with access to some or all of their pension. As discussed, such flexibility is appropriate.

National systems can also choose the links between continued work and receipt of benefits. Pensions can start at a given age only when a worker has completely stopped working (or has low earnings), or they can start at a given age whether or not the worker has stopped working. Or there can be an age-varying rule—a range of ages where benefits are paid only if work stops, after which benefits are paid irrespective of a person's labor market activities (as in the United States). In addition, a worker who is eligible for a pension might be allowed to defer benefits so as to have larger benefits once he or she does start (as in the United Kingdom) or allowed to have partial benefits, deferring the rest (as in Sweden).

In sum, there are two elements to the relationship between pension benefits and the age at which a pension is first received:

- The pension should be larger for a worker who is older when benefits begin in order to preserve incentives to work until a suitable age for stopping work.
- Either benefits should start at a given age without requiring an end to work or they should increase significantly for a delayed start.

3.3 The balance between mandatory and voluntary pensions

An important element in any pension system is the extent to which contributions are mandatory. Voluntary pensions accommodate more choices for workers, including workers with

- different preferences about the time path of saving for retirement and about the balance of living standards in old age compared with their working years;
- differences in the timing of key life events, for example, whether children are born earlier or later;
- different degrees of risk aversion;
- different working conditions so that industries in which people work in harsh conditions, or where working life is short for other reasons, can provide for earlier retirement; and
- different regional and private initiatives.

The mix of voluntary and mandatory must strike a balance between, on the one hand, the inefficiencies that arise from a uniform mandate that takes incomplete account of differences in preferences and constraints, and, on the other hand, the gaps that arise if the mandatory system is small. Consideration of the appropriate size of the mandatory system focuses on the adequate provision of retirement income and on the system's impacts on the labor market, both of which will vary across workers.

Chapter 4

Finance and Funding

Finance and funding[1] are areas of intense and wide-ranging controversy.[2] After briefly touching on some background issues in section 4.1, this chapter concentrates on three areas: implicit and explicit debt (section 4.2); the relationship among funding, saving, and growth (section 4.3); and the proper way to compare returns to PAYG and funded systems (section 4.4).

4.1 Background issues

Some countries finance mandatory pensions entirely from dedicated revenue (for example, Sweden and the United States, both of which use a payroll tax and draw from general revenues according to earmarking rules), others wholly from general taxation (Australia and New Zealand), and others from a mix (Chile, which has a defined-contribution system financed from a payroll tax and a defined-benefit element financed from general revenue, and Italy, which has regularly covered pension deficits from general revenues). The most common source of dedicated revenue (also commonly

1. We use the term *financing* to refer to the cash flow used each year to pay benefits and the term *funding* to indicate financial assets held by the pension system.

2. See Barr 2000, Diamond 2004, Diamond and Orszag 2005*a*, 2005*b*, and, for contrasting views, Feldstein 2005 and Holzmann and Hinz 2005. For an attempt to summarize the core of the dispute, see Barr and Rutkowski 2005.

called earmarked revenue) is a payroll tax, the proceeds of which are used to pay current benefits, to purchase assets for a trust fund, or to buy assets to be held in individual accounts. But there are variations. For example, the Netherlands has an earmarked tax in the form of an addition to the income tax paid by people under age 65 for a pension benefit based on length of residency, not on a record of contributions. In the United States, some of the dedicated revenue of the Social Security system comes from part of the taxation of Social Security pension benefits. Arguments in favor of at least some dedicated revenue include insulation from the annual budget cycle, greater worker security, a longer planning horizon, and possibly greater political sustainability.

There are also arguments for at least some reliance on general revenues to support the elderly either within or outside of the pension system. A pure defined-contribution system will provide inadequate benefits for many workers, including those with fragmented careers, careers divided between covered and uncovered work, or low lifetime earnings. The same holds for a strictly proportional defined-benefit system without any explicit redistribution. If a pension system is to provide effective poverty relief, these pure cases need to be modified. The adequacy of benefits for workers with a limited contributions record can be increased either within the mandatory pension system (for example, through a minimum pension or a progressive benefit formula) or outside it (for example, through social assistance). If it is done within the system, the increased benefits can be financed either from inside the system (using part of the dedicated revenue) or from outside (from general revenues). Different countries have chosen widely from among these options. The method of financing has important distributional effects within and across generations, as discussed in chapter 5. Choices about the source of financing are part of the political process and will have different implications in different political environments.

The main argument for financing part of benefits from general revenues is that this approach can support the adequacy of benefits. The main argument against it is that it may render benefits vulnerable to short-term budgetary exigencies. A potential further argument against it depends on the coverage of the system: use of tax financing may be regressive if taxes are collected from the population broadly but benefits limited mainly to urban, middle-class workers in the formal sector. The main arguments for dedicated revenue are the potential for insulation from short-term fiscal trends, which enhances the security of covered workers, and the potentially greater robustness of the political settlement. Thus a mix of dedicated and general revenue, used for explicitly different parts of the system, may be a good design.

Coexisting with arrangements to improve adequacy within the pension system are antipoverty programs for the general population or the elderly.

These are typically financed from general revenues, often include an income test (see glossary), and also may include an assets test. Since income from pensions is part of an income test, there is an interaction between programs.

4.2 Implicit and explicit debt

"Implicit pension debt" has become part of the vocabulary of international dialogue on pensions—unfortunately without a standard definition, making it a source of much confusion. The core argument—quite correct—is that the pension promises of government have a future cost. However, there are multiple measures reflecting the long-term financial position of a pension system.

MEASURING THE FINANCIAL POSITION OF A PENSION SYSTEM. From the perspective of financing a system, one wants to look at the present discounted value (PDV) of expenditures minus revenues as a measure of whether current law is plausibly sustainable over a reasonable length of time. A central issue is the choice of an appropriate time horizon. Traditionally the United States has used a 75-year horizon, long enough to allow considerable time for adjustment if the finances are thought to be out of balance. Recently there has been a push for focusing on an infinite horizon. One of the arguments for doing so is that with a 75-year horizon imbalances in annual flows beyond the end of the horizon mean that later calculations—using a 75-year horizon that then extends further into the future—will find imbalances even if the current picture shows balance. On the other hand, projecting beyond 75 years involves such uncertainty that the relevance of the approach for setting current policies is not clear. A useful and widely used compromise is to preserve the 75-year horizon but add the condition, referred to as sustainable solvency, that projected finances not be deteriorating at the end of the horizon.

From the perspective of the treatment of future generations, the use of a year-by-year calculation can be supplemented by a cohort-by-cohort calculation for all cohorts already part of the system. The former is referred to as an open-group measure; the latter, as a closed-group measure. Such a calculation is instructive about distribution, though evaluating any particular outcome requires consideration of the different positions of different cohorts in terms of earnings levels and life expectancies.

A third perspective is the cost of the system as a whole relative to the economy as a whole. That is, even if the financing of a system is sustainable from dedicated revenues, one might conclude that the system is either too large or too small. Consideration of size needs to reflect the needs of retirees relative both to their earlier earnings and to the positions of contemporaneous younger cohorts and the alternative uses of the resources being raised to finance the pensions.

Whatever frame is used, there are three natural measures of pension spending: dollars, percentage of payroll (or taxable payroll), and GDP. The direct measure in dollars is not a good way to communicate the position of a system—it is hard to distinguish among different very large numbers. The other two measures are appropriate for the different frames of financing the system and its role within the economy.

Since pension systems are to be relied on by workers, legislated changes should be infrequent and should have reasonable lead times. Hence the importance of projections and measures that make the public aware that a change of some type will be needed, even if cash flows are positive in the near term. A calculation of financial imbalance is thus important.

ANALYTICAL ERRORS. Determining when implicit debt is a useful way of communicating the financial position of a pension system is a separate issue. The term *implicit debt* is useful because it reminds people that explicit debt is not the only claim being made on future generations. However, it has led some analysts to treat implicit debt as fully (or nearly fully) equivalent to explicit debt. In particular, some analysts who favor individual accounts have argued that government should issue new debt equal to the amount of implicit debt in order to place assets into individual accounts, viewing such a step as creating accounts with no cost. This argument is problematic. It is important to recognize that such an action has real economic effects. Government can lower implicit debt as part of a pension reform by lowering benefits, and many governments have done so. In contrast, once explicit debt has been issued in place of the implicit debt, placed in individual accounts and treated the same as other debt, the value of the debt can be lowered only by actions, such as repudiation or increased inflation, that affect more than just the initial owners of the debt.[3] Moreover, unless issued as consols,[4] for which the market is unclear, explicit debt needs to be rolled over repeatedly, creating vulnerability to bond market conditions. With a genuine difference in government options, it is not surprising that markets are likely to perceive explicit debt as different from implicit debt and hence to respond with some reluctance to a large and rapid increase in the supply of bonds, thus increasing the interest rates at which the government borrows. Uncertainty

3. Taxation of benefits financed by this debt could be increased, decreasing the net cost of the debt, but the politics of doing so are different from the politics of restoring sustainability to a pension system. Increased contributions to a defined-benefit system reduce the implicit debt. In a system of funded accounts, however, increased contributions are meant to go to individual accounts and do not decrease the cost of the debt.

4. That is, government bonds of infinite duration.

about future conditions in bond markets is far more important when there is considerably more debt outstanding, as would follow from converting implicit debt into explicit debt. In short, implicit and explicit debt are not equivalent.

In assessing implicit debt, a central observation is that fully funding implicit pension debt is never required, just as a country does not ever need fully to pay off its explicit national debt. With explicit debt, it is critical that the ratio of debt to GDP does not rise to the point where it induces large increases in interest rates and becomes unsustainable. Indeed, confidence in the future ability to control the debt is critical for its interest rate and depends on projections. Similarly, what is critical with implicit debt is that the contribution rate needed in the future does not rise so much that the system becomes economically or politically unsustainable. Giving some assets to a social security trust fund to reduce implicit debt may well be sensible, but allocating enough assets to bring the implicit debt down to zero is not a necessary condition for good policy; yet again, policy (in this case with respect to implicit debt) should be to optimize, not minimize.

IN SUM. The cost of pensions matters considerably. Excessive pension spending can reduce investment and cause major distortions that interfere with economic growth. Thus it is important to project future pension costs, but such projections must be interpreted correctly. Implicit debt is a useful concept but should not be given excessive weight.

4.3 Funding, saving, and growth

Two sets of strategic arguments are frequently made for funded pensions: that funding increases growth (a macroeconomic argument) and that people regard their property rights as more secure if based on the ownership of financial assets (a political economy argument).

In principle, funding increases growth if it increases national saving (section 4.3.1) and/or improves the effectiveness of capital markets (section 4.3.2). A separate argument, also discussed below, is that funding assists adjustment to demographic change (section 4.3.3). Funding and property rights are discussed in section 4.3.4.

4.3.1 Funding and national saving

THE SOURCE OF FUNDING. The link between funding and national savings is not simply a matter of having a fund but, rather, depends critically on the source of the funding (discussed in box 4.1). The purchase of assets for a

Box 4.1 Government bonds and national saving

Consider the following quotation:

> Note that domestic government bonds do not provide a demographic reserve since they are claims on future tax payers just as pay-as-you-go pension claims are claims on future contribution payers. In fact, financing a pension system through domestic government bonds is macroeconomically equivalent to a pay-as-you-go system (Diamond 1965; Pestieau and Possen 2000). Using foreign government bonds effectively internationalizes the pay-as-you-go system by securitizing claims on taxes paid by future foreign citizens. (Börsch-Supan 2005, p. 30, writing about Finland)

The statement is correct that a swap of Finnish government bonds held by the pension system for U.S. government bonds held by its pension system would alter the risk-sharing characteristics of both pension systems. But the statement is potentially misleading in failing to distinguish between *holding* government bonds and *issuing* government bonds.

Consider a PAYG system with no assets, financed by a payroll tax. If the government issues new bonds and gives them to the pension system, that shifts future liabilities from payroll taxpayers to general revenue taxpayers, which will involve some shifting of liabilities among members of the same cohorts even if the timing of payments does not change. Issuing bonds in this way does not directly alter national saving, though the different responses of different taxpayers may result in different levels of national saving. Following such a move with a swap of government bonds for, say, corporate stocks or bonds or bonds of another country still does not directly alter national saving.

In contrast, increasing taxes and using the additional revenue to purchase existing government bonds from the public to transfer to the pension system does directly increase national saving, although the full effect depends on private responses to the tax and transfer. Thus the impact on national saving depends not on the type of asset being held, but on how the asset is acquired—through increased debt or increased taxes or reduced government spending.

Similarly, moving assets (whether government bonds or other assets) from a trust fund to individual accounts does not directly alter national saving. In contrast, raising taxes to purchase assets for individual accounts does directly increase national saving. In both cases, the overall impact depends also on the responses of private savers and resulting changes in government taxes or spending.

trust fund or individual accounts can be financed by increased contributions, through decreased benefits, or by issuing additional government debt, perhaps together with a shift in existing contribution flows. If the government uses workers' contributions to pay benefits while simultaneously placing into workers' accounts a matching value of newly issued government debt, the effect on national savings is similar to that of continuing a PAYG system. It is therefore important to distinguish between funding for the purpose of increasing savings (sometimes referred to as *broad funding*) and funding based on newly issued bonds (called *narrow funding*), which does not increase savings.

Thus a central analytical question is whether the funding of pensions comes from

- newly issued bonds (narrow funding) or
- a reduction in the number of bonds held by the public. This reduction can come about as a result of higher taxes or lower government spending such that the government has a larger surplus and can buy the bonds from the public or a smaller deficit to finance, correspondingly reducing the need to issue new bonds (broad funding).[5]

There often is a failure to distinguish between the implications of different types of assets and the implications of different ways of acquiring those assets. It is the latter that matters for the impact on national saving, as box 4.1 explains.

EFFECTS ON SAVING AND INTERGENERATIONAL DISTRIBUTION. At a given level of output, an increase in national savings requires a decline in someone's consumption. Adjusting the pension system by raising contribution rates or cutting benefits now will lower the consumption of today's workers or today's pensioners, making possible lower contribution rates or higher benefits in the future. In this case, increased funding that increases savings raises the burden on current generations in order to lower the burden on future generations, similar to a budgetary decision to increase taxes or cut public spending so as to reduce public debt.

The process of building a fund can add little or a lot to national savings. There are two questions: does funding increase saving and, if so, is the result welfare enhancing? On the first, the impact of an increase in funding on national savings can be anything from negative to large positive depending on the reaction of private savers and of the rest of the government budget.

5. A government could also sell assets and use the proceeds to buy back bonds, which would not improve the government's financial position.

- Workers' responses: if workers are obliged to pay new contributions into funded accounts, they will to some extent reduce their voluntary savings; thus the introduction of a mandatory funded element has less effect on national savings than the accumulation in the accounts. If contributions are shifted from a central fund to individual accounts some workers may save less because individual accounts bear a stronger parallel to voluntary savings, which would make the impact negative. The overall outcome will depend on the balance of different responses by different groups of workers as well as on the source of the funds.
- Government responses: it is necessary also to consider government responses of changing taxes or spending in areas other than pensions. New revenues going into individual accounts may lead the government to spend more in other areas so that, again, there is little or no increase in national savings. Transfers of revenue from a central fund to individual accounts may be financed by additional government borrowing so there will be no substantial increase in savings.

While we have considerable evidence on the responses of individual savings to pension design, it is much harder to reach a conclusion that is well supported for the response of the rest of the government budget. Some have argued for transferring revenues from a central fund to individual accounts based on the political argument that doing so would induce lower spending of the rest of the budget. This argument is not well supported empirically. In addition, we think that pension policy should be designed to provide old-age security, not primarily to influence nonpension policies.

If funding does raise national savings, is the outcome beneficial? Specifically, does it make sense for an economy to raise contributions or to reduce benefits now in order to have lower contributions or higher benefits in the future? Increased funding through lower benefits or higher contributions necessarily redistributes across generations. Thus, there can be no universal answer about whether funding raises welfare. Each country must consider the question in the context of its own circumstances and priorities, including its current saving rate and anticipated growth in earnings. If the saving rate is already high and growth rapid, it may make little sense to adopt a policy to increase savings even further to help future cohorts who will have much higher earnings.

ANALYTICAL ERRORS. Discussion of funding is prone to errors. Analysis often starts by comparing alternative long-run steady-state outcomes with different degrees of funding and then follows with a comment that there is a transition cost to reach a steady state with a higher level of funding. This approach can be misleading. It gives little insight into the trade-off between the benefit of having a larger fund and the cost of building one. Indeed, the term *transition cost* suggests something small, even for a transition period of decades (as in Chile). It is more informative to analyze funding as above, by considering the implications of increasing funding today in order to have some combination of lower taxes or higher benefits in the future. This way of posing the issue does not focus on funding per se but on the tax, benefit, and debt decisions that should underpin any decision to increase funding.

A separate, widely made but incorrect case for funded accounts is the argument that a funded system is better if the rate of interest (i.e., the return on pension funds) exceeds the rate of growth (i.e., the return to a PAYG system). Once the analysis is done fully, there is no gain for everyone from funding per se, but there is an intergenerational redistribution, as explained in section 4.4. That is, the comparison is basically the same incomplete analysis of considering only the steady state without considering the adjustment to a new steady state. Moreover, such comparisons sometimes ignore the need to recognize differences in risks with different pension systems and the administrative costs of organizing the funding.

Another suspect argument is that "a multipillar structure allows for tactical sequencing, strategic bundling, packaging, and compensation and thus is useful for overcoming resistance to reform" (Holzmann and Hinz 2005, p. 42). This argument suggests that a gain for everyone is available by bundling analysis of static efficiency improvements in pension rules with funding. But those efficiency gains are available without funding, by better design of a PAYG system, so this is misattribution, unless it really is the case that the efficiency gains are not available politically without such bundling. In politics bundling does matter but may not be necessary for reform and indeed may make reform more difficult, as appears to be the case for Germany. In any event, political arguments are separate from economic arguments and should be clearly labeled as such.

Finally, some analysis implies that funding necessarily requires individual accounts. The view that funding requires individual accounts is mistaken. If policymakers want more funding, they have many ways to bring it about, not only through the individual accounts as pioneered by Chile. Sweden has funded a diversified central portfolio within a defined-benefit system for years (and are continuing that alongside their funded accounts), and similar arrangements have been started in Canada and Switzerland. Funding a central fund within a defined-contribution system has been done by the provident funds of Malaysia and Singapore. Thus, choosing a level of funding and a degree of portfolio diversification is economically unrelated to the choice between defined-benefit and defined-contribution systems or between individual and more broadly based accumulations.

4.3.2 Funding and capital market development

Alongside any effects on saving, funding assists growth if it helps to improve the efficiency with which savings are channeled into investment.

In two polar cases the argument clearly fails. In advanced countries, financial markets are highly developed so that mandatory pension savings are unlikely to bring about substantial further improvements. Contrariwise, in countries with very limited institutional capacity, the existing financial infrastructure is too weak to risk the pensions of large numbers of workers by mandating funded individual accounts.

Between the two is a range of country capacities in which there is the potential to improve capital markets but also the risk, without enough improvement, that workers will not get good returns on their contributions or that government will have to bear the cost of bailing out the pension system. The risk is easy to comprehend: inadequate markets can yield low returns. They also have much higher costs than better developed ones, a point of particular relevance to small accounts. Adequate markets require significant government regulation. Indeed, reference to "free markets," suggesting that regulation is necessarily bad and that Chile's success came without heavy regulation, is wrong. The mutual fund and insurance markets that handle Chile's individual accounts are heavily regulated, as is the U.S. capital market. This is not to suggest that all regulation is good. Indeed, what generally is needed are more good regulations and fewer bad ones. It also helps to have a large market, by being based in a large economy. As discussed shortly, poor markets not only hurt pensioners; they also may imply a worse allocation of investment than would occur with less formal ways of allocating savings to investment. The possibility of gain is also easy to comprehend, since better functioning capital markets increase economic efficiency and so economic growth. What is critical to the possibility of gain is a sustained effort to improve the regulation of markets and the functioning of the economy generally, an effort that may be enhanced by committing the funds of workers and so their political interests.

An alternative approach is to encourage voluntary pensions as a stimulus to market development, particularly where the economy is large enough that voluntary savings can reap economies of scale.

Exploring the issue in more detail, there are four channels through which savings are allocated to investment:

(a) market transactions—purchasing newly issued bonds and stocks (as opposed to trading existing ones);
(b) intermediation—deposits in banks and other intermediaries, which are then lent to investors;

(c) direct pairwise loans: to people starting small businesses from friends, families, and others seeking direct investments; to people one transacts with through trade credit; or through seller-provided credit more generally; and
(d) saving to finance ones own investment.

In a country where market structure is weak and the banking system functions poorly, progress is not likely to come through (a) or (b). Individual accounts, by taking more money from workers, cut down pairwise loans and workers' own investments, with no structures in place whereby pension funds could be allocated better in the short run.

A second set of arguments about the role of pension funds in improving the efficiency of capital markets is whether transferring shares of newly privatized state-owned enterprises to the social security trust fund (as in some of the former communist countries in Central and Eastern Europe) improves corporate governance, a key ingredient in economic efficiency and economic growth in market economies.[6] High-quality governance needs good legislation, effective oversight by the regulatory authorities, and effective oversight and exercise of voting rights by share owners. In advanced countries, centralized pension funds (e.g., defined-benefit or provident funds) can result in additional players in corporate governance, which can influence outcomes for better or worse.[7]

4.3.3 Funding and demographic change

Although the point was shown to be flawed many years ago, the argument that funding removes concern about the impact of demographic change on pension finance is wrong. The argument needs to be considered in the context of a decline in both fertility and elderly mortality.

Suppose that a large workforce is followed by a smaller workforce. In a pure PAYG system the revenue from a given social security contribution rate falls, creating upward pressure on the contribution rate, downward pressure on the level of pensions, or both. This problem is well understood and not controversial. Adding some funding, as has been done in the United States, can assist the adaptation to the changed demography through tax smoothing.

But even a fully funded system is affected by demographic change. Continuing with the example of a large workforce followed by a smaller

6. See the symposium on corporate governance in the *Oxford Review of Economics Policy*, vol. 21, no. 2 (2005).

7. The California Public Employees' Retirement System (CalPERS), for example, with over $150 billion in assets, takes an active shareholder interest.

one, we can consider the impact on the pension system. If each member of the large workforce in period one builds up pension savings; if the defined-contribution pension available for a representative worker is exactly what can be covered by those savings; and if there is a large number of such workers, this is not a problem, it is argued, because each worker accumulates enough, on average, to pay for his or her own pension. This argument is correct in terms of *finance* (i.e., the system is not out of balance) but may fail to provide workers with the *consumption* they expect in old age. The argument is set out more fully in box 4.2. With PAYG, the shortfall comes through a decline in pension contributions. With funding the mechanism is less direct but has

Box 4.2 How falling output affects holders of individual accounts

Falling output creates problems for individual accounts independent of whether the account holds cash-like assets or equities. If a large generation of workers is followed by a smaller one, suppose that pensioners of the large generation seek purchasing power over future production during their retirement by building up bank accounts. Their desired consumption (the amount that they wish to spend out of accumulated savings in retirement) may exceed what the smaller generation of workers wants to save, given fiscal and monetary policies. This can lead to excess demand in the goods market, causing price inflation, thus reducing the purchasing power of nominal annuities. Anticipation of the possibility of such an outcome will generally affect the interest rates used to attract bank deposits. Hence the impact of demography, which is visible to savers and investors, gets spread over a long time.

Suppose, instead, that workers seek purchasing power over future production by accumulating nonnominal assets, such as equities. In that case, as retirees they must finance their consumption by selling their financial assets. But because the next generation is smaller, there will be relatively less aggregate demand, hence less need for productive assets, leading to excess supply in asset markets, leading in turn to lower asset prices than if generations were of equal size. (To see this, suppose that every couple has one child; thus each couple of the next generation will inherit two apartments and, other things equal, apartment values will fall.)* This will reduce the value of pension accumulations and hence of the resulting annuity. In practice, asset prices would show slower growth (or even decline) much earlier, as investors anticipate the effect of asset sales by larger cohorts of retirees.

Under either outcome, retirees may not get the real pension they expected.

* We are indebted to András Simonovits for this example.

the same cause: unless a decline in the number of workers has no effect on output, output will be less than if the workforce had not shrunk; if output is less, consumption and/or investment must be less. Lower rates of return or higher prices would deny pensioners the consumption they expected; or the increase in the combined consumption of workers and pensioners is at the expense of investment and hence puts future growth at risk. As noted earlier, PAYG and funding are both mechanisms for organizing claims on future output; since demographic change generally affects that output, it generally causes problems for pension systems however they are organized.

An even closer parallel exists if the birth rate is stable but the life expectancy of pensioners increases. The effect is to increase the number of pensioners per worker. With pure PAYG this increase requires a higher contribution rate or lower monthly benefits to maintain the balance of the system. With funding and no change in interest rates, the sustainable level of monthly benefits is lower if the retirement lifetime is longer.

What matters is not financial accumulation, but increased output, which makes it easier to meet the claims of both workers and pensioners. The solution to population aging lies not in funding per se, but in output growth.

4.3.4 Funding and property rights

In a country with a public defined-benefit system, the legislature generally has the authority to change the benefit formula. Thus—for better or worse—protection for current and future beneficiaries comes from the properties of the political process, though the desire to be reelected and to avoid street demonstrations generally limits the extent to which politicians will make large, sudden downward changes in pension benefits and accruals.

It is sometimes argued that the political salience of property rights makes private individual funded accounts less prone to government depredation. The most recent contradictory example, discussed in section 9.1, is Argentina. In 2008, Argentina eliminated its system of mandatory individual accounts, transferring the assets to the government PAYG system. This illustrates a point that is too-often overlooked—that a fund accumulated over a number of years is a larger target for alternative government uses than the annual revenue flow of a PAYG system.

Even in countries where property rights are respected, having the assets in individual accounts does not eliminate the government's ability to lower the value of current or future pensions. This can happen in multiple ways. The government can:

- lower the value of government bonds through unexpected inflation;
- raise taxes on corporate profits, thus depressing stock values;

- increase taxes on incomes, including pensions, or on consumption spending, thus reducing the value of benefits to current and future retirees;
- reduce any tax advantages given to pension accumulations.

It is not uncommon for advocates of individual accounts to point to political risk with defined-benefit systems without mentioning the political risks with individual accounts.

In the United States, the taxation of Social Security benefits has been changed twice: in 1983, when up to 50 percent of benefits became taxable for some retirees, and again in 1993, when the taxable portion was raised to 85 percent for some of these already taxed retirees. Another example is the reduction of the tax privileges of U.K. pension funds in 1997. The tax rates and the income levels at which taxation starts are both variables that may properly be changed by legislation that is not a violation of property rights.

Thus the value of anticipated benefits can be changed by legislation, both in a national defined-benefit system and in a system where assets are held in individual accounts. Should this be regarded as a problem? Is the ability to change future benefits simply a source of risk to workers and retirees, or is it an opportunity to do a better job of sharing the risks inherent in pension systems—an opportunity that may be used well or badly? As discussed in chapter 5, whatever the other arguments for or against them, defined-benefit arrangements, unlike defined-contribution arrangements, have the ability to spread risks across cohorts. This spreading can have substantial value.

In sum, the role of property rights in protecting the expectations of workers and retirees is not as simple as some analysts would make it appear.

4.3.5 Conclusion

The relationship between funding and growth is neither simple nor automatic.

One: Does funding increase saving? As discussed, it will fail to do so if an increase in mandatory pension saving is offset by a decline in voluntary saving or a decline in the saving of government elsewhere in the budget. Thus saving may or may not increase; the amount of increased national savings has a complex relationship with the amount of increased funding and the way it is financed.

Two: How much will an increase in saving increase output? The simplest argument is that a move to funding (a) increases savings, which (b) increases investment, which (c) increases output by the marginal product of capital.

These links hold in many circumstances but not always or necessarily and not with a simple connection.

- As noted, a move to funding does not necessarily increase saving.
- The link between an increase in saving and increased investment is complex; some savings will simply increase prices of existing assets. Part of increased saving can drive up the prices of assets in limited supply, such as urban land.
- An increase in investment may not increase output by much. Inefficiencies in capital markets may make the marginal product of investment low, as in the communist countries in Central and Eastern Europe and the former Soviet Union, all of which had rates of investment that were exceptionally high by Western standards yet had growth that stagnated and in some countries turned negative. Moreover, returns on financial assets include an adjustment for bearing risk. Thus it is wrong to use financial returns as a measure of the return to society without incorporating an adjustment for differences in risk and administrative costs, and hence it is wrong to use the expected return on stocks as the gain from increased funding.

Three: Is such a policy optimal? That an increase in funding may increase output does not mean that the policy is necessary welfare improving. Beneficial effects will depend on country-specific features.

- Are savings in the country lower than optimal, and/or are pension funds likely to improve the allocation of savings or corporate governance?
- Intergenerational issues are another aspect of the previous point. Increased investment through increased funding implies lower consumption in the present. Thus funding that increases growth necessarily reduces current consumption and raises future consumption—redistribution that may or may not be good policy.

Four: Is such a policy feasible? The answer will depend in part on whether the country has the necessary institutions. Does it have the necessary skills in allocating pension funds, skills in administering pension accounts, and the capacity to regulate financial markets?

In sum, the argument is not that funding is bad policy, or that it cannot help with population aging, but that its helpfulness is contingent on beneficial effects on growth and on country-specific factors. Funding may be important for economic growth, but the case has to be made in each country, not just assumed or asserted.

4.4 Comparing the returns to PAYG and funding

Some analysts compare the long-run return on assets with the rate of growth, which is the long-run return in a PAYG system.

> In contrast to the 2.6-percent equilibrium return on Social Security contributions, the real pretax return on nonfinancial corporate capital averaged 9.3 percent over the same...period....[As a result], forcing individuals to use the unfunded system dramatically increases their cost of buying retirement income. (Feldstein 1996, p. 3)

Since long-run rates of return exceed growth rates, the higher stock market return is sometimes presented as a pure gain. This argument is flawed because it does not compare like with like. A fuller analysis considers (a) the costs of the transition from PAYG to funding, (b) the relative risks of the two systems, and (c) their respective administrative costs.

4.4.1 Inappropriate comparison of steady states

If proper account is taken of the costs of transition from a PAYG to a fully funded system there is generally an equivalence between the rates of return in the two systems.

The flaws in the argument that pensioners are better off under funding if the stock-market return exceeds real wage growth can be seen clearly if policymakers are considering establishing a pension system in a brand new world. In a funded system, in contrast with PAYG, the first generation of pension age will not receive a pension; thus it is mistaken to present the gain to pensioners after the first generation as gain to everyone (a Pareto improvement). Mostly, however, what is being discussed is a move from an existing PAYG system toward funding. In that case, including the transition costs of the change gives the same picture—some are helped and some are hurt. A central question, discussed in box 4.3, is where those costs will fall.

The fundamental point in box 4.3 is that there is a zero-sum game between the first and subsequent generations. The cost of the gift to the first generation can be placed entirely on the transition generation of pensioners (generation B) by reneging on PAYG promises; or entirely on the generation of workers at the time of transition (generation C) by financing generation B's pension out of taxation; or spread over succeeding generations by financing the transition through borrowing. It is possible to alter the time path of the cost but not its total. Again, the only way out of the impasse is if a move toward funding leads causally to higher rates of growth, an issue on which, as discussed earlier, controversy continues.[8]

8. The analysis in the text has considered a simple setting, in particular without taxes on the return to capital. Such taxes complicate the analysis but do not alter the need to consider winners and losers in any reform.

Box 4.3 Who pays the transition costs of a move from pay-as-you-go (PAYG) to funding?

Case 1: constant benefit rules; transition costs financed by public borrowing: in table 4.1, each generation pays $1 in contributions when young and receives $1 in pension when old. In period 1, the $1 pension of older generation A is paid by the $1 contribution of younger generation B. In period 2, when generation B is old, its pension is paid by the contributions of young generation C. Now suppose that the real rate of return on assets, i, is 10 percent, and imagine that we are generation C. Under a PAYG system we pay $1 in contribution in period 2 and receive $1 pension in period 3; the real rate of return is zero. In contrast, with an individual account we save $1 in period 2 and get back $1.10 in period 3; the real rate of return, it appears, is 10 percent.

The flaw in the argument is that if generation C contributes to its own funded accounts, generation B's pension must be paid from some other source. If that source is government borrowing, generation C receives a pension of $1.10 but has to pay interest of 10¢ on the borrowing that financed generation B's pension. The real return—as under PAYG—is zero. The lower return on the PAYG system is not the result of some inherent flaw but is precisely the cost of the initial gift to generation A. Formally, there is an equivalence between the two systems if the move to funding is considered not in isolation, but alongside the cost of financing the change. Thus generation C is not made better off by a move to individual accounts.

> Falling money's worth in this model is *not* due to the aging of baby boomers, increased life expectancy, or massive administrative inefficiency, but rather to the simple arithmetic of the pay-as-you-go system (Geanakoplos, Mitchell, and Zeldes, 1999, p. 86; emphasis in original).

Case 2: constant benefit rules; transition costs financed by taxation: suppose that we are generation C: in period 2 we put our contribution of $1

Table 4.1 A simplified pay-as-you-go system

	Generation			
Period	A	B	C	D
1	+$1	−$1		
2		+$1	−$1	
3			+$1	−$1
4				+$1

Source: Orszag 1999, p. 9.

(continued)

Box 4.3 (Continued)

into an individual funded account, and the $1 pension of generation B is paid in part from a tax on generation C. The pension we receive as generation C is $1.10. But generation C paid part of generation B's pension through a tax and so has less wealth to finance retirement. The real return on the assets is 10 percent, but this does not imply a return of 10 percent on the combination of the mandatory savings and the tax paid toward generation B's pensions.

Case 3: no benefits to the transition generation: another way to finance the transition is to throw generation B out of the lifeboat by not paying their pension at all. Generation C and onward enjoy a 10 percent real return, but those gains are at the expense of generation B, on whom the entire cost of transition is concentrated. In this case, the cost of the gift to generation A is offset by the negative gift to generation B.

As discussed in box 4.4, the improper comparison of steady states is a more serious error than is often realized.

4.4.2 Adjusting for differences in risk

The cost of financing the transition is only part of the comparison between PAYG and funding. A second element is risk, the key point being that the real return to PAYG and to funded systems should be adjusted downward to account for risk. The simplest approach to risk adjustment is to assume a bond rate of return on stocks, although this understates the value to those with no outside assets.

Alongside market risks are political risks, which are present with both kinds of systems. It is true that government action can increase risk through various forms of government failure. Equally, however, some adjustments by governments are precisely to address, at least partially, the risks that individuals face. Formal analysis of such political risks and how they differ across systems has not advanced very far.

4.4.3 Controlling for administrative costs

The evidence that the administrative costs of individual accounts are higher—often considerably higher—than PAYG systems is well established. The importance of administrative costs should not be underestimated. As shown in table 7.1, under plausible assumptions, over a working life, an annual administrative charge of 1 percent of a person's pension accumulation will reduce the total accumulation by about 20 percent.

Box 4.4 Inappropriate use of steady-state analysis: More than a trivial intellectual error

The errors that result from inappropriate use of steady-state analysis are more profound than is immediately apparent. Consider the following statement: "Some of the problems—such as the inevitability of intergenerational transfers and low rates of return to later cohorts—are inherent in pay-as-you-go systems" (World Bank 1994, p. 236). It is correct that PAYG systems, through their gift to the first generation, reduce the rate of return to later generations. However, the unqualified statement that this is a problem is mistaken.

First, in referring to the gift to the first generation as a "problem," the statement makes an implicit assumption that the transfer to the earlier, probably less well-off, generation was a mistake.

Second, the argument leads to invalid claims for the Pareto superiority (see glossary) of some policies. The point is most obvious if policymakers are establishing a brand new pension system where there was not one before. If they introduce a PAYG system, the first generation of retirees receives a pension, but returns to subsequent generations are lower; if they introduce funding, later generations benefit from higher returns, but the first generation does not receive a pension. Thus it is mistaken to present the gain to pensioners in later generations as a Pareto improvement, since it comes at the expense of the first generation. The same argument applies in a country that already has a PAYG system: a decision to move toward funding redistributes from the current generation to future generations. The claim that a move to funding is a Pareto improvement is invalid.

Finally, the argument is wrong in that it is generally optimal to have a PAYG element in a pension system because the resulting possibility of intergenerational risk sharing is welfare enhancing (see, for example, Dutta, Kapur, and Orszag 2000). The argument that paying off implicit pension debt is necessarily beneficial makes the same error.

4.4.4 Conclusion

In assessing proposals for pension reform a central analytical point is to be clear what question is being asked. Feldstein 2005, for example, argues that Social Security in the United States reduces savings. The analysis makes a steady-state comparison, that is, compares the economic situation in the United States today with what it would have been in an alternative steady state with funded pensions. Thus the underlying question is: how does welfare in steady-state B differ from that in steady-state A? Most of the analysis in this book is about a different question: what are the welfare effects of moving from steady-state A to steady-state B? Either question (and answer) is legitimate. What is not legitimate is to apply the answer from one question to the other; having a better steady state does not necessarily imply that it is worth the cost of moving to it.

The conclusion is not that a move to funding is always bad policy, but that its desirability cannot be established by simple comparison of rates of return.

- A move from PAYG toward funding should take proper account of the costs—both their total and their distribution—of transferring from one steady state to another, of differences in risk, and of any discrepancy in administrative costs.
- All three adjustments remain relevant to the choice of pension regime in a hypothetical new country where the issue of transition costs is replaced by the issue of whether to give benefits to people who have already retired or are close to doing so.

Atkinson (1999, p. 8) points out that critics of the welfare state tend to consider its costs without taking account of its benefits.

> The emphasis by economists on the negative economic effects of the welfare state can be attributed to the theoretical framework adopted..., which remains rooted in a model of perfectly competitive and perfectly clearing markets. [This] theoretical framework incorporates none of the contingencies for which the welfare state exists.... The whole purpose of welfare state provision is missing from the theoretical model.

The point here is precisely similar: that the benefits from a move to funding should not be considered in isolation, but alongside the relevant costs.

Chapter 5

Redistribution and Risk Sharing

There are many ways in which a country can raise the income of people who, for whatever reason, enter retirement with low pension benefits. Some countries offer a minimum income guarantee, such as means-tested social assistance for which all elderly people are eligible, whether covered by the pension system or not. The discussion here concentrates on the impact of the pension system itself on the income distribution, ignoring the complementary role of social assistance. In addition to direct poverty relief, public pension systems in some countries provide people on lower incomes, but who are not necessarily poor, with a pension that is a larger fraction of their previous earnings, so as to assist their consumption smoothing. As discussed in box 9.2, other countries use universal pensions, with their impact on poverty depending on the degree of targeting on poverty by age and the level of resources devoted to the pension. The underlying idea is that age can be a good indicator of poverty for the reasons set out in box 5.1.

This chapter discusses three aspects of redistribution and risk sharing: redistribution across generations (section 5.1), sharing risks (section 5.2), and adjusting pension systems over time, the mechanisms for which can have an important bearing on both redistribution and risk sharing (section 5.3).

Box 5.1 Targeting benefits: Income test or indicator targeting?

Well-targeted poverty relief should aim to assist everyone who is poor (sometimes referred to as horizontal efficiency) and only, or mainly, the poor (vertical efficiency). There are different ways of targeting benefits (see Barr 2004, pp. 217–19). In the present context two are especially relevant: income testing and indicator (or proxy) targeting. Another option, not discussed here, is self-targeting, which awards benefits on the basis of an incentive structure (for example, subsidies for goods consumed mainly by poor people or requiring time-consuming activities) that induces only the targeted population to claim the benefit.

Income testing seeks to identify poor people by their incomes. Its advantage is that, at its best, it can target benefits tightly. If the poverty line is, say, $100 per month, it is in principle possible to pay a benefit that brings the monthly incomes of poor people up to $100, thus spending nothing on anyone whose monthly income from any source is over $100.

Income testing, however, has significant disadvantages. If benefits are tightly targeted, as above, a person who receives an extra dollar from earnings or asset income loses a dollar in benefit. This creates a serious disincentive against work and saving. If benefits are less tightly targeted, either some people are not raised above the poverty line or some benefits are paid to people above the poverty line or both. In addition, income testing is typically based on family income, creating disincentives for family formation. Income testing is also administratively demanding, even in developed countries, and raises even more serious measurement problems in developing economies, where much income arises in the informal sector or through household production. Finally, in at least some countries the receipt of income-tested poverty relief and, in particular, the operation of the income test itself is regarded as stigmatizing.

Any use of income or asset testing to determine benefits weakens the incentive to save for old age. Indeed, one argument for mandatory retirement saving is that it limits the free riding that occurs when people choose not to save, given the larger transfers they will receive if they have few assets and, hence, little income from assets.

Indicator targeting seeks to identify the poor not by their income, but in terms of other indicators. The idea is best illustrated by example. Assume that only redheads are poor, that all redheads are poor, and that there is no hair-dyeing technology. In these circumstances it is theoretically possible completely to eliminate poverty, as defined by the poverty line, by paying a redhead benefit. Additionally, because benefits go only to the poor, expenditure is minimized, and because identification is easy, the administrative demands are small. Thus the ideal indicators are highly correlated with poverty, to ensure accurate targeting; beyond the control of the individual,

(continued)

Box 5.1 (Continued)

to minimize disincentives; and easy to observe, to assist administration. In practice, useful indicators are the presence of children in the family and sufficiently old age.

The great advantage of indicator targeting is that it avoids some of the worst effects of income testing. Although it can discourage saving for retirement (since people anticipate future pension benefits), it does so in a nondistorting way in that it does not alter the amount of income generated by additional saving. But the approach is no panacea. First, as with all transfers, benefits are financed from distortionary taxes. In addition, measurable characteristics are in practice not perfectly correlated with poverty: some benefits will go to people who have the relevant characteristic but are not poor but not to some people who lack the relevant characteristic but are in fact poor. And the indicator, for example, age, may not be accurately measured. Finally, the use of family structure to determine either eligibility or the benefit level again creates disincentives for family formation. Thus in practice, a system based on indicator targeting needs to be supplemented by a system of income-tested benefits.

Some programs do exactly this, for example, paying disability benefits only to poor people and earnings-related benefits only to people with children. The United States has two disability programs, one for covered workers that is not income tested and one for poor people that is.

In developing countries (see Coady, Grosh, and Hoddinot 2004), a pension awarded on the basis of age can be implemented without heavy administrative requirements; in particular, the approach avoids the need to keep a history of contributions. Such a pension will generally be well targeted and, if pensionable age is sufficiently high, may also be fiscally feasible.

5.1 Sharing burdens across generations

As discussed in section 4.3.1 and boxes 4.3 and 4.4, choices between PAYG and funding (or the degree of funding more generally) are inescapably also choices about the intergenerational distribution of income. If the additional resources generated by any increase in savings are used to raise future benefits or to reduce future contributions, the policy redistributes across cohorts.

To evaluate whether such redistribution is worthwhile, one needs to consider not only the return on the additional capital but also the extent to which consumption would have grown anyway. One also needs to consider the distribution within each cohort of the decreases in consumption now as well as the increases in the future.

More specifically, consider increasing the contribution rate now so as to have a lower contribution rate later. Workers, paying a higher contribution rate, have lower consumption. Later workers, paying a lower contribution rate, have higher consumption. How should we evaluate this redistribution from today's workers to later cohorts of workers? There are three parts to the comparison.

- How much does each worker value the change in consumption? With diminishing marginal utility, the higher the level of consumption the lower the value of an increase. Thus, moving consumption into the future is less valuable to future pensioners after rapid growth than after slower growth in consumption. Similarly, a country with a high savings rate has a low consumption rate today relative to its income. If the savings rate is lower in the future, as the country moves to a higher living standard, then again the increase in consumption lowers the gain from delaying consumption.
- The greater the investment needs of the country, the greater the marginal product of capital is likely to be, assuming adequate markets for allocating investment. But a country with a high savings rate, and so a high investment rate, is likely already to be investing in opportunities with the highest rates of return. Thus the return to yet higher rates of saving may not be so high.
- The pure public weighting of different cohorts: it is common to discount across cohorts as well as, separately, discounting for consumption during a worker's life.

These distributional effects across cohorts should not be ignored in evaluating proposals for pension reform. Equally, they should not be ignored in interpreting past reforms: an earlier decision to use PAYG pensions (as in the United States after 1935 and the United Kingdom after 1946) raises the consumption of the elderly by providing more in benefits than their own contributions could finance and thus implies less investment at the time and so lower consumption later. This is not an unanticipated or unlucky outcome of policy but a necessary part of the implied redistribution.

5.2 Sharing risks

5.2.1 Benefit design and risk sharing

Different pension designs share risks differently. As discussed in section 2.2.3, there are wide differences between pure systems. In a pure defined-contribution system the individual faces most or all of the risks discussed in section 2.3. In a pure defined-benefit system the risks are borne by the sponsor (an employer or taxpayers for a public system). In practice, however, systems differ from the pure cases both in design and in adjustments (including government guarantees in defined-contribution systems and adjustment of benefits—sometimes even benefits in payment—in defined-benefit systems). It is important also that through government saving and borrowing, risks can be shared with future generations. With social insurance or (partial or total) tax finance, the institutional structure should be designed explicitly to spread risk, rather than being an afterthought for poor outcomes.

5.2.2 Indexing pension benefits to prices or wages

The way that pensions are indexed also has important implications for sharing risk. Section 3.1.3 discussed how benefits at retirement are determined from a worker's previous earnings. Here we discuss the way benefits are indexed after a worker has retired.

If benefits were based on nominal earnings, a worker's initial real benefit would bear an erratic relationship to past earnings, depending on the pattern of past inflation rates. If benefits themselves were set in nominal terms, real benefits would decline over time and in an erratic pattern, as inflation rates vary. This section considers proper and improper ways of indexing pensions, discussing in turn

- what indexation rules should apply to a worker's history of earnings or contributions in determining the worker's initial benefit;
- what indexation rules should apply after initial benefits are determined; and
- some problems that can arise from faulty rules.

INDEXING A WORKER'S HISTORY OF EARNINGS OR CONTRIBUTIONS. A defined-benefit system relates benefits to a worker's history of earnings (or, in the case of NDC plans, contributions). Typically, as described above, an average is taken of earnings in some number of highest earnings years or across all years. To avoid the ill effects of subjecting benefits to the vagaries of inflation, benefits can be indexed in one of two pure ways or in a mix:

- *Price indexation:* If a worker's past earnings are indexed to changes in prices (such a system is known as a real system), then initial real benefits are based on the worker's history of real earnings. Thus the initial pension depends on the worker's nominal earnings in each of a number of years, adjusted by the increase in the price level from each year up to the year when initial benefits are calculated.
- *Wage indexation:* In a wage-indexed system, initial benefits are based on the history of a worker's earnings in each year relative

to economywide average earnings in that year. Thus the initial pension depends on the worker's earnings and on average earnings in each year.

- One way to have a mix of price and wage indexation is to use a proper weighted average of the price and wage indexes (defined below), as in Finland.

The relationship between benefit levels and the method of indexation is not simple. For a given benefit formula, if real wage growth is positive, a worker's initial benefit generally will be higher with wage indexation than with price indexation. In practice, however, a country chooses an indexing method and a benefit formula together. Thus, even though past earnings upgraded by wage growth will typically be larger than past earnings upgraded by price growth, the pension need not be larger if the formula is different. If two systems, one price-indexed and one wage-indexed, would give equal benefits on average for a cohort, some workers will do better under one system and some under the other. Those with relatively higher earnings early in their careers will do better with wage indexing, which gives more weight to earlier years, and those with relatively higher earnings late in their careers will do better with price indexing. Matters are yet more complex if the system of indexation is faulty.

If the benefit formula is stable across cohorts, and if the rate of wage growth varies over time, wage indexation will tend to result in the same replacement rate (relative to final pay) across cohorts, whereas price indexation will produce varying replacement rates. But a full analysis would need to take account of possibly shifting relative wages of cohorts that overlap in the labor market (and so in the determination of average wages), which would be far more complicated.

With a funded or notional defined-contribution system, benefits depend also on the pattern of earnings.

- With a funded system, the impact of contributions on benefits depends on the cumulative rate of return on assets from the date of contributing to the date at which the benefit is determined. Since returns on assets tend to be larger than rates of wage growth, this gives more weight to early years than with a wage-indexed defined-benefit system.
- With a notional system, the weighting of different years depends on the notional interest rate. This might equal the growth of average wages or the growth of the wage bill. The former is the same as with a wage-indexed defined-benefit system. The latter is anticipated to be smaller in countries anticipating a shrinking labor force.

INDEXING PENSIONS AFTER RETIREMENT. In some developed countries, benefits after retirement are indexed to inflation rates, in some to the change in average wage rates, and in some to a proper weighted average of the two ("proper" meaning that the weights sum to one). For example, in Finland benefits increase at 80 percent of the growth of prices and 20 percent of the growth of wages. Another approach is illustrated by Sweden, where benefits are indexed to wage growth minus 1.6 percentage points. The choice of an index involves two related issues: the average expected rate of increase in benefits over a retiree's remaining life and the risk characteristics of different methods of adjustment. (The discussion here does not consider adjusting benefits for changes in life expectancy, a topic discussed in section 5.3.1.)

The choice of indexation method has wide-ranging implications.

Cost v. adequacy. For a given initial pension, the more rapidly benefits grow, the more expensive the system; the less rapidly they grow, the further retirees fall behind average living standards over time. Thus price indexation places greater emphasis on containing costs and preserving purchasing power; wage indexation, on the relative adequacy of benefits. Policy needs to strike a balance between these two concerns while recognizing their different distributional impacts. Moreover, wage-indexed benefits will be more variable in real terms than price-indexed benefits. Thus the ability of retirees to bear risk is also relevant.

Another way to think about the growth of benefits is to recognize that, at a given long-run cost, there is a trade-off between the average level of initial benefits and the rate of growth of benefits thereafter: the more rapidly benefits grow, the lower the initial replacement rate must be to hold costs constant. This is how initial benefits are determined in a system that sets initial benefits on an actuarial (or quasi-actuarial) basis, for example, in funded defined-contribution systems that purchase annuities from insurance companies, and in the NDC system in Sweden as well.

Distributional effects. Since workers differ in life expectancy, different combinations of initial benefit levels and growth rates of benefits with the same aggregate long-run costs will affect different workers differently. Those with shorter expected lives will prefer higher initial benefits with slower subsequent growth. Both men and women with higher earnings tend to live longer than others of the same sex; thus the choice of growth rate of benefits has important ex ante distributional effects. Since on average women live longer than men, there is also the issue of gender equity. Some workers may make their retirement decision based on initial benefits rather than paying adequate attention to their entire future. This focus of attention may be encouraged by newspaper reports of initial benefit levels. For such workers, a lower benefit that grows faster may encourage later retirement.

Poverty relief. The pattern of measured poverty among the elderly depends on design features of the pension system and on how poverty is measured—whether poverty is measured in absolute or relative terms. The choice of indexation method affects relative consumption, that is, of retirees relative to that of workers. Since wages tend to rise faster than prices, a given real benefit over time declines relative to average wages.[1] In the absence of other sources of antipoverty insurance, an increase in pension benefits over time may be useful, for example, to finance long-term care.[2]

There is an association between aging and poverty in the United States due primarily to the increasing number of widows as a cohort ages rather than to a pure aging effect, family structure held constant. Generally, poverty will be affected by the rules governing survivor benefits.

Risk. Wages tend not only to rise faster than prices but also to fluctuate more than prices. Thus the choice of method of indexation also has a risk dimension. Consider two systems with the same initial benefit, one that is price-indexed and one (similar to Sweden's) that is indexed to the change in wages minus a constant set equal to the anticipated growth rate of real wages. The two systems have the same expected cost but different degrees of risk. Choosing a wage index minus a constant, meant to keep retirees in roughly the same position, involves the real possibility that the chosen constant will not track average real wage growth over a period of a decade or even longer and may stray far from it. Historically, some countries have seen extended periods with quite different real wage growth. Thus the use of real wages minus a constant involves more risk than a weighted average of price and wage changes with the same expected cost.

That additional risk matters. It is good to share risks widely, but those who are more risk averse should bear less of the aggregate risk. Employed workers have a greater capacity to bear risk than retirees: they can adjust both their earnings and their consumption, and because their remaining life expectancies are longer, they can more easily smooth consumption following an unexpected income shock, by making smaller adjustments over more years. These considerations suggest that if benefits adjust by less than wages, this should be done through a mix of price and wage indexation rather than by relying on wages less a constant.

POTENTIAL PROBLEMS. What is clear is that the real value of a person's pension benefit should not vary erratically with the level of inflation, all the more because inflation rates can vary significantly across years, even consecutive

1. From the late 1980s the U.K. basic state pension was indexed to prices and thus fell increasingly behind average earnings. The more widespread poverty among pensioners that resulted was one impetus for the creation of the U.K. Pensions Commission.

2. On the financing of long-term care see chapter 5 of Barr 2001.

years. If pensions are fully indexed for price inflation, their real purchasing power is preserved, but over time retirees will fall increasingly behind general living standards, assuming wage growth exceeds inflation. If instead pensions are indexed to nominal wage growth, they will be adjusted for inflation insofar as wages keep up with inflation and will preserve the position of retirees relative to workers; however, since over time wage growth generally exceeds inflation, the system will be more expensive for a given level of initial benefits. In this situation there is some risk sharing between workers and retirees over the impact of inflation on wages, at least in the long run. Either of these rules, or a proper weighted average, is reasonable, given different objectives. What is not reasonable is to use improper weights when indexing for inflation, that is, weights that do not add up to one. As discussed in section 10.2, this is the case in China. Boxes 5.2 and 5.3 give two illustrations of other faulty methods of indexation that were (but are no

Box 5.2 Overindexing initial benefits for inflation: United States, 1972–77

Faulty indexation can affect both a person's initial pension and the increase in benefits in payment. The experience of the United States in the 1970s provides an example of the former. Box 5.3 has an example of the latter.

Before 1973, the U.S. Social Security system did not adjust benefits automatically in response to inflation. Instead, Congress periodically voted changes in the benefit formula to reflect concern about the extent to which prices had risen since the previous change. These changes applied both to benefits paid and to the formula for future initial benefits. Legislation in 1972 called for automatic adjustment for inflation, both of initial benefits and benefits in payment, roughly incorporating the practice that Congress had previously followed. As a result, the benefit formula used a worker's average nominal earnings while also increasing the benefit formula for inflation. So high inflation affected benefits in two ways: directly through changes in the benefit formula and indirectly to the extent that higher inflation raised wages.

This overindexing was recognized at the time of the legislation, but it was thought that the progressivity in the benefit formula would be sufficient to offset the rising cost. Although the method would have kept costs in line with projections had inflation remained within a narrow band, actual inflation was rapid. As a result, the real value of benefits grew far more rapidly than Congress had intended, contributing to a financing crisis. The system remained overindexed until legislation enacted in 1977 introduced wage indexing of initial benefits while continuing price indexing of benefits in payment.

Box 5.3 Overindexing benefits in payment for inflation: United Kingdom, 1975–80

The United Kingdom provides an example of faulty indexing after initial benefits have been determined. Under 1975 legislation, the U.K. basic state pension was indexed to the higher of wage growth or inflation but with each year's decision made strictly on its own. Thus, if wages doubled in year 1 with no change in prices, and prices doubled in year 2 with no change in wages, real wages afterward would not have changed, but the pension would have doubled in year 1 (in line with wages) and again in year 2 (in line with prices). This created an unintended upward bias, which was significant given the high rates of wage and price changes in the later 1970s.

longer) used in the United States and United Kingdom. Also of concern is the use of a cap on the extent to which benefits adjust to inflation. Although this may assist the finances of the system, a cap undercuts the social purpose of indexing.

Proper indexing avoids this sort of erratic response to inflation. Depending on concerns about the initial level of benefits, the relationship between benefits and average wages, variation in life expectancy, and the financing available for pensions, different countries can reasonably make different choices.

5.3 Adjusting pension systems over time

How should a pension system be adjusted to reflect differences across cohorts, considering, for example, that people born later are likely to have higher earnings and longer lives? Specifically, how should the relationship between contributions and benefits vary, and how should the earliest eligibility age and the adjustments for early and late retirement vary? We discuss adjustments with respect to greater life expectancy, a changing labor force (notably the effects of declining fertility), and changing social risks.

5.3.1 Adjusting for longer life expectancy

Although mortality rates are likely to continue to decline, there is debate about the speed of the decline. History suggests that, even if current projections are on average accurate over long periods, significant deviations should be expected from time to time. In 1981 the U.K. Government Actuary projected that male life expectancy at 65 in 2004 would be 14.8 years; it turned out to be 19 years, an error of 28 percent. Thus the second report of the U.K. Pensions Commission (2005, p. 90) notes that

> around the 2003-based [Government Actuary's Department] principal projection of life expectancy for a man aged 65 in 2050 of 21.7 there was a wide and asymmetric range of uncertainty stretching at least from 20.0 to 29.0, but with small probabilities of still wider divergence.... It is therefore essential that both state pension policy and occupational pension provision, in both the public and private sectors, is designed to be robust not just in the face of increasing life expectancy but of major uncertainty about how fast that increase will proceed.

Thus projected mortality improvements face a widening funnel of doubt about future outcomes. If current legislation sets future adjustment factors, they generally will not match actual mortality rates. It is, of course, always possible to change the adjustment factors. But legislating change may be difficult and may include an asymmetric transition: slow if larger benefit decreases are needed but rapid if smaller benefit decreases are sufficient and can be financed. Thus there is considerable advantage in designing a system that, at least up to a point, responds automatically as uncertain outcomes eventuate. For example, in its NDC system, Sweden includes automatic indexing for benefits at the earliest eligibility age and for the increase in benefits for delayed retirement but has not included automatic adjustment of the earliest eligibility age itself.[3] A further issue is that mortality improvements in the United States (and presumably elsewhere) have not occurred at the same rate across the earnings spectrum. Those with higher lifetime earnings, among both men and women, have enjoyed more rapid improvements in mortality than lower earners of the same gender. This issue is particularly important when considering the earliest eligibility age and is a further complication in trying to predict the future. Changes in the distribution of mortality are of limited importance for their effect on the costs of a pension system but are of considerable importance for the distribution of sensible retirement ages and, so, for the choice of earliest eligibility age.

In a defined-contribution system an increase in life expectancy has no effect on the finances of the system, since benefits at any given age are lowered to meet the level that can be financed. If people continue to retire at the same age as those in earlier cohorts with lower life expectancy, replacement rates will be lower if rates of return are the same. Individuals can offset this effect by

3. Thus the endogenous variable is not the earliest pensionable age, but the size of the pension. In a world of rationality this would not be an issue. However, a person whose personal discount rate exceeds the rate of actuarial adjustment of the pension will retire as soon as possible, creating potential pensioner poverty. Thus consideration needs to be given to adjusting the minimum pensionable age as well.

working proportionally longer. But historically they have not done so: retirement has been a normal good, that is, one for which demand increases as people's incomes rise; thus retirement ages have generally decreased until recently, and growth of female labor force participation has not been rapid enough to represent a fully offsetting trend. Since on their own accord many workers may not respond to longer life expectancy by working longer, an increase in the earliest entitlement age may help to protect some workers from retiring too soon. Reconsideration of the contribution rate may be warranted as well.

With a defined-benefit system, increased life expectancy has an adverse effect on pension finances if there is no adjustment for life expectancy. If the increase in benefits for the age at which they start is roughly actuarial, this adverse impact is not helped by longer average careers. Indeed, adjustments to benefits can become too large as life expectancy rises. Thus a defined-benefit system needs to adjust the benefit formula.

A process of automatic adjustment that relies heavily on projected mortality rates could easily become politicized. Thus a system may function better if it adjusts benefits on the basis of realized mortality information. In Sweden this is done by using historic mortality data in calculating pensions, with no adjustment for anticipated improvements in mortality after a cohort has retired. Another approach is through year-by-year adjustments based on year-by-year changes in mortality.

When aligning a system over time to changing life expectancies, several separate (and fully separable) instruments are available. It is possible to

- reduce the average monthly benefit at the earliest eligibility age to reflect the increased cost of providing given benefits as life expectancy increases. This can be done automatically and is so done in defined-contribution systems that rely on market provision of annuities;
- raise the earliest eligibility age over time, either automatically or through periodic review, thus reducing the average duration of benefits while removing the offsetting increase in the monthly benefit for a start delayed past the previous earliest entitlement age. This combines the first option with an increase in earliest eligibility age;
- adjust the increase in benefits for later retirement; since the value of an increase in benefits is greater when remaining life expectancy is longer, the increase in the benefit for delaying retirement by one year might be reduced as life expectancy increases.[4]

4. A typical plan adds a fixed percentage of earliest or full benefits for each year by which the start of benefits is delayed. This results in a declining percentage increase of currently eligible benefits as a worker ages. A constant percentage increase would result from *multiplying* the benefit by one plus a fixed percentage increase rather than from *adding* a fixed percentage. However, mortality rates increase with age, and so the percentage addition to benefits should rise if the aim is to provide actuarial adjustment.

However, it is not necessary, and neither does it seem optimal in all circumstances, to place all adjustment on the side of benefits. An additional option is to

- increase contributions.

The increase can be indexed to the cost of increased life expectancy.

The first and third options were the choice of policymakers in Sweden and are inherent in a standard, fully funded, defined-contribution system, such as Chile's. The first option was also one of the proposals for the U.S. Social Security system put forward by the commission appointed by President George W. Bush. The second option is being pursued for the basic state pension in the United Kingdom. A different approach would combine the first option with an increase in contributions, the balance of the two depending on the existing contribution level and available resources. This has been proposed for the United States, where contribution and replacement rates are low by international standards, by Diamond and Orszag (2005*a*, 2005*b*). In general, it is likely to be good policy to make use of a range of these instruments.

As discussed in section 3.2.3, adjusting the earliest eligibility age raises complex issues because the factors determining how many workers gain and how many lose from such a change vary not only with increases in average life expectancy and the average level of earnings but also according to individual circumstances and decisions. A simple rule making the earliest eligibility age proportional to life expectancy has advantages in terms of transparency but may be suboptimal in theoretical terms: people are living longer, adding to the cost of pensions, but that effect is partially offset by the fact that people are better off than in the past and so can afford to spend more on retirement; and, as noted, improvements in life expectancy can be very different across income classes. Thus periodic adjustment of the earliest eligibility age—perhaps based on recommendations from a nonpartisan commission—may be better than automatic adjustment. Or a given change in life expectancy may be presumed to call for an adjustment while still requiring legislation to enact it.

Once a government has decided to adjust pension benefit and eligibility rules regularly, the decision should be implemented on the basis of the principles set out in box 5.4.

5.3.2 Adjusting for a changing labor force

Apart from the postwar baby boom period in some countries, there has been a long-term declining trend in fertility rates in much of the world. For some of that time, declining child mortality more than offset the decline in fertility,

Box 5.4 Principles for adjusting pensionable age

If benefits and eligibility are to be adjusted for mortality changes, automatic adjustment should be based on three principles.

- The rules should relate to date of birth, not to the date of retirement; otherwise there will be a wave of retirements just before any reduction in the generosity of benefits goes into effect. Such an incentive to retire is inefficient.
- Changes should be made annually to avoid large changes in benefit levels across nearby cohorts. Large changes are inequitable and politically difficult, since benefits could differ significantly between people born in successive years, sometimes only days apart. The combination of large changes and rules determined by date of retirement would exacerbate the inefficient incentive to early retirement.
- As far as is sensible, rules for changing benefits should be explicit. The case for explicit rules for adjusting benefit levels as life expectancy changes is clear, since the cost of benefits depends primarily on life expectancy. Automatic adjustment with explicit rules leads to greater predictability and decreased political pressure. Automatic adjustments may function better if based on actual mortality outcomes rather than projections. Nevertheless, as with the indexation of income tax brackets, there always remains the option of legislation to change whatever the automatic rules produce.

The case for an explicit rule automatically adjusting the earliest eligibility age is weaker than the case for periodic reevaluation, since the normative analysis of the choice depends on much more than just life expectancy.

The legislated increase in women's pensionable age in the United Kingdom, announced in 1991, illustrates all three of the above principles. The key date is April 6, 1950. For women born before that date, the state pensionable age will continue to be 60. The pensionable age for a woman born on May 6, 1950 (one month after the key date) will be 60 years and one month, which will occur in 2010, 19 years after the legislation; for a woman born on June 6, 1950, 60 years and two months, and so on. For women born on or after April 6, 1955, the pensionable age will be 65.

leading to rapid growth of the working-age population. But in many countries child mortality rates are now sufficiently low that the scope for further decline is limited, and consequently growth of the labor force is slowing, a trend that we anticipate will continue.

Such a slowdown affects the economy in general and pension systems in particular. If that were the only change, it would be expected to lead over time to higher wages and lower rates of return on assets (see the discussion in box 4.2). In practice, however, the impact of slower labor force growth on the age-earnings profile or on the growth of wages across cohorts is not simple. Some analysts have hypothesized that an older labor force will result in slower technical progress and particularly less of what is called learning-by-doing. In addition, for the next few decades those effects may be more than offset by the effects of globalization. Meanwhile, empirical studies have found little reliable connection between demography and rates of return. Nevertheless, one can consider how an economy should react to a fall in interest rates. We begin by considering a fully funded defined-contribution system before going on to analyze a less than fully funded defined-benefit system.

With a fully funded defined-contribution system, if interest rates fall while everything else remains the same, workers are less able to replace earnings levels after retirement, since retirement consumption becomes more expensive relative to earlier earnings—more savings will be needed to finance a given level of replacement rate at a given age. Although there could be a legislated increase in mandated saving rates, there will be no financial pressure for such a change, apart from a possible increase in the cost of providing a minimum pension. The same conclusion holds for the earliest eligibility age. In the absence of an increase in the mandate, some people would save more, others not, and some people would work longer, others not. By its nature, a fully funded defined-contribution system does not redistribute across cohorts and might continue that pattern.

With a partially funded defined-benefit system, in the absence of automatic adjustments, a slowdown in the rate of growth of the labor force has both a direct impact on the financing of the pension system and an indirect effect insofar as there is a decline in interest rates. Thus some response is necessary: reduce benefit levels, raise contribution rates, raise ages of eligibility (with no compensating adjustment in benefit levels), or use a mix of these policies. The direct effect can be addressed automatically in an NDC system by relating benefits to the growth in the total wage bill (as opposed to the growth in average wages), by including a "braking mechanism" reducing benefits when liabilities outstrip explicit and implicit assets (as in Sweden), or by adjusting benefits for the dependency ratio (as in Germany). As to the indirect effect, with lower interest rates a given increase in consumption today costs less in terms of lower consumption in the future. Other things being equal, this lessens the value of funding. Since a less-than-fully funded system got that way by redistributing across cohorts, a legislative package should take account of the further redistribution inherent in any change in policy.

5.3.3 Adjusting for changing social risks

As stressed repeatedly, pension systems have multiple objectives that extend beyond consumption smoothing. For example, Chile, which has a fully funded defined-contribution system, also provides poverty relief, historically through a minimum pension guarantee and from July 2008 through a noncontributory basic pension; there also are legislated constraints on the speed with which a family may draw down its pension accumulation, and life and disability insurance are available to help protect families. In the United States, as discussed in boxes 6.1 and 6.2, Social Security provides supplementary benefits for spouses, surviving spouses, and divorced former spouses. Interestingly, in Sweden the separate parts of the pension system treat spouses in different ways: the funded system allows individuals to purchase joint-life annuities with their accumulations, whereas the NDC system does not. Many countries have benefits for surviving spouses, with a wide variety of rules covering eligibility and benefit levels.[5]

The circumstances leading to such rules change over time, as do social attitudes. Rates of marriage, divorce, and remarriage have changed. Attitudes toward cohabitation and same-sex marriage also have changed. Male and female life expectancies have diverged and may diverge further (or become more similar) in the future. The level of a minimum guarantee thought to be socially appropriate may shift relative to average earnings. It is natural to think that changing circumstances and attitudes call for changes in the details of pension systems. But we have seen no proposals calling for automatic responses to measurable changes of this kind, and we have none to offer. Thus we simply note that it may be useful from time to time to review the design of pension systems relative to social objectives—and that such a review may be easier politically when combined with adjustments needed to accommodate, or made possible by, changes in the financial position of the system. In the United States, for example, reforms made necessary by financial shortfalls—and, in earlier years, reforms made possible by financial surpluses—have both been recognized as times to address certain social issues. Thus, for example, the commission appointed by President Bush called for greater financial protection for some vulnerable groups along with broad benefit cuts to address the projected financial shortfall. Our focus here has been to point out the value of reviewing the details of pension systems that relate to social objectives, not to discuss such objectives directly; we discuss some of the issues related to male-female differences in chapter 6.

5. We draw a distinction between a temporary widow benefit for an adjustment period and a benefit that lasts from retirement age until death.

Chapter 6

Gender and Family

Living arrangements are diverse, and a person's living arrangements change over time. At any given time there are adults who are single and living alone, others who are single and sharing housing and other consumption, and others who are married or in other unions that governments recognize in different ways. Married couples differ in the extent to which they share resources. Some stay married until one of them dies, other marriages end in divorce after varying lengths of time, and many people remarry after a divorce or the death of a spouse. This chapter explores some of the implications for the design of pensions posed by these living arrangements. Section 6.1 frames the issues, and section 6.2 discusses general aspects of pension design. Thereafter discussion turns to pension credits for child care (6.3), individual versus family pensions (6.4), survivor pensions (6.5), and divorce (6.6). Section 6.7 offers some conclusions.

6.1 Framing the issues

THE BACKDROP. Three types of government programs recognize living arrangements in different ways, both across programs within a country and across countries:

- *Transfers of income or of goods and services in kind (or both) to poor people:* Such programs take into consideration the incomes of spouses and in some cases also the presence of others sharing living arrangements.

- *Taxes to provide general revenue:* Countries differ in the extent to which taxes are based separately on the individual earnings and capital income of each spouse or allow or require recognition of the earnings and capital incomes of both spouses so that couples pay different amounts of tax in total than if they were single.
- *Pension systems:* Countries differ in how their public pension systems treat couples. Some require joint-life annuitization (see glossary); in others decisions about the type of annuity are voluntary. In some systems the public pension is based only on a person's individual record; in others the public pension takes account of a person's marital status.

All of these programs need to combine various equity and efficiency concerns. As the 2006 Report of the Chilean Presidential Advisory Council, discussed in section 10.1, put it, there is a need to recognize both personal autonomy and solidarity within the family, "recognizing that women have their own rights as citizens and not only rights derived from their position in the family."

In this chapter we examine how the rules of pension systems can affect men and women differently, focusing on three aspects:

- whether the pension system has different rules for men and women (this was common historically, but many countries have changed their rules in the direction of uniformity);
- how, even if they are uniform, rules can affect men and women differently on average; and
- how governments recognize that many individuals live as couples, sharing resources to varying degrees and later bequeathing them.

Because the labor market behavior and outcomes (labor force participation and wage rates, for example) of men and women tend to differ, uniform pension rules typically lead to different distributions of pension outcomes for the two sexes. For example, in the United Kingdom in 2005, about 85 percent of recent male retirees were entitled to a full basic state pension (which at the time required over 40 years of contributions or contribution credits); the comparable figure for women was 30 percent. In addition, the overall financial positions of men and women in old age tend to be quite different. In most countries poverty in old age is more common among women, especially widows and divorcees. Since women have longer life expectancies and typically are younger than their husbands, women are more likely then men to be the survivor of a couple, and so the pension treatment of survivors is an important element in differences in the impact of pensions by gender.

PUBLIC POLICY AND FAMILY BEHAVIOR. The design of taxes and pensions inescapably affects the behavior of family members in a wide variety of ways, of which the following are only examples (to put it more bluntly, it is not possible to have a policy that does not affect incentives in these and other areas):

- Gender-neutral tax rates have different effects on husbands and wives, on average, because men and women have different labor supply elasticities.
- Consumption behavior can differ depending on whether benefits are paid to the husband or the wife. For example, evidence suggests that if child benefits are paid to the mother rather than the father a greater fraction will be spent on children.
- Policy design can encourage or discourage marriage. Taxes may be higher or lower on two people if they remain single than if they marry. Similar issues can arise with pensions.
- Policy design can encourage or discourage mothers with young children from taking paid work, depending on the design of child-care subsidies or income tax deductions, the length of school hours, and the employment rules applicable to people with small children. Also relevant is the subsidized provision of pension credits for those caring for young children.

RESULTING QUESTIONS. These policy impacts suggest a series of questions, the answers to many of which are outside the remit of this chapter:

- How is consumption shared within the family? How should it be shared?
- How should the earnings of husband and wife be taxed?
- How much should taxes, current benefits (such as subsidized child care or child benefits), and future benefits (such as pensions) encourage mothers with young children to accept paid work or discourage them from doing so?
- Should taxes and benefits be designed to encourage marriage? If other policy goals can be met only by rules that discourage marriage (for example, if some benefits are lost upon marriage), how much weight should be given to that disincentive when designing such policies?
- How do the policy rules affect the outcomes for children?
- How should survivor pensions be organized?
- How should pensions be arranged for couples who divorced?

IMPLICATIONS. The primary reason for posing these questions is to make it clear that none of them has an unambiguous answer. Adopting horizontal equity (see glossary) as a starting point restricts the range of policy options, but the remaining set of policies is still very wide. And horizontal equity has multiple definitions. As with other aspects of pension design, therefore, the task is to optimize in terms of the weights given to different objectives; and since those weights reflect differences in individual tastes and in social values (for example, between paid work and care activities), views about policy are likely to differ more over gender issues than for other aspects of pensions. The matter is complicated because often it is not clear whether a particular outcome, for example, a woman forgoing paid work to look after young children, is the result of choice or constraint.

The conclusion to which this leads is that, in this aspect of pensions as in others, there is not—and cannot be—a single optimal policy that applies to all countries. The rest of this chapter has the more modest aim of discussing policy options that make sense in different contexts, with no pretense at identifying a definitive set of answers.

6.2 The design of pension systems

The overrepresentation of women among the elderly poor arises in part because of their lower earnings and fewer and smaller contributions while of working age and in part from their greater likelihood of surviving their husbands than vice versa. The latter is important because the fraction of the family's pension benefits that continue after the death of a spouse may not be sufficient to maintain the survivor's consumption and also because ill health in old age—particularly if it involves long-term care—can be financially costly for the family. In this context, the design of survivor pensions matters.

CONTRIBUTORY PENSIONS VERSUS NONCONTRIBUTORY UNIVERSAL PENSIONS. Some countries provide a pension benefit for which eligibility or the size of the benefit is conditional on the number of years of residence in the country; in others the benefit depends on the number of years of contributions to the pension system. Rules based on residence tend to result in larger pensions for women relative to men than do rules based on contributions.

CONTRIBUTION REQUIREMENTS. Some countries give no benefit unless a person has contributed for at least a minimum number of years (10 years in the case of U.S. Social Security), whereas others provide benefits after any contribution. Since women on average contribute for fewer years than men, the latter approach tends to provide at least some pension for more women.[1] For the same reason, the fewer the years of contributions necessary to qualify for a full benefit, the (relatively) higher the pensions that women tend to get. In Chile eligibility for the guaranteed minimum pension used to require 20 years of contributions, a level reached by relatively more men than women. (On reforms of the Chilean system, see section 10.1.)

A provision that years spent in child care count toward meeting contribution requirements, discussed in section 6.3, helps women, relatively speaking. The U.K. government has announced that it "will radically reform the contributory principle, by recognizing contributions to society while retaining the link between rights and responsibilities" (U.K. Department for Work and Pensions 2006, Executive Summary, para. 38). As a result, "all those who have worked or cared for 30 years will get full entitlement to the basic State Pension" (para. 47).[2]

BENEFIT FORMULAS. Details of benefit formulas affect men and women differently. For example, the formula used in the U.S. Social Security system relates benefits to the average level of indexed earnings over the highest-earning 35 years of a career, with zeros included if needed to reach 35 years. In response to a proposal to extend the averaging period to 38 years, analysts noted that, on average, women would add more zeros than men to reach 38 years, subjecting women to a relatively larger decrease in benefits. On the other hand, unlike most countries, Social Security has a progressive benefit formula. Since, on average, women have lower earnings than men, this progressivity benefits them relatively.

RETIREMENT AGE. Although it is less common today, in the past many countries set the statutory retirement age for women lower (typically by five years) than for men. A lower earliest eligibility age favors women, assuming that the pension at that lower age is the same as that at the higher earliest eligibility age for men. Past thinking included this option to reflect in part different social perceptions of the roles of women and men and in part the typical pattern of women being younger than their husbands. (A lower earliest eligibility age for women allows a typical couple to retire more nearly simultaneously.) However, this opportunity can generate social pressure for women to retire early and can lead to lower actual retirement ages, which may not be in the best interest of some women. In contrast, a lower *mandatory* retirement age unambiguously disadvantages women, in terms of both

1. The 10-year minimum in the United States has less impact than it might since there are auxiliary benefits and a person receives the largest benefit for which he or she is eligible.

2. Under the U.K. proposal, a person is entitled to a full basic (flat-rate) state pension upon satisfying two conditions: 30 years of actual or deemed contributions *and* attaining state pensionable age, currently 65 and set to increase in future years.

earnings opportunities and pension benefits if the latter would be larger with longer work. A lower actual retirement age for women than men, either because retirement is mandatory or as a consequence of social attitudes, will reduce benefits for women in many pension arrangements. Also relevant is whether other rules, such as eligibility for disability benefits and the opportunity to contribute to tax-favored retirement accounts, are based on the earliest entitlement age. In such respects also, a lower retirement age can place some women at a disadvantage.

Incentives to continue work past the earliest entitlement age can vary between men and women depending on the structure of the benefit formula and the differences in the typical earnings histories of men and women. For example, if there is a large jump in benefits upon crossing some threshold number of contribution years, and if more women than men are just below the threshold when reaching the earliest entitlement age, the incentive to work up to the threshold will be more important for women than for men. And systems that incorporate family structure in benefit determination create different incentives for the lower and the higher earner in a couple. (Box 6.1 discusses the case of U.S. Social Security.)

Where pension benefits depend on the number of contribution years, as in many defined-benefit systems, earlier retirement implies fewer contribution years and hence a smaller pension. Where benefits are actuarially related to a person's pension accumulation, as in defined-contribution systems, women's benefits can be lowered in multiple ways. First, if a woman retires earlier, she contributes for fewer years, and so her accumulation and hence her monthly pension benefit are smaller. Second, having retired earlier, she collects a pension for longer than an otherwise identical person who retires later, further reducing her monthly benefit; if the pension calculation takes account of women's longer life expectancy, the effect is even stronger. Separately, women may prefer not to be forced or pressured to retire at a younger age than that for men. In some countries the pressure to raise women's eligibility age came from women.

GENDER-SPECIFIC VERSUS UNISEX MORTALITY TABLES. Governments can provide annuities based on uniform pricing for a given birth cohort or require private providers to do the same. In such a system a man and a woman with the same pension accumulation and retiring at the same age receive the same monthly pension, and a man and a woman with the same accumulation who happen to have the same life expectancy receive the same expected lifetime benefits. On average, however, with uniform pricing, men receive less in present discounted value of pension benefits per dollar of accumulation than do women because of the lower average life expectancy of men.

Box 6.1 Auxiliary and surviving spouse benefits in the United States

In the U.S. Social Security system, persons 62 and older with at least 10 years of covered earnings are entitled to a worker benefit provided their current earnings are not too high (in other words, there is a retirement test; for details on how the benefit is determined, see section 9.10). If a worker has claimed benefits and is married, the worker's spouse, if also at least 62 and with low or zero earnings, is entitled to a spouse benefit equal to one-half of the worker's benefit, adjusted for the age at which the benefit starts. However, a person may receive only the higher of the spouse benefit or a worker benefit based on his or her own record. So, if a couple are both over age 62 and both claim benefits, the husband receives the higher of a benefit based on his earnings record or half of the worker benefit to which his wife is entitled (both adjusted for the age at which benefits start). Similarly, the wife receives the higher of a worker benefit based on her earnings or a spouse benefit equal to half of her husband's benefit. (Technically, each spouse receives a worker benefit based on his or her own earnings, plus an additional benefit to reach the higher of the two benefits. A person with ten years of coverage whose spouse benefit exceeds his or her worker benefit is referred to as a dual-benefit recipient.)

When one member of a couple (say, the husband) dies after retirement, there is a new calculation, giving the survivor the higher of the worker benefit based on her own earnings record or a survivor benefit equal to 100 percent of her deceased husband's worker benefit; again, these benefits are subject to adjustments for the ages at which they start. When a covered worker dies before retirement, there is a similar calculation once the survivor reaches the eligibility age for benefits.

With this structure, a married person with sufficiently low average lifetime earnings compared with the earnings of the spouse receives no additional benefit as a consequence of additional earnings. Thus the implicit tax on earnings (the payroll tax minus the value of additional future benefits) is equal to the full payroll tax rate for pensions, with no offset for anticipated benefits. With somewhat higher earnings, so that there is potential eligibility for a survivor benefit (based on 100 percent of the deceased worker's benefit) but not to a spouse benefit (based on 50 percent of the deceased worker's benefit), the implicit tax is still quite high. This system, which goes back to the early days of Social Security, thus creates adverse incentives for labor market participation and for additional hours of work for a person with low career earnings and a spouse with much higher earnings, since additional earnings bring no additional pension benefit, given eligibility for a spouse pension. The labor market incentives

(continued)

Box 6.1 (Continued)

for the higher earner in the couple also depend on the earnings level of the spouse, being greater if a higher worker benefit also raises the benefit received as a spouse benefit.

The Social Security benefit formula is progressive (see section 9.10) to provide a higher replacement rate for those with lower earnings, who on average are more needy. This underlying logic calls for comparing the degree of need of an individual with that of a couple with the same total earnings. Consistent with this approach, some adjustment is called for when two people rely on a given benefit rather than one.

Note that, with this structure, a survivor receives between one-half and two-thirds of what the couple were receiving when both were alive (ignoring adjustments for the ages at which benefits start). If husband and wife had the same average earnings, the survivor receives one-half. In the case of a one-earner couple (or with a spouse receiving a spouse benefit), benefits go from 150 percent of the higher earner's benefit to 100 percent of the worker benefit—a reduction of one-third. This pattern of survivor replacement rates has no apparent logic.

A further set of incentives relates to remarriage, if a person who remarries loses his or her pension based on the previous spouse's earnings.

Alternatively, governments may allow pension providers to base annuities on gender-specific mortality tables, in which case, given their different life expectancies, pensions for men and women will be priced differently: a man and a woman with the same accumulation and retiring at the same age would receive different monthly pensions, the man receiving a larger one. This practice occurs in countries in Latin America but is outlawed in employer-organized systems in the United States and the European Union, and many countries require unisex life tables not only for the mandatory system but also for voluntary pensions.

In sum, different pricing rules result in different patterns of benefits, hence different patterns of returns relative to contributions—a part of the redistribution occurring in a plan. Since higher earners tend to live longer than lower earners of the same gender, uniform pricing will tend to benefit them; additionally, market pricing will reflect administrative costs so that people with higher benefits may get better pricing. And the relative benefits of men and women will differ with differing annuity pricing. The different patterns of benefits with uniform pricing relative to nonuniform pricing need to be viewed within the context of the entire system, which generally will contain other redistributive elements, notably for poverty relief (for example, if pensions are partly financed from progressive taxation) or where there is a flat-rate benefit or a minimum guarantee.

6.3 Pension credits for child care

A system in which entitlement to a pension recognizes years spent caring for children or for elderly dependents helps women relative to men because women in general bear the greater share of the care burden. We discuss first the different ways in which such entitlements might be organized and then the broader question of whether this approach is good policy.

DIFFERENT FORMS OF PENSION CREDIT. There are different ways of recognizing care activities, with different distributional and incentive effects. One approach is to credit a woman's pension record with a fixed amount for each year she provides care, as in Sweden's NDC system. Sweden also credits a caregiver's individual-funded account. Thus her pension is larger because of additional deposits into her account paid out of general revenue. In some countries pensions are based on career average earnings, typically incorporating people's highest earning years. In this case a uniform level of credit per year of child care raises the pension of someone with a short career or sufficiently low earnings while providing less (or no) help to someone with a long career and high earnings. In other countries, including Canada and the United Kingdom, years spent in caregiving may be dropped from the calculation, thus reducing the number of years used to calculate career average earnings. With an earnings-related pension, this approach implicitly credits a higher earning woman with a larger amount than it does for a lower earning woman for a year of out of the labor force for child caring.[3]

There are other types of pension credits. Some countries give credits for time spent in college, thereby giving an advantage to those who obtain more education than does a system based only on earnings. Since more education tends to generate higher incomes, it is not clear that this is a good rule. Some countries protect people in military service; this can be done either by counting

3. To see this, suppose a pension is normally based on a person's 40 highest earnings years. For someone who has 30 years of earnings and who spent 10 years caring for children, the average will be based on those 30 years of highest earnings with the next highest 10 years of earnings dropping out of the calculation. Thus those 10 years are credited with the average of the highest-earning 30 years rather than zero. This is worth more to a woman with higher earnings in those 30 years than to one with lower earnings. For women with more than 30 years of positive earnings, the gain depends on earnings in the highest-earning 30 years relative to earnings in lower years.

years of military service as contribution years or by making explicit pension contributions from the defense budget during a person's military service.

The broader question is when credits for time spent in caregiving are good policy. Note first that a pension credit is a blunt instrument, which does not distinguish between cases where labor supply is affected by the credit and cases where it is not. For example, some parents in well-off households may have no paid work, and hence are eligible for a credit, but also employ a full-time nanny. That is, a pension credit for people with young children and low or no earnings does not distinguish between those who look after the children themselves and those who do not. And unless the credit is added to any pension contributions paid by working parents, it does not distinguish between those who look after children and do not work and those who manage both to look after children and to work (possibly earning less than they would without providing child care).

Pension credits for child care pose a series of questions:

- To what extent should society share in the costs of raising children?
- What should be the mix of providing income at the time of caring and providing pensions in the future after caring?
- What is the desired balance of incentives between labor market activities and caring for children?
- What should be the relative treatment of different types of families?

We set the first two, very broad questions to one side and concentrate on the latter two.

BALANCING INCENTIVES BETWEEN PAID WORK AND CARING. Decisions about the optimal design of consumption smoothing have to be set alongside policy preferences about the balance between paid work and caring for children. Incentives to take paid work are stronger where subsidies for child care are conditioned on the caregiver being in paid work and where taxation of secondary earners[4] is lower. Incentives to take paid work are weaker where caregiving is recognized through a pension credit. In contrast, a child benefit paid independent of work (as is typical) has an income effect on labor supply but no substitution effect.[5]

The relative sizes of these elements determine the balance of incentives between paid work and caregiving. To maintain a given level of incentive for paid work, the presence of a pension credit needs to be balanced by an offsetting change in one of the other incentives. Policy design needs to consider

4. The secondary earner is the spouse with the lower earnings.

5. By increasing parental income, the child benefit reduces the incentive to take paid work; however, the benefit has no effect on the net return to additional work and thus creates no disincentive via the substitution effect.

also the balance of incentives between paid child care and care by the parents themselves or other family members. The following are some options:

- The incentive to stay at home to care for children can be strengthened by making child benefits or pension credits, or both, available only to people with no (or little) earnings.
- To strengthen the incentive to take paid work, a subsidy for child-care costs could be conditioned on working at least a minimum number of hours. Such a subsidy encourages the use of paid child care by those who earn income and therefore the willingness to accept work that will have them use paid child care.
- It is possible to separate the incentive to work from the incentive to use paid child care when working by changing the balance between (a) the child-care subsidy and (b) lower taxes or higher pension credits for those working. Design can make part-time work more or less attractive relative to full-time work.

Of course, in practice the desire to avoid undue complexity will affect the design of policies that support children and encourage (or do not encourage) paid work.

BALANCING THE RELATIVE TREATMENT OF DIFFERENT FAMILY TYPES. The choice of balance between different instruments has important distributional effects. A greater emphasis on pension credits or child benefits assists families with children relative to those without (assuming the tax on secondary earners is the same whether or not the family has young children). A greater emphasis on lower taxation of secondary earnings benefits couples with children relative to single parents. Unless the lower taxation of secondary earnings is available only to those with small children, it does not match a pension credit. And a pension credit does not perfectly match a child-care subsidy, since use of child care is not universal among those who work. Thus the distributional effects of the various instruments are diverse and complex and may require some offsetting adjustments.

There are also potential distributional effects between better- and worse-off families. A critical question is the overall financial position of recipients of a pension credit. If the credit goes primarily to members of high-earning families (perhaps because they are the most likely to be able to afford to have someone not in paid work) who will have sizable pensions, the situation is very different from one where the credit goes primarily to low-income single parents, who otherwise would have very small pensions. Thus the case for a pension credit needs to be evaluated on a country-by-country basis with a focus on who receives it and on the extent to which that fits policymakers' distributional objectives.

6.4 Individual versus family pensions

The design of pension systems, like the design of an income tax, is no accident; rather, it heavily depends on the social philosophy underpinning it. Specifically, does policy regard a woman primarily as an adjunct of her husband, hence covered by his pension contributions, or primarily as an autonomous individual earning a pension in her own right? The former view was common in the past but has been rejected in many countries in favor of a view that recognizes autonomy. Recognizing autonomy is not inconsistent with recognizing a person's role as part of a family. Given historic patterns, the latter view prompts a policy drive to adjust labor market and pension institutions to strengthen women's earnings and to encourage labor force participation; it also influences views about how an equitable pension system might look. Such views are in part a matter of social values, on which countries differ, just as they differ in the mix of one- and two-earner couples and the prevalence of marriage and the degree of recognition of other forms of union.

As with an income tax, a related social consideration is whether to think of the family or the individual as the economic unit for policy design. This is a major issue in any program aiming at redistribution. Should a person in a rich family with low earnings or low pension benefits be eligible for the same redistribution as someone with similar earnings or benefits in a poor family or on their own? Most people would say no, but one thing that complicates this evaluation is that family structures have become more fluid: more than in the past, the family at the time of benefit receipt may be different from the family at the time when its members worked and made pension contributions. And divorce settlements may or may not have taken into account future pension benefits.

Organizing pensions on an individual rather than a family basis, with women having pensions *only* in their own right, is argued by some to be a better fit for societies with such fluidity in structure. On the other hand, as in the context of income taxation, family structure affects available resources and the demands on those resources. Moreover, adjusting pension benefits after a divorce (discussed below), which is a way of recognizing family structure, may be important for relative pension levels. As an example of the role of family structure, box 6.1 discusses the current public pension arrangements for spouses in the United States and the resulting labor market incentives.

6.5 Survivor pensions

Studies have found that a single survivor of a couple typically needs more than half of the couple's income—commonly 65 to 70 percent—to maintain a broadly constant standard of living. Thus, in the absence of other resources and survivor benefits, if two spouses are the same age and have identical earnings histories and identical pension benefits, the death of one may lower the living standard of the other, depending on the level of nonannuitized wealth available to the surviving spouse. This is part of the mechanism that results in greater poverty among widows than married elderly women. Survivor pensions are therefore an important element in preserving the living standards of the elderly. Although we discuss only the case of surviving spouses, the issue is broader: a well-designed system also has benefits for young survivors, notably young children. Our focus is on consumption over the rest of life for widows beyond retirement age, not just transition needs.

There are many ways of organizing and financing survivor pensions. In either a funded defined-contribution or an NDC pension, the accumulation could be used to purchase a joint-life annuity with a suitable fraction for the survivor. In a two-earner couple this can be done by both earners. Of course, with mandatory annuitization, differences in the perceived life expectancy of people who are the same age imply that there are perceived winners and losers from such a mandate. In contrast, if joint-life annuitization is voluntary, there are issues of adverse selection: couples who think that one spouse will live considerably longer than the other are more likely to purchase such annuities. Voluntary joint-life annuitization is the approach taken with the funded portion of the pension system in Sweden (although not with the NDC portion, which does not allow that option). The balance of influences on the decision could be tilted toward a joint-life annuity by making that the default and, more strongly, by requiring both members of a couple to agree before the default is replaced by a single-life annuity for the worker. Regulation of employer-provided pensions in the United States includes these rules. A further step could make joint-life annuitization mandatory.

A defined-benefit system could offer a similar set of options, based on the actuarial conversion of a single-life annuity into the relevant joint-life annuity. Alternatively, survivor benefits might be provided out of the overall revenue of the pension system, as in the U.S. Social Security system, thus benefiting couples at the expense of single people. Such an arrangement involves transfers to couples that are greater the higher the worker's pension benefit, a feature that has been much criticized. Thus it may be better to use a more complex rule covering survivor benefits, such that they are partly financed out of the worker's benefit and partly out of the resources of the pension system, with the proportions depending on the level of benefit.

If pensions are proportional to earnings, the underlying logic of this portion of the pension system is that it does not attempt to adjust for differing needs at different levels of earnings; that is, it makes no attempt to redistribute between richer and poorer pensioners. Any redistribution takes place in other portions, or outside the system, and so the proportional pension system does not need to adjust redistribution where there is joint-life annuitization. Thus, when benefits start for a couple of given ages, the expected present discounted value of benefits, including benefits when both are alive and when only one of them survives, should be determined by the defined-benefit formula or the balance in a (funded or notional) defined-contribution account.

In contrast, with a progressive benefit formula, as in the United States, the system adjusts replacement rates to reflect need. Under a progressive income tax, a single person is usually seen as better able to pay taxes than is a couple with the same total income; analogously, a couple has a greater replacement need than a single person with the same aggregate earnings history. Thus the replacement rate for a couple (reflecting the earnings of both) might be matched with that of a single person judged to have the same need. But a further complication arises because one member of a couple generally survives the other. Thus "replacement need" should be considered on a lifetime basis, including recognition of the "survivor replacement rate," the ratio of the benefit paid to the survivor to the benefit paid when both were alive. It is common in employer plans for the worker to receive some benefit independent of the survival of his or her spouse, whereas the spouse receives a smaller benefit if he or she survives the worker. It is not clear that such an asymmetric arrangement makes sense.

6.6 Divorce

The increased fluidity of marriage increases the salience of rules for pensions when a couple divorces. There are social rules, often involving the courts, on the division of accumulated assets (including sometimes human capital) of the couple upon divorce, with particular focus on accumulations during the marriage. Entitlements under a public pension system might be part of what gets divided as part of the general settlement, or they might be regarded as implicit assets that cannot be divided. The rules of the pension system might determine the division, or they might merely limit the division that a divorce settlement or divorce court ruling may make. The issue is important: without some adjustment, divorce after many years of marriage can result in very low benefits for a person with a limited earnings history. Indeed, in the United States poverty rates are high for elderly divorced women who do not remarry.

There are different strategies for providing benefits after a divorce, strategies that are implemented through decisions at the time of retirement or at the time of divorce. One strategy is to provide benefits when a divorced person reaches retirement age. This can be done as a transfer of benefits between spouses. For example, when a worker starts to draw a pension, benefits are adjusted to provide some benefits not only to a current spouse but also to previous spouses, using a formula relating to the lengths and timing of the marriages. Future availability of such benefits could be factored into a divorce agreement. Alternatively, benefits for a divorced spouse could be financed from the resources of the pension system generally, without reducing the benefit of the worker entitled to the pension, as in the United States (see box 6.2).

A second strategic approach is to transfer explicit or implicit pension wealth between spouses at the time of a divorce based on their earnings records (and realized rates of return if there are assets) during the marriage. In Canada, when a marriage or common-law partnership ends, the entitlements to the Canada Pension Plan built up by the couple during the time they lived together may be divided equally between them as part of a divorce settlement.

A third approach is to divide earnings records on an annual basis during the marriage, for example, with individual accounts, where each year the earnings of husband and wife are divided evenly between them. These accounts belong to the individual and would be carried through a divorce.

Box 6.2 Auxiliary and survivor benefits for divorced spouses in the United States

In the United States, if a couple divorces after being married for 10 or more years and at least one has not remarried before starting benefits, a Social Security benefit may be payable to one spouse based on the other's earnings record. The rules parallel those for the spouse and survivor benefits described in box 6.1: a divorced person is entitled to the higher of a worker benefit based on his or her own earnings record or a divorced spouse benefit equal to 50 percent of his or her spouse's worker benefit. (An amendment to the Social Security Act in 1965 provided benefits to divorced wives and widows if they were dependent on the wage earner's support and if their marriage had lasted 20 consecutive years or more; this was reduced in 1977 to 10 years). Because the system does not decrease a worker's benefits because of auxiliary benefits provided on the basis of his or her earnings record, such payments come from the pension system as a whole, subject to a maximum family benefit for a single earnings record. If that maximum applies, the worker benefit is not affected, but the other auxiliary benefits are reduced. Similarly, there is a surviving divorced spouse benefit of 100 percent of the worker's benefit, again subject to a family maximum.

However, when the ages of husband and wife are significantly different and they have had very different earnings (and the higher earner is older), such a division of pension assets undercuts their ability to finance their retirement if they remain married. This is clearest in the case of a one-earner couple. When the worker reaches retirement age, only half of the benefit is available until the younger spouse has reached retirement age.

6.7 Conclusion

This chapter has put forward three sets of arguments about gender and family issues in pension design:

- There is no unambiguously best design. But some designs are unambiguously bad.
- Policy should not focus only on the design of the pension system itself; it should also be cognizant of the impact on eventual pension benefits of other policies concerning, for example, the taxation of earnings, subsidies for child care, all-day schools, and regulations about flexibility of work for parents of young children.
- We do not argue that women ought to work or ought to care for children; rather the argument is that tax and pension systems (and other policies) inevitably create incentives that affect decisions about paid work, care activities, and leisure and therefore should be chosen to reflect social values, individual preferences, and constraints, all of which will differ within a country and across countries.

More concretely, pension design needs to be sensitive to the differing impacts on men and women. To that end it should

- consider what recognition is appropriate, and in what form, of years spent in socially valued activities, such as caring for children, disabled people, and elderly dependents, balancing such recognition with incentives to participate in paid work;
- set common rules for pension eligibility and determination;
- require the use of unisex life tables if the system converts account balances to annuities; and
- ensure that satisfactory pension arrangements are in place for surviving spouses and after a divorce.

Chapter 7

Implementing Pensions

Chapters 2 through 6 set out the economic theory that underlies good policy design, recognizing that many different designs are possible and identifying examples of poor design. Moving beyond general economic analysis, this chapter emphasizes that what constitutes good design for a particular country depends also on the country's capacity to implement it. A system that cannot be implemented more or less as designed is not well designed. Numerous cleverly constructed reforms—of pensions, the finance of health care, student loans, and many others—have failed because their administrative requirements were underestimated or exceeded what was possible or because political support for the reform was lacking. The issue is not unique to developing countries. Examples abound of government projects in developed countries that were late, over budget, or failed altogether.

This chapter considers the conditions for the feasibility of pension designs. The analysis is selective, both for reasons of space and because neither of us is an expert in implementation: neither of us has ever run a pension system or studied implementation in detail. Our central point—obvious but often overlooked—is that a country's choice is constrained by its fiscal, political, and institutional capacity. Ignoring or underestimating the task of implementation dramatically increases the likelihood that a reform will fail to achieve its objectives.

Effective reform requires at least three sets of skills: policy design, administrative and technical implementation, and political implementation. Although we will have less to say about the last of these, it is of coequal importance with the more technical aspects. Experts in one set of skills frequently do not grasp the importance of the other two. There is much lip service but little real understanding. Experts in policy design tend to ignore implementation or to underestimate its difficulty; politicians may give insufficient weight to the coherence of policy or to meeting its administrative requirements, for example, by not allowing enough time or by not including an adequate administrative budget; administrators and other technical experts may overestimate the difficulty of change, may take a blinkered approach, or may be reluctant to reform for other reasons.

A key point is that implementation requires skills additional to and different from policy design. The idea that if one understands the policy one can establish a program for implementing it is generally false. Implementation skills are an integral element in reform, not an add-on. These skills must be involved at the stage of policy design, not bolted on after policy is set. There is a deeply flawed view that policy involves "higher" skills: higher-level people design policy, which is then handed over to the apparatchiks to implement. This is, quite simply, wrong: the three sets of skills—policy, technical, and political—are neither hierarchical nor sequential. Effective implementation needs the right skills from the outset.

Section 7.1 sets out the tasks that a government must be able to carry out if a pension reform is to succeed, tasks that clearly vary with the type of pension system. Section 7.2 describes the capacities that private pension providers need to have in order to implement voluntary or mandatory privately organized individual accounts effectively—that is, to ensure that the supply side is working well. Section 7.3 considers the demand side of the market for individual accounts, notably the extent to which workers are well informed about the decisions they need to make, the characteristics of different pension arrangements, and the quality of different pension providers. Section 7.4 pulls together the discussion of implementation in this chapter and the theoretical discussion of chapter 4 to consider the circumstances in which funding is, or is not, desirable.

7.1 The capacity of government

Pensions—large or small, simple or complex—must respect three sets of constraints: financial capacity, administrative capacity, and broader institutional requirements. Consumption by retirees is at the expense of consumption by workers, or spending on investment, or both. From a macroeconomic perspective, therefore, pensions are in part a device that helps to divide output between workers and retirees. Clearly, total spending on pensions must be compatible with a country's financial capacity. Although all pension systems make significant demands on government capacity, some are considerably more demanding than others. The following options for public pensions are listed in ascending order of their fiscal and administrative demands.

NONCONTRIBUTORY SYSTEMS. The limited budgets and administrative capacities of very poor countries restrict them to providing modest, administratively simple poverty relief, for example, through locally based discretionary benefits, means-tested social assistance, or a flat-rate, tax-financed pension for the very elderly. Even the simplest of such arrangements requires that government have at least a limited capacity to collect tax revenue and be able to distribute benefits to the intended recipients (which requires, for example, that government can ascertain people's ages).

SIMPLE DEFINED-BENEFIT CONTRIBUTORY ARRANGEMENTS. A somewhat greater fiscal and public administrative capacity makes possible a national system of income-tested social assistance, or a simple PAYG pension (for example, a flat rate per year of contribution), or both. The pension can be financed in a range of ways: from a dedicated social insurance contribution or from a mix of general revenues and contributions; either is possible with a trust fund (that is, a partial accumulation to cover future pension liabilities) or without. Systems of this sort require a government that can collect contributions effectively, maintain records over the years for workers who will be mobile geographically and across firms, adjust benefit levels for the worker's age when benefits start (if the system allows a delayed start), and pay benefits in an accurate and timely way. Government also needs the ability to project future contributions and benefits so that the system can adapt slowly and with significant lead times to evolving financial capacity.

If the pension system incorporates a trust fund, government needs the ability to preserve and invest these claims on future output. Preservation starts with the ability to prevent widespread embezzlement. Also critical is a suitable macroeconomic environment. In particular, as discussed in box 7.1, bouts of high inflation can erode or even erase the purchasing power of accumulations in the absence of full indexing—and the ability to fulfill indexed promises. Trust funds may hold a portfolio that consists entirely of government debt, or they may hold private assets as well. If funding is to strengthen the ability of the economy to provide consumption to pensioners in the future, any additional government borrowing through purchases of government debt by the trust fund must not be used primarily for current consumption. If private assets are purchased, there needs to be an adequate capital market in which to invest. Although investments abroad can substitute for investments in domestic capital markets, they may or may not be good choices at different stages in economic development.[1]

1. Developing countries may have to pay a country risk premium to induce capital inflows, and such inflows can increase vulnerability to capital flight by foreign investors.

Box 7.1 The importance of avoiding high inflation

Governments must have the capacity to avoid high inflation because rapid, unanticipated inflation erodes the real value of nominal bonds, including those held in pension funds. The impact on stocks is generally negative as well, though stock values, like the value of the underlying companies, may return to the previous relationship to the economy. A single burst of rapid inflation at any time during a person's working life (if assets are not fully indexed) or during retirement (if annuities are not fully indexed) will cause a sharp decline in his or her pension benefits, as the example below illustrates.

Two points are noteworthy about inflation after retirement. First, any loss of value due to inflation is permanent; retirees have little opportunity to make up any of the lost ground, since they have far less ability than workers to adjust to inflation through additional earnings or increased saving. In addition, with rising life expectancy, people live much longer in retirement than previously. Thus even low inflation can have a considerable cumulative impact on a retiree's standard of living. For example, with 2 percent annual inflation, the real value of a nominal benefit after 10 years is only 82 percent of its original value and only two-thirds after 20 years. Note that these losses are stated in terms of the original benefit, which is a fixed proportion of the worker's previous real earnings (the replacement rate); the decline relative to rising average real earnings of current workers is generally considerably larger.

As an example of the ill effects of inflation on pensions, the price index in the United Kingdom in January 1974 was 100; by September 1978, in the wake of the first oil shock, it was 200. Most individual annuities in the United Kingdom were not indexed to inflation at the time, and so their real value was halved. Most U.K. private pensions are now required to compensate for annual inflation of up to 5 percent (so-called limited price indexation). Had that rule been in place in the 1970s, the nominal value of pensions would have increased from 100 to about 133, still well short of the 200 needed to preserve their real purchasing power; in other words, pension benefits would have lost one-third of their value.

Separately, pensions may require effective coordination between national and subnational levels of government if all are to have a role in supporting the elderly. This is a matter both of broader constitutional arrangements and of the specifics of pension design. As with all systems, it is also a matter of implementation. For example, the software to run the pension system should be provided centrally, with subnational levels of government unable to make any modifications except (if the system allows such variation) to set a local level of benefit within a nationally determined formula. Experience shows that excessive customization is a likely outcome unless strictly prevented.

EARNINGS-RELATED PUBLIC PENSIONS. Earnings-related pensions require, in addition, that government can measure people's earnings effectively and keep the more detailed records needed for calculating benefits. Examples of such systems include NDC pensions, which take into account all of a worker's earnings in all years, although the accumulated balance is a sufficient statistic for calculating benefits. Without detailed records, however, it is difficult to correct errors once workers approach retirement and attempt to verify the accuracy of calculations. Hence earnings-related pension systems require that government undertake the following tasks:

- track and record a worker's earnings accurately across his or her entire working life, which requires identification of and record keeping for each individual worker;
- do so for workers who are mobile across jobs, employment status (employed, self-employed, or unemployed), and geographical regions;
- in the case of an NDC system, make actuarial calculations that accurately convert notional accumulations in accounts into benefit levels;
- assist workers' planning by keeping them informed through regular (ideally annual) statements of the relevant earnings records (or, in an NDC system, balances in their accounts) and the implications for retirement income of those records or balances and future contributions, based on a range of assumptions;
- pay benefits accurately and promptly;
- make the calculations and adjustments necessary to keep the system financially sustainable, either automatically or by legislated changes.

Merely listing these requirements is sufficient to emphasize their stringency.

PUBLICLY FUNDED DEFINED-CONTRIBUTION SYSTEMS. This type of arrangement can vary greatly in the extent of administrative capacity needed. Such systems hold assets and therefore require the capacities discussed earlier to maintain trust fund investments. What the system needs beyond that depends on its design. Perhaps the simplest is a provident fund system, which has a single fund that determines all benefits on the basis of its realized earnings. Thus the administrative needs are similar to those of an NDC system. It may be possible to rely on private insurance firms rather than a government program to actually calculate and pay benefits. But this, in turn, relies on adequate regulation of those firms.

More sophisticated systems can allow workers to choose different portfolios. This approach greatly increases the demands on communication and record keeping, since the government has to keep track of each worker's portfolio in order to credit accounts appropriately and must maintain a system that allows workers to change their portfolios, either by changing the mix of new purchases or by rearranging existing portfolios. The greater the amount of choice allowed, the greater the administrative complexity and administrative cost. And since some workers may fail to choose a portfolio, it is necessary to set up a well-designed default portfolio, as discussed in section 7.3.

PRIVATE PENSIONS. Significant government capacity is needed if a country is to have well-running private pensions. Government has three interests in the functioning of employer-provided pensions and individual accounts: to ensure that the pensions fulfill the expectations reasonably held for them; to encourage lower earners to save for retirement; and, in many (but not all) countries, to encourage retirement saving generally, both to promote old-age security and to bolster economic growth.

The achievement of those objectives requires that government has the capacity

- to maintain macroeconomic stability (box 7.1);
- to set suitable incentives, for example, through such devices as autoenrollment; and
- to regulate financial markets effectively.

Even voluntary private funded pensions require nontrivial government capacity to regulate and supervise financial markets, including insurance markets. Voluntary plans can contribute to a political environment that encourages better regulation of markets as well as serve as a test phase in any move toward mandatory plans that will cover a much larger fraction of the labor force, including more vulnerable workers. Moreover, the extent to which pensions fulfill social goals depends on how well the plans themselves are regulated. Mandatory private funded pensions require significant fiscal capacity, plus strong public *and* private institutional capacity.

7.2 Implementing mandatory individual funded accounts

Given the great interest in mandatory individual funded accounts since their introduction in Chile and their adoption in various other countries, we pay particular attention here to the implementation requirements of this type of arrangement. Two sets of questions arise:

- Is private sector capacity adequate? As discussed below, private pensions depend on administrative expertise to keep track of individual contributions and pension accumulations across a working

life as well as on financial market expertise to manage pension funds and payouts. A lack of either capacity runs the risk that administrative costs, administrative breakdowns, or incompetent or corrupt fund management will erode the benefits to pensioners from investment returns. Since administering an individual account has a fixed-cost element (it does not cost much less to administer a small accumulation than a large one), the issue is of particular concern for small pensions. At worst, deficient administrative capacity and expertise in fund management put at risk the viability of the entire system of private accounts.
- Even if private sector capacity is adequate, is its deployment in administering private pensions its most welfare-enhancing use? A key issue is whether a developing country is willing to let firms from developed countries take on tasks that domestic firms might find too demanding, thus avoiding a situation that risks the retirement security of vulnerable workers.

For fully funded individual accounts the major tasks include:

- collecting contributions;
- keeping records and informing workers;
- selecting portfolios;
- investing funds, and
- determining and paying benefits.

As discussed in section 7.3, the process of educating workers—about what they have at a given moment, what they can expect to have at retirement, and how to think about the choices they can make—also is important. In an economy where most workers have no experience in making such financial decisions, it is critical to provide education on the implications of different choices.

All these tasks have costs that vary with the design of the system and with the quality of services provided.[2] All involve government as well but in different ways with different design features.

Although all these tasks are essential, this section illuminates the issues by focusing on the third bullet in the list above. With any system of asset accumulation, the design of the institutions involved in making portfolio choices is important. It is important to ensure that the choices are made for the benefit of current and future retirees, not for other objectives. It is important to have rules that encourage efficient portfolio choices. Such

2. There are significant one-time costs in setting up a system and ongoing costs once the system is mature. This section discusses only the ongoing costs but also serves as a guide to the initial costs of creating the necessary institutions.

rules will naturally differ in different circumstances. It is one thing to have a centralized trust fund run by professional fund managers effectively insulated from political pressures and highly motivated to do a good job. But in some countries it may be necessary to restrict portfolio choices so as to insulate portfolio managers from outside influences. And the rules will be very different if the portfolio choices are made by individual workers themselves: both the administrative costs and the difficulty inexperienced investors face in making good investment decisions call for restricted choices.

Three elements are important in considering how much choice workers should have. First, how well are they likely to choose? (discussed in section 7.3). Second, among workers with the capacity to choose well, how much are those choices likely to vary, and how much does the variation matter? Third, what are the costs associated with wider choice? The argument for limiting choice—in the number of portfolios made available to workers and in the frequency with which a worker may change funds—is precisely that consumers do not always choose well so that transactions and other costs may outweigh the potential gains from wider choice. Since costs are a central part of the argument and raise complex issues of measurement, it is helpful to start by discussing different measures of cost as a prelude to discussion of choice.

EVALUATING CHARGES. The different arrangements described below tend to have systematically different levels of cost, as more choice tends to cost more. These costs need to be allocated across accounts (or outside the system of accounts). There are multiple options for allocating costs across different accounts (in a centralized system) or regulating charges (in a decentralized system). The charges could be made proportional to annual contributions or to a person's total accumulation, implying that all workers with the same portfolio receive the same rate of return. Alternatively, the charges could include a fixed component reflecting the underlying structure of costs, implying that workers with larger accumulations have higher rates of return net of charges. The importance of this choice depends on the dispersion in the earnings of the covered population.

For any given system of allocating costs to accounts, there are many ways to report the resulting charges. Some of these are described in box 7.2. Consideration of costs and comparison across systems require recognition of the compounding nature of costs: different ways of allocating costs will affect workers with different lengths and timing of their careers. Because of the effects of compounding, it is easy to underestimate the importance of charges. A comparison of up-front charges and annual charges is shown in table 7.1.

The table reports charges for a 40-year career, evaluating the charge right at the end of the career. Many workers have shorter periods of covered employment, and those periods might be early or late in their careers. With annual charges, the length of time that a contribution is growing matters for the importance of the charges. For a dollar that is contributed one year

Box 7.2 Measuring charges

Comparing the costs of individual accounts is complex. Some set-up costs are independent of the size of the system, whereas others depend on the number of participants. Ongoing costs are mostly fixed costs per account, and for that reason estimating costs is often approached in those terms. For all but the smallest plans the cost of managing the aggregate portfolio is small relative to the costs of record keeping, including communication with account owners. For example, in the U.S. Thrift Savings Plan, described in box 9.4, investment management fees represent about 10 percent of total administrative costs.

Account charges come in different forms in voluntary private markets. There can be charges when deposits are made (called a front-end load or sales charge) or when money is withdrawn (a back-end load or deferred sales charge); there are also periodic (usually annual) charges based on the value and type of assets in the account or on the rate of return, as is common with hedge funds. Similarly, costs can be measured in various ways so that a common measure is needed to allow comparison of diverse systems. The following measures are potentially useful:

- *Percentage front-end load.* The Thrift Savings Plan reports the *dollar cost* of running the accounts. Dividing this annual dollar cost by annual deposits gives a *percentage front-end load,* that is, the annual cost as a percentage of a person's annual contribution. This may or may not match the way the individual accounts are charged.
- *Annual percentage management charge.* This is the annual charge as a percentage of the account holder's accumulated balance.
- *Reduction in yield.* If the rate of return in a given year was 5 percent before charges and is 3 percent after, the reduction in yield is 2 percentage points.
- *Charge ratio.* This is the percentage decrease in a person's total accumulation at retirement as a consequence of all administrative charges over the life of the account.

Table 7.1 shows the relationships among the percentage front-end load, the annual management charge, and the charge ratio, based on continuous time calculations.

Table 7.1 Cumulative effects on account value of sales load and management charges[a]

Up-front or annual charge	Cumulative decline in value of accumulation (charge ratio) after 40 years[a]
Front-end load	
(percent of new contributions)	
1%	1%
10%	10%
20%	20%
Annual management charge	
(percent of account balance)	
0.1%	2.2%
0.5%	10.5%
1.0%	19.6%

Source: Diamond 2000.

a. Calculations assume real annual wage growth of 2.1 percent and a real annual return on investments of 4 percent. With a larger difference between the rates of wage growth and annual return, the charge ratio with annual management fees is slightly larger.

before the start of benefits, a 1 percent annual charge takes only 1 percent of the accumulation. For a dollar contributed 20 or 40 years before the start of benefits, the charge ratio is much higher because that dollar's accumulation is subject to the annual charge each year for 20 or 40 years. Of course, with positive net real interest, a dollar deposited earlier finances a higher retirement benefit. But the point of this calculation is that for a given gross return on assets, higher charges mean lower net returns and the impact of higher annual charges is more important the longer the contribution is accumulating and the more times it is subject to an annual charge. In the face of competing pressures between cost and choice, countries have adopted a wide range of approaches.

A SINGLE, CENTRALLY ORGANIZED PORTFOLIO. The simplest and least expensive option is for government to choose the workers' portfolios for them, as was formerly done in Singapore.[3] Although this can be done by building a single, monolithic portfolio, it is also possible, without allowing individual choice, for portfolios to vary systematically across workers of differing characteristics. For example, the mix of stocks and bonds in a worker's account can be selected to vary systematically with age; the default allocation of funds in Chile uses this so-called life-cycle approach. Given fixed costs per account, a single, simple, government-designed fund can be used for a worker's account until it exceeds some minimum size, at which point the cost of

3. The Central Provident Fund Investment Plan in Singapore offers some limited choice, as outlined in section 9.7.

portfolio choice may be seen as worthwhile for workers who choose (but are not forced) to move to another arrangement, such as those described below.

CHOICE AMONG A SMALL NUMBER OF CENTRALLY ORGANIZED FUNDS. The least expensive way to give workers some choice is for the government to establish a limited menu of investment funds and to select the managers for each. Workers then divide their contributions among the available alternatives and may change the allocation of new contributions or rearrange existing asset holdings (both of which affect costs), subject to specified limits. As discussed in section 7.3, a default fund is necessary for workers who fail to make a choice. Although the government might invest directly in assets, contracting with private providers to manage the funds takes advantage of the presence of existing firms, which plausibly have economies of scale. Moreover, the commingling of pension funds with private investments in the same fund contributes to insulation from political pressures on investment. The lowest administrative cost comes from a successful selection of efficient, low-cost providers for the different funds after a process of examining alternatives, perhaps involving an auction among firms judged capable of performing. (Box 9.4 discusses the example of the U.S. Thrift Savings Plan, the pension program for federal workers that illustrates this approach.)

CHOICE AMONG COMPETING PROVIDERS OF HIGHLY REGULATED FUNDS (RESULTING IN A LIMITED SET OF FUNDS). In Chile and some other countries, pension assets may be invested only in a private, tightly regulated investment fund that engages in no other business. Entry to the business is open to any firm with the necessary capital so that in principle the industry is competitive. As discussed in section 10.1, however, in practice choice among funds in Chile has remained limited: a small number of firms transact most of the business, and there is continuing concern about the high level of charges.

Other Latin American countries have followed approaches similar to Chile's, except for Bolivia (box 9.1), which allowed only two firms to enter and initially gave workers no choice between them. Because firms had to bid for the right to be one of the chosen two, charges are lower than elsewhere in Latin America. However, it is important in settings like this, after a price has been set, to regulate the quality of the services provided, and this is not easy. Indeed, the quality of services has been a source of complaint in Bolivia. As table 7.2 shows, costs vary widely even among countries following similar strategies. Apart from Bolivia, costs range from 13 to 36 percent of a person's annual contribution, reflecting, among other factors, the small size of the accounts.[4]

4. For a broader discussion of recent experience with pensions in Latin America, see Gill, Packard, and Yermo 2005 and Arenas de Mesa and Mesa-Lago 2006.

Table 7.2 Administrative costs of private investment funds in Latin America, December 2002 (Percent)

Country	Administrative fee as share of salary[a] (1)	Contribution to fund as share of salary (2)	Fee as share of total contribution = (1)/[(1) + (2)]
Argentina	1.56	2.75	36.19
Bolivia[b]	0.50	10.00	4.76
Chile	1.76	10.00	14.97
Colombia[c]	1.63	10.00	14.02
El Salvador	1.58	11.02	12.54
Peru	2.27	8.00	22.10
Uruguay[d]	1.92	12.27	13.53
Average	1.60	9.15	16.87

Source: Gill, Packard, and Yermo 2005, table 7.3.

a. Includes only account and asset management charges that are set as a percentage of contribution or salary. Insurance premiums are excluded.

b. Includes only the contribution charge; the asset management charge varies from zero to 0.23 percent, depending on the amount of assets in the portfolio.

c. Refers only to the mandatory pension fund system for December 2000.

d. Excludes an additional commission for custody, which averaged 0.293 percent of total assets under management in December 2002.

CHOICE AMONG A WIDE SET OF CENTRALLY ACCEPTED FUNDS WITH PRICE REGULATION. In contrast with the limited options in Latin American countries, Sweden, discussed in section 9.8, makes available a wide array of funds. Sweden has both an NDC pension and mandatory participation in funded individual accounts, with 2.5 percent of payroll going into the latter. Funds meeting specified requirements may join the list of approved funds as long as they agree to pricing rules set by the government. At the end of 2007 there were 785 such funds. Workers allocate their contributions among up to five funds and inform the government of their choice(s). The government has put in place a central clearinghouse, which keeps the records, collects the contributions, aggregates the contributions going to each fund (and any portfolio transfers), and sends them to the funds. A potential problem with competition among a wide array of funds is that it encourages advertising, which adds to costs without necessarily improving consumer choice, not least because of the imperfect choices made by workers, discussed in section 7.3. After the initial startup period, the arrangements in Sweden resulted in limited advertising, in part because administration through the central clearinghouse means that firms do not know which workers have invested with them. Without price regulation, competition among many funds would be very expensive. Even with a central clearinghouse, arrangements in Sweden are significantly more expensive than the U.S. Thrift Savings Plan described in box 9.4. It remains to be seen how well price regulation will work over the long haul: historically, price regulation has not worked well over extended periods.

CHOICE AMONG A WIDE SET OF COMPETING PROVIDERS. In the United States, individuals saving in tax-favored individual retirement accounts can hold these funds with private providers who are subject to standard capital market regulation. Analyses of the U.S. voluntary mutual fund industry have found a steady downward trend in charges for different kinds of mutual funds. Yet the impact of charges remains significant. In 2007 average annual charges were 79 basis points for bond mutual funds and 102 basis points for equity mutual funds. According to table 7.1, the resulting charge ratio (loss of benefits due to the charges) for a mix of funds would be roughly between 15 and 20 percent.[5] This does not include the costs that many U.S. investors pay separately for investment advice, sometimes as much as 1 percent of assets per year in what are called wrap accounts.

The United Kingdom also allows workers who opt out of public and private defined-benefit systems to contract directly with firms in the investment and insurance markets, thereby making essentially all of the market available. As in the United States, this approach has proved to be very expensive: the charge ratio for these pensions has been estimated to be above one-third for the accumulation phase, not counting annuitization costs. That is, benefits are one-third lower than if these costs were avoided. Not least for that reason, reforms have been introduced, but administrative costs remain a concern. We are not aware of any country taking this approach to mandatory accounts.

Given the size of the fixed-cost element, the U.K. Pensions Commission (2004*a*, p. 224) questioned "whether [the level of costs] implies that there is a segment of the pension market, comprised of lower income savers and people working for small firms, to which a free market will never be able to sell pension products profitably except at [reductions in yield] which make savings unattractive." For those reasons the subsequent report (U.K. Pensions Commission 2005) recommended introducing low-cost savings plans with centrally administered individual records and fund management on a wholesale basis.

In sum, systems that offer wide choice among competing providers face two strategic problems:

- Approaches that offer wide choice have proven to be expensive. The effect of charges, often overlooked, should not be underestimated. Table 7.1 shows that even annual charges as low as 1 percent of assets

5. This includes annual fees and conversion of front-end loads to an annual charge but not to brokerage charges for transactions by the funds.

under management have a major impact on accumulations when the charges are made annually over a long period. Over a 40-year career, the typical dollar of assets remains in an account for roughly 20 years. Hence an annual charge of 1 percent reduces a person's accumulation after a 40-year career by roughly 20 percent (the charge ratio).
- In addition, many investors make poor choices, a topic to which we now turn.

7.3 The capacity of consumers

Alongside government capacity and private sector capacity, a third set of questions concerns the capacity of individuals and, in particular, whether individual consumers understand the bases for good choices. By allowing greater choice, individual accounts, it is argued, offer two sets of advantages: they increase economic growth via improved allocation of savings to investment and they increase the welfare of individual workers, who can invest according to their different degrees of risk aversion.[6]

The first potential advantage is assessed in section 4.3.2, which argues that such benefits may be real but that this will depend on country specifics. The second potential advantage also needs to be tested. The conventional argument is that choice maximizes welfare by accommodating differences in preferences across individuals. At least two sets of qualifications, relating to both the costs of choice and the extent of consumer understanding and information, are relevant.

THE COSTS OF CHOICE. Although the benefits from increased individual choice may be real, they may be offset by the costs of allowing such choice (box 7.2). This is a serious issue for individual accounts: as already noted, charges tend to be high, and they tend largely to reflect a fixed cost per account, thus bearing most heavily on small accounts and in countries where economies of scale are not available. Depending on pricing rules, this cost may hit poorer workers especially and those in poorer and smaller countries most of all.

CONSUMER UNDERSTANDING AND INFORMATION. These are central. Given the extent of risk and uncertainty, and the complexity of many pension products, over what range, if any, does increased choice make workers better off?

One potential problem is myopia. The purpose of pensions is to ensure retirement income. But some workers pay too little attention to the future: they may not attend to making a good choice and may be influenced by

6. For a consumer with considerable assets outside the pension fund, the choice of assets inside may be of little significance since the overall portfolio can be the same with different mixes of assets inside and outside.

current inducements when choosing investments, for example, from sales pressure and possibly kickbacks.

A second concern is that individuals often do not do a good job of retirement planning. For the reasons discussed in box 2.1, many people are imperfectly informed about complex financial products and hence make poor choices about financial intermediaries and portfolios for their retirement savings. For example, many people do not understand the importance of portfolio diversification, as evidenced by heavy investments by some workers in the stocks of their employers.

A related possibility is that workers will fail to make any choice at all. In Sweden, despite a massive effort at public education at the launch of the system of funded individual accounts in 2000, roughly one-third of workers ended up in the default fund.[7] Since then roughly 90 percent of new workers do not choose a fund and thus end up in the default fund. A well-designed default is therefore considerably more important than would be the case if the standard economists' model of rational choice were fully accurate.

A third concern is that even where a person does have the necessary capacity to choose well, an individual account is an ongoing relationship so that the benefits of smarter shopping (e.g., higher returns or lower charges) in any particular month are small, whereas the transactions costs in terms of time are significant. Thus workers, particularly low earners, for whom the gain in any month is smallest, have little incentive to stay on top of the changing details of alternative investments and alternative charges.[8]

Poor choices by some workers should not be surprising. The principles of finance—the advantages of diversification, the trade-off between risk and return, the identification of underlying stochastic structures, even the efficiency of markets—are not, after all, intuitively easy concepts. Indeed, cognitive psychology tells us that even much simpler statistical concepts are generally not intuitive. Given the noise in returns, moreover, it is difficult for anyone to tell whether good portfolio outcomes are the result of a manager's skill or of luck.

CONCLUSION. Box 2.2 suggests that there is good reason to be skeptical about the gains from individual choice in mandatory accounts. Will learning by doing take care of that? The evidence suggests not. U.S. experience with

7. Some of these viewed the default fund as the best choice: it was not available as a choice but only if no choice were made.

8. This is true even for the simplest financial arrangements. Banks in some countries offer higher interest rates on new types of savings accounts while leaving the terms of existing accounts unchanged, relying on the inertia of existing savers, many of whom stay in the old, lower-yielding accounts. In some other countries regulation restricts the freedom of banks to offer different interest rates in this way.

401(k) plans shows that worker education must be substantial and expensive to have a noticeable effect on investment choices. This should not be surprising, since what is involved, it can be argued, is not an information problem but an information processing problem (box 2.1). More generally, the considerable difficulty in making investment choices even in countries with generations of individual experience in investing is a major concern in countries with a limited history of individual investment.

7.4 Funding

Section 7.1 described the capacities governments need to have to implement alternative ways of funding pensions, while sections 7.2 and 7.3 examined implementation issues for funded individual accounts. The analyses in these sections complement that in chapter 4, which sets out some of the economic theory relevant to the desirability or otherwise of funding. Box 7.3 pulls the two elements together by setting out the key questions that policymakers should ask in considering a move to funding.

Box 7.3 Funding is not a no-brainer

A move to funding is not always and self-evidently the right policy. Such a move may be good policy or may not. Which is the case depends on the answer to a series of questions.

Is a move toward funding optimal?

Would a move to funding increase output by increasing saving?

- Is higher saving the right objective? The answer is often yes, but not always. As discussed in section 10.2, saving in China is too high.
- Does funding increase saving? As discussed in section 4.3.1, an increase in mandatory saving can be reduced by an offsetting reduction in private saving, or because the necessity to finance the transition to funding may lead to higher government borrowing.

Would a move to funding increase output by strengthening capital markets? As discussed in section 4.3.2, it does not do so in advanced economies, nor in countries below a threshold of development. For countries in between there may be gains, although that is dependent on the quality of implementation and improvements in the regulation of capital markets. However, policymakers should consider the extent to which the gains could come through encouraging voluntary pensions.

(continued)

Box 7.3 (Continued)

Would a move to funding have beneficial effects on the intergenerational distribution of income? As discussed in section 4.4.1 and box 4.3, any decision about PAYG and funding is necessarily also a choice about the intergenerational distribution of income. Such redistributive effects may or may not be good policy. As discussed in section 10.2, a move toward funding in China is likely to redistribute from today's poorer workers to tomorrow's richer ones.

Once these questions have been answered, a separate question follows.

Is a move toward funding feasible?

The simplest approach is to have a single, government-organized provident fund, the management of which could perhaps be outsourced.

Individual accounts make much greater demands on institutional capacity.

- Public sector prerequisites include the capacity to collect contributions, maintain macroeconomic stability, maintain effective regulatory capacity, and maintain political sustainability.
- Private sector prerequisites include having a well-informed population, trust in the competence and the integrity of the private sector, financial assets, financial markets, and private sector capacity both to administer accounts and to manage funds.

In sum, the counterargument to the proponents of competitive pension provision is that achieving the advantages visualized in idealized competition is contingent on sufficiently strong institutional capacity and sufficiently good decision making. Administrative weakness and the scale of uncertainty, risk, and other consumer information problems do not *necessarily* rule out consumer choice as welfare improving but should be seen as a counterpoint, especially in poorer countries where government and citizens have little financial market experience.

Chapter 8

International Diversity and Change since 1950

Countries have choices about pension systems, choices that widen as their economic and institutional capacities grow. Section 8.1 discusses some of the reasons why systems today rightly look different from systems 50 years ago. Section 8.2 considers developments in pension systems and their design and economic and political responses to long-term trends. Some of the responses in some countries worked well; others fared badly, not least because of policy errors, as section 8.3 illustrates. The next chapter illustrates the variety of possible choices through brief descriptions of pension systems in a range of countries.

8.1 Changes over the past fifty years

Pension systems have been changing and with good reason: many of the earlier structures were no longer well suited to social and economic environments that have changed profoundly. And, in light of advances in understanding the workings of pensions, some were not well designed. Thus countries should continue to pay attention to current practice and what best suits their current situation and not indulge in nostalgia for earlier approaches that have been appropriately discarded.

LONG-TERM TRENDS. The backdrop to the discussion that follows is the long-run trends discussed in chapter 1.

- Demographic change: life expectancy has been rising for a very long time (figure 1.1) and is projected to continue to rise (figure 1.2). A second long-term trend, declining fertility (figure 1.4), is evident in industrialized and in poorer countries. Both trends have been significant and widespread.
- Declining labor force participation is in large part a response to higher living standards—as people become richer, they can afford more leisure. Figures 1.7 and 1.8 show the long-run trend. Figure 8.1 illustrates the situation in 2002: the labor force participation of older workers (men and women combined) is lower, and in many countries considerably lower, than that for younger workers. Earlier retirement and longer life combine to increase the duration of retirement, which ranged from 15 years for men in Japan in 1999 to nearly 21 years in Italy, with even longer durations for women. In some countries, however, the trend to early retirement ha s halted.
- Increasing economic and political rights for women is central to pension design for the future. Increasing numbers of women work for pay, and for an increasing number of years, and the view that women's old-age security should come solely through their husband's

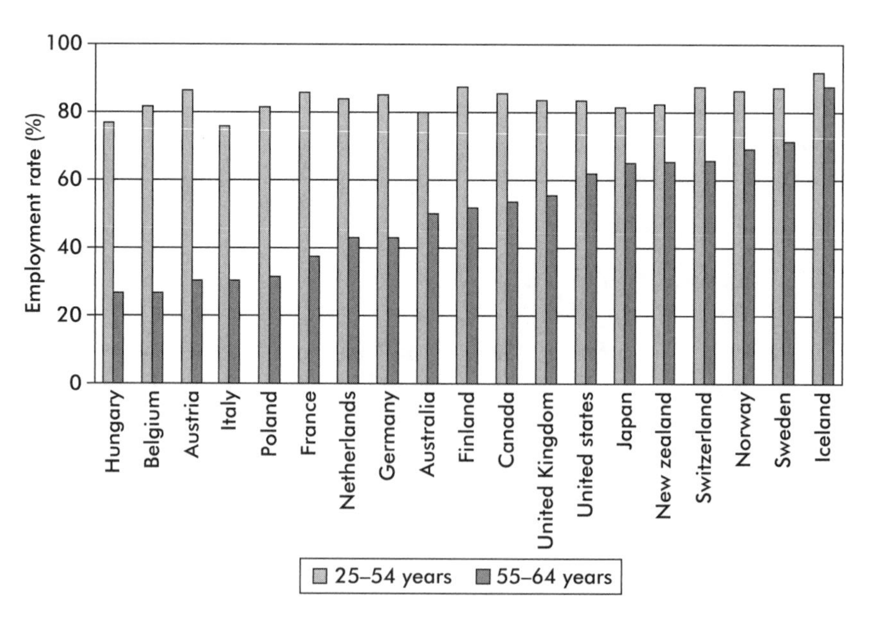

Figure 8.1 Employment rates by age group in selected OECD countries, 2002
Employment rates are for both sexes. *Source:* Sigg 2005, figure 8.2.

pension contributions is increasingly regarded as out of place.
For these reasons and others, more women have pensions in their own right. In addition, as discussed below, pension design must accommodate a greater variety of living arrangements.

CHANGES OVER THE POSTWAR PERIOD. Superimposed on these very long-term trends is a series of changes that have taken place over the past half century.

- Growth and maturity in pension systems: even in the developed countries, most pension systems before World War II covered relatively few people and provided relatively modest benefits. The extension of pension systems, both in their coverage and in the replacement rate they offer, has been a widespread feature of postwar policy, making systems more expensive and increasing the importance of the politics of reform. Contributions have tended to rise in most countries through higher contribution rates or higher ceilings on the income on which contributions are levied. Advanced countries have PAYG systems with nearly universal coverage; thus further expansion of coverage is not available to ease financial problems.
- The baby boom: the post–World War II baby boom is a fairly widespread phenomenon and, when combined with other demographic trends, has had powerful effects in some countries. Its importance, however, should not be exaggerated: as figure 1.5 shows, the age pyramids projected for 2050 are not strikingly different in the United States from those in India and China, neither of which had a baby boom.
- Growth of female labor force participation: throughout the Western countries over the postwar period, women in increasing numbers not only have taken on paid work, as shown in table 1.2, but have also pursued lifelong careers. One implication is that the presence of more workers eases the short-term finances of a PAYG system by increasing the contributions base. Another is that many systems needed to be redesigned to recognize the entitlements that a woman builds on the basis of her own earnings record.

All of these elements—the long-term trends and the postwar changes—have direct and obvious implications for the costs of pension systems. Two further changes have important implications for other aspects of pension design.

A CHANGING INTERNATIONAL ENVIRONMENT. Alongside reduced restrictions on international trade and finance has come increasing awareness of international labor mobility. The practice of migrating to another country, working there, and sometimes returning to one's country of origin has a longer history than these other manifestations of globalization. How pension systems deal with prime-age immigrants, who naturally tend to have shorter careers in the destination country than do the native born, has received relatively little attention. But as pension systems have grown, incomplete entitlements become a greater perceived problem. Thus the treatment of migrants and—a related issue—the international portability of pension rights are becoming, and will continue to become, more salient. A major manifestation is the unresolved issue today of how to organize pension rights within the European Union.

MORE FLUID FAMILY STRUCTURES. In many countries the nuclear family has neither the stability nor the numerical dominance it had 50 years ago. At a time when most people married and stayed married, the most common reason for women being single was widowhood, which could be addressed by including widows' benefits in the pension system. Today, in addition, many women are single after a divorce or never marry at all. In the United Kingdom something like 40 percent of mothers can now expect to be single mothers for some part of their adult lives. Pension systems need to be redesigned to accommodate the greater diversity of living arrangements, both across individuals and across a single individual's life. In countries where support for the elderly was largely through the extended family, rural-urban migration and, in some countries (such as China), much smaller families increase the importance of pension systems in filling the growing gaps.

8.2 Issues and responses

The economic and social context in which pensions operate today is thus very different from that of 1950. In this section we consider some issues arising from these factors that policymakers in many countries have faced over the past 60 years. We discuss in turn developments in pension systems and design (section 8.2.1), the menu of economic options for adjusting pension systems to long-term trends (section 8.2.2), and political aspects of adjustment (section 8.2.3).

8.2.1 Developments in pension systems and design

Notwithstanding considerable differences across countries, a number of developments since World War II are common to many, including growth in the scale of pension systems, measures to address gaps in coverage, the indexation of pension benefits to rising wages and prices, adjustments to achieve gender balance, and, in some countries, the introduction of notional defined-contribution pensions (see glossary). Alongside these changes, which mainly concern public systems, are three further developments: measures to address the administrative costs of individual accounts, efforts to strengthen the governance of private pensions, and a growth of employer-organized defined-contribution plans in place of defined-benefit plans.

GROWTH IN THE SIZE AND EXTENT OF COVERAGE OF PENSION SYSTEMS. As noted above, systems have expanded in terms of both coverage and level of benefits. This trend has been accompanied by increasing contribution rates.

ADDRESSING GAPS IN COVERAGE. A major goal of mandatory pension systems is the reduction of elderly poverty, often accompanied by decreased reliance on means-tested programs, which involve stigma and have higher administrative costs. Lower poverty rates have been an important accomplishment of systems with wide coverage, and the expansion of coverage beyond urban employees was an important part of the accomplishment. But the need for income-tested support for the elderly remains. Incomplete coverage arises in countries with immature pension systems and in developing countries with limited institutional capacity, a large informal sector, or both. However, it also comes from fragmented careers even in countries with nearly full coverage. Thus it is no accident that even in developed countries not all workers have a full contributions record—the United Kingdom's record was noted in section 6.1.

As the Presidential Advisory Council in Chile correctly realized, it is thus mistaken to imagine that better administration is a complete solution to problems of coverage.

> The prevailing image at the time of the pension reform [in Chile in 1981], of a workforce composed mainly of male heads of household, with permanent jobs, contributing continuously throughout their active lives, has become less and less representative of the real situation of the country and will become even less so in the future. This means that the system designed at that point in time is also gradually losing its ability to respond to the needs of the population as a whole. (Chile Presidential Advisory Council 2006, p. 6)

The implication is that the design of pension systems should recognize that gaps in contributions will occur. One approach has been to adjust the rules of the contributions regime, for example, by granting contribution credits to people who are unemployed or caring for young children. Another has been to reduce the number of years of work necessary to qualify for a pension. Also under this head, to reflect migration, a few countries now take account of contributions to public pensions in other countries.

A different approach, recognizing that gaps in contributions are unavoidable in a modern economy, is to introduce a noncontributory universal pension to assist in covering women, people with fragmented careers, and workers in the informal sector. Australia, Canada, New Zealand, and the Netherlands have adopted this type of pension, and Chile introduced one in 2008. South Africa (box 9.2) illustrates how a noncontributory universal pension can work in a developing country and be extended to the rural population. Box 9.2 also discusses a number of other countries, including developing countries which have such systems.

INDEXING BENEFITS TO RISING WAGES AND PRICES. The use of indexing to offset the impact of inflation on the purchasing power of pension benefits during retirement is key to ensuring that benefits can be relied on to maintain a given level of consumption. Over time, countries have incorporated such indexing, sometimes to prices, sometimes to wages, and sometimes to a mix. In its absence, inflation alone can "cure" the financial shortages of pension systems—and went a long way toward doing so in some of the former communist countries—but obviously that is bad policy.

In addition to indexing benefits during retirement, countries now also index contribution records or earnings records during working life, usually to wages, thus taking account of wage growth over a worker's career when determining his or her initial benefit and avoiding the uncertain impacts of inflation on the real value of initial benefits. Again, as a result, the political process has to address explicitly any financial shortfalls in the pension system rather than rely on inflation to take care of imbalances.

A change in the basis of indexation can have significant effects. For example, in the latter part of the 1980s, reforms in the United Kingdom indexed the basic state pension to changes in prices rather than (as previously) to wages. As a result, the replacement rate offered by the basic pension fell from around 20 percent of average earnings in the mid-1980s to 16 percent in 2002 and is anticipated to continue to fall as long as price indexing remains in effect.

ADJUSTING GENDER BALANCE. Growing concern for the position of women has led many countries to move their pensions either toward or all the way to gender neutrality in legal structure.[1] We think that pension systems should seek to be gender-neutral but should also recognize the existence of families. Thus pension design should protect the living standards of spouses after

1. For example, in the United Kingdom until 1978, a married woman could opt to pay a greatly reduced national insurance contribution, which gave no entitlement to a pension, on the grounds that she was covered by her husband's contribution. Today such an arrangement would be unthinkable as well as a violation of EU law.

the death of one member of a couple and after divorce. A separate issue, discussed in section 6.3, is whether, how, and to what extent a pension system should recognize years spent caring for children. Several countries have done so explicitly, including Canada, Sweden, and the United Kingdom. There are different ways of designing such recognition.

INTRODUCING NOTIONAL DEFINED-CONTRIBUTION PENSIONS. A recent innovation in pension design, NDC pensions (i.e., PAYG pensions run on a quasi-actuarial basis, described in section 2.2) were invented and implemented roughly simultaneously (but somewhat differently) in Italy and Sweden. Several other countries, including a number of the reforming former communist countries, have since introduced pensions organized on that basis. The innovative parts of this design are the use of a defined-contribution vocabulary within a PAYG system and the related adjustment of benefits for life expectancy.

INTRODUCING FUNDED DEFINED-CONTRIBUTION PENSIONS. The growth of mutual funds and the decline in their charges in some countries has increased the fraction of the population for whom retirement savings using capital markets is worthwhile. In turn, this has increased the fraction of the population in some countries who are familiar with the workings of capital markets. This combination of lower costs and greater familiarity has increased the practicality of funded defined-contribution pensions.

REPLACING DEFINED-BENEFIT PLANS WITH FUNDED DEFINED-CONTRIBUTION PLANS. While it is common for workers to think that both accrued rights and anticipated benefits in defined-benefit plans are safe, in practice they are not. Anticipated benefits are subject to changes in the rules of the plan. Accrued benefits may not be paid because of financial shortfalls of the sponsors. As discussed in box 8.1, it is difficult to guarantee payments. Attempts to do so in both the United Kingdom and the United States have been, at least in part, the reason many firms closed their plans to new members and, in some cases, moved future contributions of existing members to a defined-contribution basis.[2]

ADDRESSING THE ADMINISTRATIVE COSTS OF INDIVIDUAL ACCOUNTS. Administrative costs, though seemingly a narrow technical matter, have important policy ramifications. As illustrated in table 7.1, an annual management charge of 1 percent reduces a person's pension accumulation, and hence that person's

2. Blake (2006) concludes that in the United Kingdom a combination of piecemeal reform and inadequate regulatory impact assessments created a situation in which individuals ended up with weaker pension promises than 30 years earlier and firms faced solvency problems arising from their legacy defined-benefit plans.

Box 8.1 Difficulties in regulating private defined-benefit plans

The long-run security of workers and retirees requires long-run financial stability of pension arrangements. When a firm or industry with an unfunded or inadequately funded defined-benefit pension gets into financial trouble, its workers and retirees lose much, and possibly all, of the pension they were expecting. Countries have found this highly unsatisfactory and have responded in a range of ways.

One approach is through government-provided guarantees. However, if guarantees are insufficiently generous, they do not protect workers and pensioners adequately; conversely, the more generous they are, the more they may lower the incentive to provide funds and manage them prudently (that is, they may create moral hazard). For example, risky pension investment may become attractive since, with defined benefits, the pension fund keeps for itself the high returns if the risk pays off, and the guarantee covers the losses if it does not.

With or without a guarantee, another approach is to impose requirements about funding. Such requirements, and particularly the speed with which any shortfall needs to be made good, can create problems. When asset values fall, firms need to increase their contribution rates if they are to restore adequate funding rapidly. But this demand on a firm's revenue typically comes at precisely the time when the firm is experiencing low profitability: low profitability and declines in asset values are highly correlated.

One outcome of stringent funding requirements is that sponsors may close defined-benefit plans. This trend is accentuated when other requirements are imposed that add more to the cost of the pension than firms think is worthwhile: for example, that the rights accrued by workers who have left a firm be fully protected and that pension benefits cover spouses.

In sum, policies designed to ensure the long-run stability of defined-benefit plans face an inherent tension: too little regulation leaves workers with inadequate protection, but too much imposes excessive costs on plan sponsors, often at inopportune times, leading to withdrawal of the plans, at least for new members. Given this tension it is worth considering whether substituting employer-provided defined-contribution plans for employer-provided defined-benefit plans might improve the social outcome. Countries that do not have defined-benefit plans are probably wise to not encourage them through tax policies.

monthly benefit, by about 20 percent over a full career. When Chile introduced funded individual accounts in 1981, some analysts thought that market competition would result in low administrative costs. That has not been the case in either Chile or the other countries that imitated Chile, except for

Bolivia (box 9.1), which did not follow Chile's reliance on the market but instead established government-organized bidding for the right to handle workers' accounts. As a result, policy in Chile has seen repeated changes in the regulations for individual accounts in the hope of reducing costs. For the reasons discussed in box 2.2 and section 7.3, the sluggish response of consumers to charges is not surprising.

In response to increasing awareness of both the existence of these costs and their size, countries have explored other ways of reducing them. Sweden has centralized much of the administration of pensions, which it combines with price controls. The United States has combined centralization with very limited individual choice but only for federal civil servants, not the entire working population (box 9.4).

The quality of investment in government-selected portfolios historically has been very mixed. In the past some countries have done poorly with centralized investment.[3] But with a greater recent focus on the incentives and transparency of the process of such investment, some countries have seen returns comparable to those of private investors. Good quality investment is more likely with full and transparent accounting, including a clear and explicit mandate, independent nonpolitical management, and detailed, published, audited accounts. However, it is inherently difficult to put in place a system that can ensure sound investment, particularly where experience with such investment is limited.

STRENGTHENING THE GOVERNANCE OF PRIVATE PENSIONS. Strengthening the regulation of financial markets generally has been an ongoing and necessary process in all countries, including the most developed. In parallel, many countries have increased the requirement that private pensions be funded and have strengthened their regulation. Some countries have introduced mandatory insurance.[4]

8.2.2 Economic adjustment to long-term trends

When coverage is far from complete, the demography of a country and the demography of its pension system can develop very differently. Once coverage is close to complete, long-term trends in demography become central to the financial functioning of the system. Thus the trend of increasing benefits

3. See, for example, World Bank 1994, box 4.5, which shows negative real rates of return over extended periods in a range of countries, the worst being Peru, with a real loss of 37 percent between 1982 and 1988.

4. Examples include the Pension Benefit Guaranty Corporation in the United States, created by the Employee Retirement Income Security Act of 1974, and the Pension Protection Fund in the United Kingdom, established by the Pensions Act 2004.

has been reversed in a number of countries in recognition of the financial imbalances in their pension systems, imbalances that result primarily from demographic pressures and the long-run decline in labor force participation by older male workers. Few governments would claim that the process is complete.

Faced with ever larger numbers of pensioners, some policymakers (for example, in some EU countries) at first ignored the problem, paying the increasing deficits out of general taxation. A range of other possible policy directions—higher contributions, lower monthly benefits, and later retirement—are generally more realistic. Economic growth also assists adjustment, and therefore policies designed to raise output—for example, through increased national saving—are an important part of the picture.

HIGHER CONTRIBUTIONS. The long-term trend of rising contributions, through higher contribution rates and higher ceilings on the income on which contributions are levied, has been part of the response to financial imbalances in many countries. Although there is room for variation, contribution rates face the constraint of adverse incentive effects, an issue to which countries have become more sensitive in the face of international competition. Given the extent of population aging in many countries and high existing contribution rates, higher contributions on their own do not always provide a satisfactory complete solution. Indeed, some countries have avoided significant further increases in contribution rates when undertaking reforms.

LOWER MONTHLY BENEFITS. If people live longer and the average retirement age and available financing do not change, the average pension benefit will have to fall. This approach avoids fiscal problems but risks increasing pensioner poverty. Many countries have responded to the rising cost of pensions by reducing real monthly benefits; the United Kingdom, for example, moved to a less generous system of indexing benefits; the United States phased in an increase in the age for full benefits, starting long after the legislation. Countries that made major changes in their systems, for example, by introducing NDC systems, could readily change the size of benefits in the distant future. On an ongoing basis, in countries with NDC systems, such as Sweden and Poland, benefits fall automatically in response to increased life expectancy. Because an NDC system is quasi-actuarial, people can offset the decline in benefits by working longer, an option that is relevant also in countries with defined-benefit systems that increase benefits sufficiently for a delayed start. Some workers will respond to lower benefits and actuarial (or nearly actuarial) benefit increases by working longer, thereby mitigating some or all of the decline in replacement rates.

Key to lowering pension benefit levels is spreading the decline suitably across cohorts and giving adequate advance notice while also preserving the opportunity for increased saving, more work, or both, to raise replacement rates. The politics of benefit reduction are easier when reductions are not imminent—an opportunity when long-run problems are addressed early.

LATER RETIREMENT. If benefits are roughly actuarial, longer work does not affect the long-run finances of the system. But it does increase the replacement rate, affecting the adequacy of pension benefits. Concern remains about the replacement rates of some workers who would continue to retire as soon as they can. When pensions are being lowered for any given retirement age, it is possible to limit the decline in replacement rates by increasing the earliest entitlement age. With and without benefit changes countries have been changing early entitlement ages, primarily increasing them. As Turner (2007, pp. 88–89) notes:

> Over the years 1993–2004, nearly two-thirds of the [OECD] countries (15) raised the pensionable age for at least one gender (Table 2). Nine of those 15 had lowered the pensionable age for either men or women or both during the period before 1993 and then subsequently raised the pensionable age after 1993.
>
> In ten of those 15 countries, the effective date of the increase occurred during the relatively brief 1993–2002 period. From 1993 to 2035, based on legislation as of 2004, the median pensionable age will rise from 62 to 65 for men and from 60 to 65 for women in the 23 OECD countries.

PENSIONS, SAVING, AND GROWTH. Policies to promote economic growth are an important part of the response to demographic trends. One approach is through higher saving out of additional revenue. The Norwegian Government Petroleum Fund, for example, uses some of the revenue from oil taxation as a buffer against demographic change. The United States has built up a trust fund, with payroll tax rates set above what was needed to cover expenditure, to be drawn down as part of accommodating the retirement of the baby boomers.[5] Chile switched to funded individual accounts while financing benefits under the old system out of general revenue.

A parallel concern is to devise broader strategies to promote growth:

- Measures that can increase worker productivity include policies that encourage investment in more and better capital equipment, improve the allocation of capital through better capital markets and tax policies, improve the quality of the labor force through more education and training, and improve labor mobility to allow a more productive allocation of labor.

5. The extent to which the build up of the trust fund has added to national saving, given the politics of the rest of the government budget, is unclear and a matter of dispute.

- Measures that can increase the number of workers from each age cohort include policies to increase labor supply (for example, that of married women by offering better child care facilities), to raise the average age of retirement, to encourage higher fertility, and to import labor.

The message for policymakers is to consider the entire menu of pro-growth policies.

8.2.3 The politics of adjustment

Political cultures vary widely: politics can be more adversarial or more consensual as well as more top down or more grassroots; public willingness to become seriously engaged in debates about policy can be higher or lower. The United Kingdom and the United States share an adversarial tradition, whereas debates in countries like Norway and Sweden, with their more consensual political culture, have taken a different form. The Swedish reforms that in 1998 resulted in their NDC system were based on a long period of political debate and public discussion. Interestingly, Sweden held two parliamentary votes: the first on the principle of moving to NDC pensions and the second, at a later stage, on the specific system to be implemented. This approach is intended to avoid the situation where a reform fails because although everyone supports the whole, a majority votes against the specific part that affects them negatively—just as everyone supports the need for garbage dumps but not in their own back yard.

Pensions affect many people over many years, and therefore changes require a clear strategy supported by much detailed work. But raising taxes, reducing benefits (even future benefits), and increasing the earliest entitlement age are all politically difficult. Having apolitical projections of future pension costs that are accepted by the public can ease some of the political difficulty. Thus governments often find it useful—both to garner the necessary expertise and to provide political insulation—to set up a commission headed by persons other than elected officials to assess the situation and make recommendations and so to help with the adversarial political process. We briefly review four such commissions, two in the United States and one each in the United Kingdom and Germany.

UNITED STATES: THE GREENSPAN COMMISSION. From the creation of Social Security in 1935, many rounds of legislation expanded coverage and raised benefits and taxes. Legislation in 1972 included the first automatic indexing of the system for inflation. However, this indexing was not done correctly. Thus by 1977 a projected Social Security deficit would have forced benefit cuts within 5 years, and the projected deficit over the standard

75-year projection period would have required a 75 percent increase in the payroll tax rate to provide the legislated benefits. The clear need for reform in the short term and the recognition of error in the 1972 legislation contributed to a bipartisan approach to reform, resulting in 1977 in legislation that created the basic structure of the current system. However, because the financial imbalance was so large, the intention was to squeeze through the short term and to cover a substantial period but less than the full 75 years. The legislation might just have met this goal but for the deep recession of the early 1980s, which made the short-run finances untenable. It thus became necessary only a few years later to review benefits and taxes again.

This time the process was more contentious, and several attempts to generate legislation failed. By 1983 the long-run projected financial shortfall was roughly one-quarter what it had been in 1977, but the system was expected to run short of money, and hence to have to cut benefits, that spring. Some combination of benefit cuts and tax increases was needed quickly, pointing to a bipartisan approach. In reaching a political compromise, a key role was played by a bipartisan commission headed by Alan Greenspan (at the time a little-known figure), which included members appointed by both parties who stayed in close contact with party leaders.

The bipartisan solution included measures to increase revenue and measures to reduce benefits in roughly equal proportions. Some of these changes were needed in the short run given the precarious short-run finances. Others were phased in over decades to achieve balance over the traditional 75-year horizon.

This experience offers three possible lessons for countries with adversarial two-party politics. First, the political momentum to respond to a financial shortfall in the public pension system will generally be lacking until the impact on financing is imminent. Second, a bipartisan (or, in some countries, multipartisan) commission can be useful in breaking the political impasse. And third, the approach to legislation needs to be genuinely nonpartisan.

UNITED STATES: THE COMMISSION TO STRENGTHEN SOCIAL SECURITY. The 1983 legislation was barely sufficient to cover the standard 75 projection, and large annual deficits loomed just beyond the projection horizon. Thus the rolling 75-year projections again showed a deficit, but with adequate balances until well into the future.[6]

6. This experience has led to a revision of the standard criterion of 75-year balance, referred to as actuarial balance, to the criterion of *sustainable* actuarial balance, which supplements the standard criterion with the further condition that the trust fund not be declining at the end of the projection period. It also led to more attention to infinite-horizon projections to supplement the 75-year projection.

During the 2000 presidential campaign, Governor George W. Bush said he would appoint a commission to propose a reform that complied with a number of principles, including funded individual accounts and no tax increases. After his election, Bush appointed a commission that was bipartisan in the sense that its membership included both Republicans and Democrats, but unlike the Greenspan commission, all were appointed by the administration, and thus the commission did not really represent both political parties. Because of the terrorist attacks of September 11, 2001, Social Security reform was largely set aside until after the 2004 election. President Bush then made it his primary domestic policy goal and launched an intensive campaign to present his approach to the public. Although he did not put forward a complete plan, Bush drew heavily on the recommendations of the commission and brought commission members to attend his public appearances. However, public support for his approach was never widespread or durable, and it decreased through the period of his public advocacy. Thus, in addition to confirming the three political lessons already mentioned, and redefining the meaning of "bipartisan" in "bipartisan commission," this experience may have illustrated that replacing part of the U.S. defined-benefit system with individual accounts, in the absence of additional financing, was not acceptable to the American public.

THE U.K. PENSIONS COMMISSION. In 2002 a commission was established to address problems in the U.K. pension system, notably the high rate of pensioner poverty, the heavy and growing reliance on means testing, and low rates of pension saving. The commission's core recommendations were a phased increase in the level of the basic state pension; a phased increase in the pensionable age to 66 in 2024, rising thereafter by one year every decade; and the introduction of simple personal accounts with many of the characteristics of the U.S. Thrift Savings Plan for federal employees (box 9.4), limited choice for workers from a small number of funds, centralized account administration, and wholesale fund management. The commission also recommended automatic enrollment, which is on the way to being added to the Thrift Savings Plan as this book goes to press.

The commission offers some useful lessons:

- It took a strategic view, looking at the pension system as a whole; thus its recommendations were likewise strategic.
- It drew some of its staff from the Department for Work and Pensions and thus had a capacity for detailed analysis.
- The commission's first report, published in 2004, focused on diagnosis and potential options. This was politically astute. One of the options was an increase in the pensionable age, hitherto a political minefield. The measured tone of the first report and the commission's subsequent public discussion were instrumental in changing attitudes.

- The increase in the pensionable age recommended in the second report, published in 2005, was sufficiently far in the future that, in public briefings, the chair could say, "if you are over 50 this won't affect you; if you are in your forties you will have to work for an extra year." This long notice did a great deal to lower the political temperature.
- As part of its initial agreement with the government, the commission's finances allowed it to maintain a reduced staff for six months after its second report was published in order to give it the capacity to respond—and to continue to respond—to the misinformation, disinformation, and special pleading that inevitably results from such reform proposals.

THE GERMAN COMMISSION FOR SUSTAINABILITY IN FINANCING THE SOCIAL SECURITY SYSTEM. The German public pension system experienced a financial crisis in 2002.[7] The governing coalition agreed on a package with increased contributions in the short run and a review of the entire system.

The review commission, chaired by a Social Democratic academic, Bert Rürup, comprised academics, businesspeople, representatives of public interest groups (including the employers' federation and the trades unions), and representatives of the public pension administration, a total of 24 people. The commission had three working groups: on public pensions, health insurance, and long-term care insurance, each with two co-chairs chosen to represent opposing views.

The subcommissions on health insurance and long-term care insurance quickly split into two camps, ultimately issuing carefully worded summaries of why they agreed to disagree. The pensions subcommission, however, succeeded in agreeing on a recommended reform package, building on the multipillar system introduced three years earlier by then labor minister Walter Riester.

The recommendations, published in 2003, had three elements:

- Future benefits would be indexed to a weighted mix of wages and the inverse system dependency ratio (the number of workers divided by number of pensioners). This would convert the traditional defined-benefit system into one that resembled an NDC system in that population aging would automatically reduce pension benefits to keep the system in financial balance.
- The normal retirement age would be increased from 65 to 67 between 2011 and 2035.
- The rules for private pensions would be relaxed to encourage greater participation.

7. We are grateful to Axel Börsch-Supan for providing the text on which this discussion is based.

These three elements were supported by a large majority in the commission and legislated by the Bundestag in 2004; only the unpopular increase in the retirement age had to wait until 2007 to be passed.

It is hard to assess why the pensions subcommission was successful in bringing about reform while the other two subcommissions failed. One reason may have been early agreement among the academic members not to entrench themselves in extreme positions; they then tried to pull the political actors toward the same middle ground. Another possible reason is that the press focused all its attention on the bitter debate over health care, leaving little room for public discussion of pensions. Finally, the arguments in the pension subcommission quickly turned toward how to rationalize the country's rule-bound pension policy, leaving little room for ideological debate.

8.3 Policy errors

The analytical errors discussed in earlier chapters and summarized in box 11.1 are paralleled by policy errors—often the result of analytical errors—which have affected adjustment to long-term trends. Once more, the World Bank, a highly influential actor in pension reform internationally, provides illustrations. The Bank, however, was far from alone. In addition, the Bank was often right in diagnosing a clear need for reform of previous pension arrangements, which in many countries combined high fiscal costs with limited coverage and poor incentives. Finally, one of the most forceful recent diagnoses of errors is an assessment by the Bank of its own pensions work.[8] Box 8.2 encapsulates a range of errors that are largely the result of taking insufficient account of implementation capacity: examples include introducing mandatory funded systems at a time when inflation was high or the budget deficit large or doing so in countries with a limited financial sector, significant corruption, or both. In what follows we discuss policy errors and then point to some overoptimistic predictions.

8.3.1 Policy problems

INADEQUATE ATTENTION TO POVERTY RELIEF. This problem is largely a consequence of inadequate attention to the whole range of pension objectives, with distributional effects especially likely to be ignored. Policy discussion tends

8. See, in particular, World Bank 2006*a*, summarized in World Bank 2006*b*, and Gill, Packard, and Yermo 2005. See also the background papers written for World Bank 2006*a*, Rofman 2007 and Valdés-Prieto 2007*a* and 2007*b*. Also relevant are Devesa-Carpio and Vidal-Meliá 2002, Rofman and Lucchetti 2006, and von Gersdorff 1997.

Box 8.2 World Bank diagnosis of errors in pensions policy

A World Bank study identified a number of policy errors committed by the Bank in its pensions work in a range of countries; these errors are powerfully summarized in the list of figures in the study's table of contents (World Bank 2006*a*, p. v), of which the following are examples:

Figures

2.1 More Sector Work Addressed Fiscal Issues and Transition Costs, and Fewer Reports Discussed Public Administration
3.1 Many Countries Had High Inflation at Reform
3.2 Several Countries Had High Budget Deficits at the Time of Their Pension Reform
3.3 Poor Financial Sectors Characterize Some Europe and Central Asia Multi-Pillar Reformers
3.5 Many Reformers Had Poor Corruption Indexes at the Time of Reform
3.6 Corruption Ratings Are Poor among Some Potential Reformers
3.7 Some Multi-Pillar Countries Already Had High Savings Rates
4.2 Fiscal Deficits Have Grown in Many Countries with Second Pillars
4.3 Savings Rates Increased Only in Kazakhstan
4.4 Market Capitalization Remains Quite Low
4.5 Post-Crisis Pension Portfolios in Argentina Fled to Government Bonds
4.6 Pension Participation Rates Have Not Changed in Latin America and the Caribbean

to focus heavily on fiscal sustainability, leading policymakers to take their eye off the ball of poverty relief. The problem has come to be recognized:

> The main problem regarding Peru's pension system was not that it was spending 1.2 percent of GDP... but, rather, that coverage was so low that the basic goal of a pension system—to provide income security to the old—was far from being accomplished.
>
> First, and most important, the poverty prevention pillar should get a lot more attention than it has in Latin America during the last decade. (Gill, Packard, and Yermo 2005, p. 11)

Similarly, the Presidential Advisory Council in Chile recognized that

> If things go on as they are, it is estimated that within 20 years, only about half of all older adults will be able to count on a pension higher than the minimum...[leading to] about a million people with pensions below the minimum in 2025. Among those at highest risk of finding themselves in this situation are low-income workers, seasonal workers, the self-employed and a considerable proportion of women.

INADEQUATE EMPHASIS ON IMPLEMENTATION. The discussion in chapter 7 places heavy weight on the preconditions necessary for effective implementation of a pension reform, especially such a demanding reform as a move to individual funded accounts. As discussed below, many reforms have taken a more optimistic view than we would about the extent to which a country meets the preconditions.

Individual funded accounts require financial institutions that are effective enough that the added weight of pension business will further strengthen them. Yet "the Bank persistently encouraged countries such as Ukraine and Russia to institute multi-pillar reforms even when financial sector conditions were weak" (World Bank 2006*a*, p. 56); it also encouraged such reforms in countries with poor corruption indexes (World Bank 2006*a*, figure 3.5).

Insufficient weight was given to the administrative costs of individual accounts, costs that are significant even in large, developed countries with long-established systems (such as the United Kingdom's personal accounts for people who opt out of the state earnings-related pension and the voluntary Individual Retirement Accounts in the United States) and considerably higher for small accounts in small countries starting a new system.

The administrative capacity of government also is important, yet,

> the limited quality of civil records in Bolivia allowed people to change their age and even to invent beneficiaries of the...program. Second, the...state did not have a bureaucracy in place that was capable of actually distributing the Bonosol [pension benefit] to the elderly, many of whom had to travel from the countryside on foot to collect the benefit in person. (Valdés-Prieto 2007*b*, para. 3.61)[9]

Political implementation is equally important. Yet,

> The Bank, the designers of the Bonosol program and outside observers failed to see one pitfall. Future governments could increase the size of Bonosol payouts in electoral years.... In fact, the government chose to maximize the electoral impact of this reform, by paying out the first Bonosol (a single annual lump sum) just one month before the 1997 election...[so that] the 1998 payment had to be suspended. (Valdés-Prieto 2007*b*, paras 3.63–64)

9. Another example, though less important, illustrates the same point. We have mentioned the importance of adequate projections of future costs. The World Bank's Pension Reform Simulation Toolkit (PROST) model assists countries in doing this. Again, however, not enough attention was paid to government's technical capacity so that "some countries could not implement PROST because of too few trained professionals" (World Bank 2006*a*, p. xxv).

FAILURE TO ADDRESS ACKNOWLEDGED PROBLEMS. When a system is on an unsustainable trajectory, delay in addressing long-run problems increases the size of the changes that will be required later. When a system does not adequately address elements of poor design (for example, inefficient retirement incentives), the economy bears the resulting costs. Moreover, eventual reform is likely to leave in place ongoing costs from the poor design, for example, the cost of pensions for people who responded to earlier inefficient incentives to retire.

8.3.2 Overoptimistic predictions

How have outcomes compared with predictions?

REPLACEMENT RATES. "The replacement rates envisioned by policymakers setting the contribution parameters of the new multipillar systems ranged from 60 percent to 70 percent of some average of earnings prior to retirement" (Gill, Packard, and Yermo 2005, p. 225). These projections often turned out to be optimistic, in part because financial returns were lower than predicted, in part because projections were often of gross returns (ignoring administrative charges), and in part because some predictions were based on naïve arguments about the beneficial effects of competition on costs and charges. Argentina is perhaps the most striking example. But Argentina is far from alone: "In Chile in early 2002 civil servants started demonstrations demanding to be allowed to switch back to the pre-reform PAYG regime as a result of disappointing projected replacement rates from individual accounts" (Gill, Packard, and Yermo 2005, p. 15).

COVERAGE. The predicted expansion of coverage from conversion to individual accounts has not happened. "Low rates of coverage of the working population under pure PAYG systems were a strong motivating factor for pension reform" (Gill, Packard, and Yermo 2005, p. 96), the argument being that "the close link between contributions and benefits...should discourage evasion, escape to the informal sector, and other labor market distortions" (James 1998, p. 276).

For reasons of myopia, limited information, borrowing constraints, and minimum guarantees, this argument does not hold in theory and has been falsified in practice. Comparing coverage in Latin America at the time each country reformed with coverage in 2004, coverage actually declined in all countries: in Argentina from 50 percent to just over 20 percent, in Mexico from 37 to 28 percent, and in Peru from 31 to 12 percent. Coverage in Chile also fell but only slightly. Thus,

> stalled progress with ... increasing coverage, is cause for concern among the region's governments. The share of the workforce that contributes to a formal pension system remains low.... In several Latin American countries the share of the elderly population receiving pension benefits is falling. For at least some individuals the new funded, privately managed individual savings pillars are not as attractive as they are made out to be. (Gill, Packard, and Yermo 2005, p. 125)

TRANSITION COSTS. The fiscal cost of reform is important, yet there was a tendency to underestimate both the size and the duration of the costs of transition from PAYG to funded systems. Transition costs for Bolivia were projected in 1997 to peak in 1999 at about 2.6 percent of GDP and decline thereafter. In reality, "a major flaw in design encouraged a surge in early pensions and...a sequence of pension policy decisions raised the actual transition deficit by 2.6 percentage points of GDP (as of 2002) above the level planned in mid-1996" (Valdés-Prieto 2007*a*, para. 3.79).

Financing transition costs was a particular problem when a move to funding was initiated at a time of fiscal deficit: "Bolivia, Kazakhstan, Latvia, and Romania had budget deficits over 3 percent of GDP, an indicator that fiscal conditions for implementation of a funded system were not ideal" (World Bank 2006*a*, p. 22). Not least because of these fiscal costs, the International Monetary Fund has tended to be less enthusiastic than the World Bank in recommending funded pensions.

Transition costs have been high and persistent. The system in Chile, though eminently sustainable, continues to require significant annual public spending, averaging 5.7 percent of GDP between 1981 and 2004, with projected spending from 2004 through 2010 of 5 percent of GDP. These costs are higher than were forecast during the 1980s.

ECONOMIC GROWTH. Claims that pension reform would boost economic growth have mostly not been fulfilled: "The Bank has also emphasized the pro-growth aspects of multi-pillar reform—that is, increased savings and capital market development. But the...[Bank's internal] evaluation found few countries in which these promised outcomes have been achieved" (World Bank 2006*a*, p. 56).

IN SUM. Its proponents predicted that

> A mandatory multipillar arrangement for old-age security helps countries to
>
> - Achieve a close relationship between incremental contributions and benefits in the private mandatory pillar. This should reduce effective tax rates, evasion, and labor market distortions.

> - Increase long-term saving, capital market deepening, and growth, through the use of full funding and decentralized control in the second pillar....
> - Insulate the system from political pressures for design features that are inefficient as well as inequitable.
>
> The broader economy should be better off in the long run as a result. So should both the old and the young. (World Bank 1994, pp. 22–23)

What happened? While some of this has occurred, it has been far from universal:

> In many countries with multi-pillar systems ... investments in privately funded pillars are not well diversified, although rates of return are high as a result of investments in government bonds. While these bonds offer high returns, they often just compensate for macroeconomic and investment risk. In addition, privately funded systems remained open to political influence, just like PAYG plans, particularly in times of economic crisis. (World Bank 2006*a*, p. xxiv)

Chapter 9

Pension Systems in Different Countries

This chapter briefly describes the pension systems in Argentina, Australia, Bolivia, Chile, China, Hungary, the Netherlands, New Zealand, Poland, Singapore, South Africa, Sweden, the United Kingdom, and the United States, not least to show how pension systems differ widely across countries. There is no dominant arrangement worldwide. At a strategic level, for the reasons set out in box 2.3, a country's pension arrangements reflect the relative weights attached to its various objectives and the pattern of constraints it faces. One reflection of the differences in weights is the poverty rate among the elderly relative to that among the working-age population, which varies greatly, as shown in figure 9.1.

Countries have chosen systems that vary from more or less pure consumption smoothing in the form of mandatory saving with little or no insurance (for example, Singapore's publicly administered provident fund, which is in essence a savings plan) to a primary concern for poverty relief achieved through a noncontributory flat-rate pension with any consumption smoothing done on a voluntary basis (as in New Zealand). In between, a wide range of systems explicitly address both objectives, some with substantial reliance on funding (Chile), others with intermediate reliance on funding (Sweden, the United States), and others established mainly on a PAYG basis (France, Germany, Italy). The Netherlands has a noncontributory PAYG universal pension based on years of residence together with funded occupational pensions. Reforms in Chile, discussed in section 10.1, introduce a

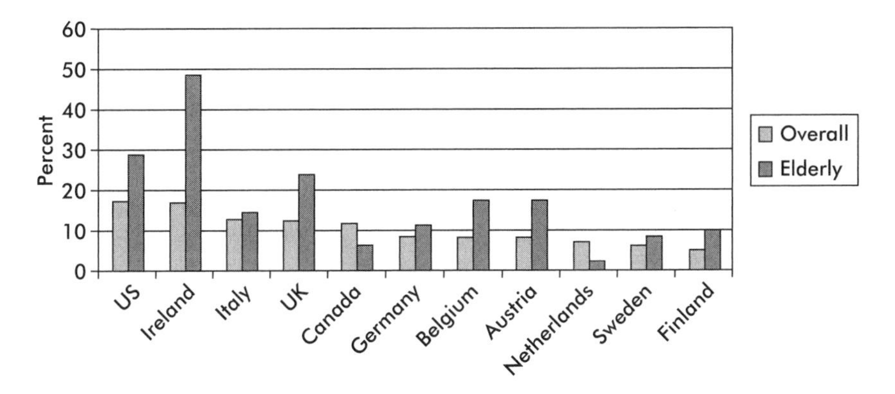

Figure 9.1 Population living on less than half the median income in selected OECD countries, 2000
Source: Luxembourg Income Study.

noncontributory PAYG basic pension alongside the existing system of individual funded accounts, thus strengthening poverty relief. In short, countries have successfully implemented pension systems using very different mixes of structures. This chapter briefly describes some of them.[1]

9.1 Argentina

Argentina reformed its pension system in 1994 using both a defined-benefit PAYG public pension and mandatory individual funded accounts. There is a statutory retirement age of 65 for men, 60 for women. The reforms made heavy demands on both financial and technical capacity, and the system was not able to withstand economic crisis in 2001.[2] As a response to the economic

1. For an international comparison that classifies systems by the extent to which pensions are earnings related, see U.K. Pensions Commission 2004*b*, appendix D; on the OECD countries and the European transition countries, see OECD 2004*c*, Queisser and Whitehouse 2006, and Whiteford and Whitehouse 2006. For recent assessments of developments in the United States and the United Kingdom, see Thompson 2006 and Hills 2006, respectively, and on the welfare state in the European Union, Pestieau 2006. On Latin America see Arenas de Mesa and Mesa-Lago 2006 and Mesa-Lago 2007. See also the other papers in the symposium in *Oxford Review of Economic Policy*, vol. 22, Spring 2006. For useful institutional descriptions, see OECD 2007 and U.S. Social Security Administration 2007*b*. For links to descriptions provided by agencies and organizations, see "Social Security in Other Countries" at the U.S. Social Security website, www.ssa.gov/international/links.html. See also resources in the AARP's Global Aging Program at www.aarp.org/research/international/map/. For an overview, see Whiteford and Whitehouse 2006, tables 2 and 3.

2. Some commentators argue that the financial demands of the pension reform contributed causally to the economic collapse, a conjecture on which the jury is still out. For

emergency, the government obliged the pension funds to swap the dollar-denominated bonds they were holding for newly issued peso-denominated bonds. The proper valuation of the new bonds created continuing problems, since their value depended on the credibility of government policies. And, in 2008, the Argentine Congress passed a law that eliminated the system of individual accounts and transferred the assets to a new PAYG Integrated Argentine Social Security System—Sistema Integrado Previsional Argentino (SIPA), which also incorporates the existing PAYG earnings-related program.

A further problem, largely inherent in a contributory system in a country with a large informal sector, is low compliance with contribution conditions. Thus many workers were unable to meet the requirement in Argentina of at least 30 years of contributions to qualify for any benefit, limiting the effectiveness of the system of individual accounts at contributing to poverty relief.

The Argentinean experience suggests three sets of lessons. It illustrates the risk of embarking on overambitious reforms or on reforms that, though plausible on the basis of optimistic assumptions, are not sufficiently robust in the face of economic turbulence. It also shows the related danger of political interference during economic crisis, which can affect both defined-benefit and defined-contribution systems. Finally, it highlights the importance of compliance for ensuring that the coverage of the system in practice does not deviate substantially from that on paper.

9.2 Chile

Chapter 10 discusses the system in Chile, so discussion here is brief. The root of the system, similar to that in Singapore, is mandatory saving. Chile, however, relies on heavily regulated competitive private supply with free entry for any firm that can meet the regulatory requirements. For the privately managed, defined-contribution individual accounts, employees are mandated to contribute 10 percent of covered earnings plus contributions for disability and survivor insurance and fees for providers. Workers may take their pensions as inflation-indexed annuities or as phased withdrawals.

The individual accounts provide consumption smoothing supported by various institutions to assist poverty relief. Until 2008, a minimum pension guarantee, financed from general revenue, was available for those who had contributed to the mandatory system for at least 20 years; in addition, a means-tested pension, also financed by general revenue, paid a benefit at

fuller discussion of the Argentinean reforms, see Bertranou, Rofman, and Grushka 2003, Arza 2006, and, for a broader assessment of experience in Latin America, Gill, Packard, and Yermo 2005.

about half the level of the minimum guarantee. Beginning in 2008, the minimum guarantee and the means-tested pension are being phased out and replaced by a noncontributory basic pension.

Notwithstanding the intentions of policymakers, private pension provision became highly concentrated, calling into question the plausibility of competition even in a medium-sized economy like Chile's. The point is of particular relevance to smaller economies, as in the case of Bolivia (discussed in box 9.1).

Box 9.1 Pensions in Bolivia

In 1996, using funds from the privatization of state-owned enterprises, Bolivia created a noncontributory pension (Bonosol) for resident citizens above age 65.* At the same time, like many other countries in Latin American, Bolivia followed Chile in setting up mandatory, funded individual accounts for salaried workers. Bolivia broke new ground by organizing the mutual funds for these accounts in a way that took cognizance of administrative costs and the small size of the Bolivian market. The system requires contributions of 10 percent of covered earnings plus 1.71 percent for disability and survivor insurance and 0.5 percent for administrative charges. These administrative charges are considerably lower than in other countries in the region; the comparable figure for administrative charges in Chile is 1.76 percent, and in Peru, 2.27 percent.

Rather than allow free entry (subject to regulation) to the industry, Bolivia decided to begin with only two pension providers, each covering half of the country, with competitive bidding for the right to be one of these two firms; the bidding was based on the average monthly management charge per account. The plan was to allow competition between the two starting in 2000 and regulated free entry starting in 2002.

This approach raises two major issues. One is whether the regulatory authorities can ensure an adequate quality of services. As a general proposition, when granting monopoly rights after a bidding process it is hard to ensure the adequacy of dimensions of service that are not readily measurable and hence hard to monitor. Second is the issue of whether, having started in this way, the introduction of competition, with the additional costs that will arise from marketing, will preserve the low initial cost structure. In a small market with entrenched incumbents, entry is likely to be limited or nonexistent, and the resulting duopoly is not likely to behave very differently from a monopoly.

* For assessments, see Escobar and Nina 2004, Leach 1998, Martinez 2004, and von Gersdorff 1997. The pension was stopped in 1998 and reintroduced in 2002. In 2007 a new program, "Renta Dignidad," replaced Bonosol, paying a higher, universal benefit, with a lower entry age (60 years).

Thus the post-1981 system in Chile gave heavy weight to consumption smoothing with some insurance through voluntary annuitization and with limited weight to poverty relief. The problems of the system—including pensioner poverty, incomplete coverage, gender-equity issues, and high administrative charges and fiscal costs—are discussed in chapter 10, as is a major set of reforms to the system in 2008.

9.3 China

Chapter 10 discusses the system in China and some proposed reforms in more detail. Since 1997, China has moved from an enterprise-based system of defined-benefit pensions based on final salary toward a unified system for urban workers. The new system has three elements: a defined-benefit, PAYG, first-tier pension (the social pool); a mandatory, funded, defined-contribution pension; and voluntary, enterprise-based pensions.

From 1999 onward, coverage was expanded with the intention of including the employees of private and other types of enterprises in urban areas, the self-employed, and (it was hoped) the informal sector. But the expansion of coverage has been limited. The system is financed by dedicated contributions, mainly from firms and workers, with some financing also from government.

This system makes long-run strategic sense but has not functioned as intended. The three elements together offer poverty relief, insurance, and consumption smoothing with some allowance for differing tastes. There are serious problems of fragmentation, system financial deficits, and administrative difficulties. These are particularly visible with the funded individual accounts.

9.4 The Netherlands

The Netherlands has a noncontributory pension of 70 percent of the net minimum wage payable at age 65. The system differs in two respects from conventional public pension systems. First, the benefit is awarded on the basis of residence, not contributions. The full pension is awarded at age 65 on the basis of 50 years of residence between the ages of 15 and 65; the full pension is reduced by 2 percent for each year of nonresidence.[3] A person with fewer than 50 years of residence is potentially eligible for social

3. In 2005, 84 percent of beneficiaries received full benefits, though with increased international labor mobility that number is expected to fall.

assistance. Second, the benefit is financed through an earmarked tax, the AOW (Algemene Ouderdomsweet or general law for the elderly) premium, which is additional to, but integrated with, the income tax. The tax base for the AOW premium is income, not earnings, and the premium is paid only by people under 65.

It is interesting to reflect on the nature of the arrangement. From one perspective the benefit is noncontributory, that is, part of a person's rights based on residence, hence addressing problems of coverage. On the other hand, it is financed from the AOW premium and so can be regarded as "earned" from contributions but through the income tax rather than a payroll tax.[4] Each of these views is valid, and each has support from a different political perspective; thus it is perhaps not surprising that the system has remained broadly stable since its introduction in 1957. The trick, from a coverage perspective, is to require contributions but not to make benefits conditional on a person's contribution record. Currently, given increasing life expectancy, policymakers are wrestling with the increasing cost of the benefit.

The noncontributory universal pension is combined with a system of occupational pensions by industry. Although in a formal sense such pensions are voluntary, once an industry chooses a plan, participation becomes compulsory for workers in the industry.[5] Over 90 percent of the workforce participate in an occupational pension (which are required by law to be funded), of whom about one-quarter were in career-average defined-benefit plans in 1998 and about two-thirds in final-salary plans. Since then, there has been a strong move from final pay to career average, which reached three-quarters of the workforce by 2004. Typically these are now hybrid defined-benefit-defined-contribution plans, with benefits based on career averages and with adjustments of both contribution rates and accrued liabilities, depending on the solvency position of the fund. This change was in response to the "perfect storm" of declining stock prices and declining rates of return along with stricter funding requirements. Thus, pension funds have responded in ways that share risks among workers, employers, and pensioners more broadly than in either a conventional defined-benefit system (where the risk in a pure plan falls on the employer) or a conventional defined-contribution plan (where the risk in a pure plan falls on the worker).The combination of a noncontributory universal pension and an occupational pension for a fairly full career aims at a total replacement rate of about 70 percent of an average worker's final salary.

4. Although there is no requirement to have had at least some level of taxable income.

5. A company can opt out of the industry plan if it starts a company pension fund with a better plan.

9.5 New Zealand

The pension system in New Zealand is in many ways the polar opposite of that in Singapore. The bedrock of the system is a noncontributory universal pension (New Zealand Superannuation) paid from general taxation to all persons over 65 who pass a residency test[6] and included in a person's taxable income. The pension is 72.5 percent of the net average wage for a married couple, more per person for singles (varying with living arrangements), and less if one of the couple is under 65. The basic pension is supplemented by voluntary savings, which, unusually among countries, for many years received no tax advantages. The country is also an outlier in that there is no mandatory earnings-related pension. However, the flat benefit is high enough to represent a high replacement rate for a sizable fraction of the population, limiting concern about consumption smoothing.

The savings regime was reformed in 2007 with the introduction of KiwiSaver, a defined-contribution plan, with tax advantages together with a flat-rate subsidy at least partly to cover administrative costs and with automatic enrollment so that a worker who wishes to opt out has to take positive action to do so. The design is simple, in part in recognition of the problems of consumer choice discussed in section 7.3.

Since the pension benefit is universal, exceeds the poverty line, and is based on residence rather than a history of paid work, it is not surprising that, as with arrangements in the Netherlands, the system is highly effective in relieving poverty. The approach also addresses the gender inequalities that often arise with contributory systems, and it accommodates diverse labor market arrangements and fluid family structures, since, for example, a woman's flat-rate pension depends neither on her own record of contributions nor that of her husband.

The system is popular. A referendum in September 1997 on replacing the tax-financed flat-rate pension with mandatory funded individual accounts (along Chilean lines) was easily defeated. Eighty percent of the electorate took part, and 92.8 percent of those voting rejected the proposal. Since 2000 the public plan has been partially prefunded so as to smooth tax rates as the population ages.[7] Box 9.2 discusses noncontributory pensions in a range of countries.

6. The pension is payable at age 65 to all New Zealanders living in the country, subject to 10 years of residency since the age of 20 and not less than 5 years of residency since the age of 50.

7. The intention is to allocate around NZ$2 billion of general revenue per year over a 20-year period. See the New Zealand Superannuation Fund website at www.nzsuperfund.co.nz/.

Box 9.2 Noncontributory pensions

High-income countries. Like New Zealand and the Netherlands, Australia also has a noncontributory pension.* The benefit is paid from general revenues and is subject not to an income test, designed to restrict benefits to the poor, but to an affluence test, which has the more limited purpose of clawing back benefits from the rich. Since 1992, workers have in addition been subject to de facto mandatory participation in individual funded accounts, an outgrowth of the country's voluntary employer-based plans, which over time the government decided to systematize.**

Middle-income countries. The new noncontributory pension in Chile is discussed in section 10.1. South Africa also has a noncontributory pension, the State Old Age Grant. The case is interesting in that it reaches effectively not only urban pensioners but also the rural elderly and is well targeted. The last point should not be surprising since old age is a good indicator of potential poverty.

The pension, paid to men at age 65 and women at age 60, is financed from general revenues with no contribution conditions. The benefit—around half of average household income—is high relative to the very low incomes of most nonwhites in South Africa but is low relative to the incomes of the better off. Originally introduced as poverty relief for whites during the 1930s, the plan was gradually expanded to cover all race groups. Research findings suggest that it is highly effective both in terms of social policy and in the way the plan is implemented:

> The South Africa social pension is an example of a transfer plan where eligibility is determined by age. In spite of the simplicity of the targeting indicator, the pension is effective in reaching the poorest households and those with children.... The South African authorities have overcome the difficulties of making cash transfers to even remote rural areas, and of checking eligibility among even illiterate pensioners. (Case and Deaton 1998, p. 1359; see also Lund 2002, and Burns, Keswell, and Leibbrandt 2005)

The administration of the system is consolidated under the South African Social Security Agency (see South Africa National Treasury 2007). In most

* For further discussion of noncontributory pensions, see Willmore 2004, 2006; on Australia, Borowski 2005; for gender aspects, Jefferson and Preston (2005).

** In 1992 the Australian government introduced a tax surcharge under which employers who did not pay contributions were liable to pay more in tax than they would otherwise have paid in pension contributions. The effect was to increase pension coverage from about 75 to 80 percent of the workforce to 92 or 93 percent. Contributions are not mandatory for self-employed workers or for extremely low paid workers.

(continued)

Box 9.2 (Continued)

urban areas, people receive the pension through bank accounts or post offices. In rural areas government has outsourced delivery to the private sector, organized at the provincial level. The system at its best is effective and innovative. In some areas vehicles fitted with cash dispensers go to predesignated places at preordained times. Pensioners enter their ID number (or fingerprint), and their pension is paid out. Notionally there is a government official on hand to provide help, but this facility is patchy.

Problems remain, however, including the potential for private sector contractors to make excessive profits, attacks on vehicles, and the disincentive to banks to move into rural areas since the system carries out what would otherwise be one of their major functions. Not least for these reasons, there has been a significant new shift to placing the cash machines inside supermarkets. Thus the cash-dispensing function of the banks is now available, as is the savings function (since pensioners do not have to withdraw the entire monthly benefit at one time) but not other banking functions.

Low-income countries. A number of low-income countries have noncontributory pensions (sometimes called social pensions), including Bolivia, Botswana, Namibia, and Nepal. Total spending is typically small (below 1 percent of GDP in Botswana, Namibia, and Nepal), and the benefit is also generally small (Willmore 2006, table 1).

Pensions of this sort have the great potential advantage of extending coverage to people with limited contributions records. This is especially important for women and for workers in the informal sector. In assessing their desirability and feasibility in a particular country, policymakers need to consider a range of factors:

- How well could the pension be targeted? The cost-effectiveness of a noncontributory universal pension depends on the accuracy of age as a targeting device. In principle, the more poor people a country has, the greater the importance of poverty relief and the better targeted a noncontributory pension will be. The extent to which age *alone* is a good indicator, however, will vary from country to country (see Kakwani and Subbarao 2007), depending, for example, on the extent to which old people live alone or as part of an extended family.
- Is administrative capacity sufficient? Even a simple pension has administrative requirements. The government must be able to establish people's ages and to guard against multiple claims by one person and claims by relatives on behalf of a pensioner who has died.
- Is the cost of delivery low enough relative to the size of pension being considered?

(continued)

Box 9.2 (Continued)

Where a government has the necessary implementation capacity, policymakers have a range of options to contain costs:

- The level of the pension can be kept low (for example, it is only 10 percent of GDP per capita in Botswana and Nepal).
- The age at which the pension is first paid can be set high (in Nepal only 1.1 percent of the population are older than the qualifying age).
- If administrative capacity permits, a further option is to pay a smaller pension to the younger old (for example, those aged 65 to 75) and a larger one to the older old (those aged 75 and above).

9.6 Poland

The system of pensions that Poland inherited from the communist era was poorly suited to a market economy.[8] A strategic problem was the large number of pensioners, partly because coverage was close to universal—one of the strengths of the system—but also because the pensionable age was low. The latter had a series of causes: many people were allowed to retire early in the waning days of communism in order to preserve social peace, and the process continued during the early transition to absorb workers left jobless by restructuring; for similar reasons, access to a disability pension was relatively easy. A second strategic problem resulted: pension spending in the early 1990s reached 15 percent of GDP, a level incompatible with other demands on scarce fiscal capacity, particularly at a time when falling output was badly eroding that capacity. Pension benefits varied unsystematically and bore little or no relation to contributions or to need. Finally, although social insurance contributions were collected, there were no records of how much each individual worker had contributed, such records being largely unnecessary with universal full employment (so that the great bulk of workers had a full contributions record) and pensions based on final salary.

A major reform in 1998 established a mandatory system with two elements. The first is an NDC pension. A person's notional fund is indexed in line with the growth of total economywide wage bill, hence in line with trends in productivity and employment; in retirement the intention is that

8. On pension reform in the former communist countries, see Barr 2001, chapter 15, Müller 1999, and Whiteford and Whitehouse 2006. On the Polish reforms, see Góra and Rutkowski 1998, Golinowska, Pietka, and Zukowski 2003, Muturi et al. 2000, Chlon-Dominczak 2002, and Chlon-Dominczak and Góra 2006.

pensions are indexed to a pensioner price index.[9] Thus a person's public pension is strictly proportional to his or her (notionally) cumulated contributions with two significant exceptions: there is a minimum pension guarantee for people with an appropriate contributions record, and credits are paid for years spent out of the labor force raising children. The second element in the system consists of mandatory, privately managed, defined-contribution pensions, which are integrated with the first tier in a number of ways. Notwithstanding the intention of the reform to equalize the minimum retirement age at 62, the minimum retirement age remains at 65 for men and 60 for women. All these arrangements apply as described to younger workers, with transitional arrangements for older workers. Thus Poland offers the example of a system that provides consumption smoothing through NDC accounts and funded individual accounts together with a poverty relief element (the minimum guarantee, pension credits for childrearing activities, and other forms of poverty relief for the elderly). Thus it resembles the system in Sweden.

Poland's example is illuminating also in terms of its implementation. Despite considerable institutional capacity and heavy emphasis during the reform process on building an adequate administrative infrastructure, the reforms almost came to grief because the system was initially unable to keep track of people's contributions. The roots of the problem were delayed implementation of the new computer system and initial compliance problems. The situation was rectified, but from the outside it looked as though a collapse was narrowly averted.

Some other countries in Central and Eastern Europe—for example, Latvia—have adopted a strategy with similarities to that of Poland. Others have taken a different approach. The Czech Republic and Slovenia decided against mandatory funded accounts, instead choosing to reform their PAYG arrangements and encourage voluntary pension saving. Hungary adopted an intermediate approach that includes mandatory funded accounts and raises the significant concerns described in box 9.3.

9.7 Singapore

The pension system in Singapore is built around mandatory, publicly managed, defined-contribution pensions provided mainly by the Central Provident Fund. Thus the core of the system is an individual savings plan with little or no insurance in the form of annuities.

9. Indexation of benefits during retirement in the years after 1998 was supposed to be based on price inflation plus 20 percent of wage growth, but in reality benefits were somewhat volatile.

Box 9.3 Pension reform in Hungary

Reform in Hungary affected two components of the pension system: parametric change to the PAYG element and a new system of mandatory, funded defined-contribution accounts. The existing system of voluntary funded accounts continued as before.

Participation in the new second tier was mandatory for workers entering the labor force after July 1, 1998, and voluntary for all others. The second tier started in January 1998 and by 2004 had assets equal to 4 percent of GDP.

The reforms raise a number of concerns, which echo earlier cautions about transition costs and implementation and administrative costs:

- Transition costs of 1.5 percent of GDP associated with the introduction of funded accounts contributed to a large budget deficit.
- A joint World Bank–IMF study found that "The average return performance of [pension funds] has been rather disappointing" (World Bank 2005, para. 30). Between 1998 and 2005, the study reported, the average weighted real net rate of return was 3.75 percent (in some years real returns were negative), lower than the average rate of growth of real wages of 5.3 percent (table 12) and lower than in any of the reforming countries in Latin America (table 13).
- Administrative costs were high. Using the same methodology as in our table 7.1 for assessing long-run costs (that is, not giving excessive weight to high start-up costs), the World Bank–IMF study estimated an annual management charge of 1.18 percent (World Bank 2005, para. 48) and a charge ratio of between 18 and 30 percent (table 20).
- For part of the period administrative charges reduced the net real return to close to zero (Augusztinovics et al. 2002; updated in Matits 2004), to the great disadvantage of people who moved to the new system toward the end of their careers. As Matits (p. 11) noted, "given workers' low level of understanding of the new private pillar, it probably would have been fairer if older workers would have not been allowed to switch."

For these and other reasons, an occasional paper issued by the National Bank of Hungary concluded that

> the performance of the pension fund sector in Hungary can be regarded as unsatisfactory.... [New] pensioners of the multi-pillar system are projected to receive significantly lower benefits than members of the pure PAYG system with an identical wage-profile and service years.... And... a major tension could arise from pensions being below any social minimum. (Orbán and Palotai 2005, p. 28)

The contributions of participants are channeled into three types of account. The Ordinary Account accumulates funds for retirement but offers earlier withdrawals for approved purposes, such as the purchase of a home. The Medisave Account covers hospitalization and allows the voluntary purchase of catastrophic illness insurance sponsored by the Central Provident Fund. The Special Account is in principle meant exclusively for retirement but can also be used in a limited way for mortgage payments. Contribution rates decline with age, on the premise that lower wages for workers older than 55 will encourage employers to hire them.[10] Alongside the Central Provident Fund, the preretirement Central Provident Fund Investment System allows individual choice from worldwide portfolios, though management costs are high.[11]

Accumulations are hampered by substantial preretirement withdrawals and by low rates of return to pension savings. Although the government guarantees a nominal interest rate of 2.5 percent a year, the real annual return over the period 1987–2005 was only 1.3 percent. A small pool of funds (about 3 percent of total balances) is contracted out to private fund managers. The real return of these funds between 1987 and 2004 was 2.9 percent, more than twice that of the Central Provident Fund.

At retirement a person can choose to buy an annuity but is not required to do so. Only a small proportion of pensioners choose the annuity option; thus most elderly Singaporeans are exposed to longevity risk. Nor are there any arrangements to address inflation risk.

In sum, Singapore's pension system relies almost exclusively on mandatory savings to provide consumption smoothing. However, the replacement rate (estimated at 20 percent of previous earnings) is inadequate, and there is no tax-financed redistributive element to provide poverty relief. Mitigation of longevity, inflation, and political risks is limited. In addition, design and governance of the system are continuing concerns.

9.8 Sweden

After major reform in the 1990s, the pension system in Sweden comprises two elements: a partially funded system of NDC accounts combined with a generous guarantee that does well at keeping elderly Swedes out of poverty; and a system of funded individual accounts, the Premium Pension. The

10. In 2007 contributions were 34.5 percent of covered wages for workers under 50, 28.5 percent between ages 50 and 55, 20 percent between ages 55 and 60, 12.5 percent between ages 60 and 65, and 10 percent for workers older than 65. The sum of participants' balances in March 2006 was equivalent to 63 percent of GDP.

11. The Central Provident Fund was introduced in 1955. The Approved Investment System was introduced in 1986 and renamed the CPF Investment System in 1997.

guarantee provides that a person who reaches retirement after forty years of residence in Sweden is eligible for a full minimum benefit. For fewer years of residence the benefit is reduced proportionately; it is also reduced in response to the level of benefit from the NDC pension. There also is an income-tested minimum pension. In addition, credits are given during working life, both to the NDC pension and to the Premium Pension, for periods when a person is out of the labor force looking after young children or collecting unemployment or sickness benefits.

The system has an 18.5 percent contribution rate, of which 16 percentage points are for the NDC element and the remaining 2.5 percent for fully funded individual accounts. The NDC element uses a notional interest rate equal to the rate of growth of average wages. However, if at any time the calculated financial balance of the system is unsatisfactory, that rate is lowered automatically; no legislative action is required. Each worker receives an annual statement with information about the notional and funded account balances and projections of future benefits.

Benefits may first be claimed at age 61, and this age is not scheduled to change; in practice, however, most people first claim benefits at age 65 (in contrast with the United States, where more people claim benefits at the earliest eligibility age than at any other age).[12] The initial benefit is set by a quasi-actuarial calculation based on the mortality of the worker's birth cohort, the age at which he or she first takes benefits, and the anticipated rate of increase in benefits. Benefits increase each year after retirement based on the difference between the notional interest rate (normally the rate of wage growth) and the anticipated annual increase of 1.6 percent.

The 2.5 percent of payroll going to the funded individual accounts is collected by the government and distributed to participating mutual funds. The number of funds is large, 785 at the end of 2007. Individuals may choose the funds in which to invest, up to a maximum of five, with a default fund for the large number of workers who do not make a choice. As discussed in section 7.3, in recent years about 90 percent of new workers made no choice and hence entered the default fund. Funds must be approved by the government and must accept the charges established by a centrally set formula. On retirement a worker's accumulated assets must be used to purchase an annuity (individual or joint-life) provided by the government. Deposits may be transferred between spouses or registered partners (subject to a 14 percent reduction for anticipated longer lives of recipients).

12. In Sweden in 2006, 7 percent of participants first took a pension at age 61, 4 percent at age 62, 4 percent at age 63, 4 percent at age 64, 75 percent at age 65, 4 percent at age 66, and 1 percent at age 67, by which time almost everyone was drawing a pension (though without necessarily stopping work). Those not working at ages younger than 65 typically are on disability benefits.

Sweden addresses the problem of administrative costs through a central clearinghouse which administers and maintains the individual accounts. Contributions to the NDC pension and individual accounts are collected together, and the funds are then channeled wholesale to individual accounts; thus fund managers know nothing about individual contributors. The average annual charge (net) is 0.73 percent of assets, equivalent to a charge ratio of about 14 percent.[13] Although this central management of funds is similar to that in the U.S. Thrift Savings Plan (box 9.4), the cost is much higher; the two sets of institutions are not fully comparable, however, since the latter severely restricts the choice of funds and deals only with a single employer, the federal government. The system shows that, even in a developed country, fully funded individual accounts can be expensive and that many workers show no interest in having a wide choice of investments.

Box 9.4 The U.S. Thrift Savings Plan

The U.S. government established the Thrift Savings Plan for federal civil servants (see www.tsp.gov) in 1986. The plan offers participants a very limited choice of portfolios. Initially there were three: a stock market index fund, a fund holding bonds issued by private firms, and a fund holding government bonds. In 2007 workers could choose from six funds, including a life cycle option. A government agency keeps centralized records of individual portfolios. Fund management is on a wholesale basis. Investment in private sector assets is handled by private financial firms, which bid for the opportunity (and which manage the same portfolios in the voluntary private market).

As a result, administrative costs are astonishingly low: as little as 6 basis points annually, or 60¢ per $1,000 of account balance. By 2007 the program had grown to include 3.8 million participants and held assets of $225 billion. The commission appointed by President George W. Bush to propose reforms for Social Security recommended that it adopt the same approach, which should be of wide interest also to other countries considering reform, in particular to developing countries where institutional capacity is limited. As discussed in section 8.2.3, the United Kingdom is adopting a similar plan.

13. Fees for the individual accounts in 2005 included an administrative fee charged to all accounts of 0.3 percent of assets; an average fund fee (including the default fund) of 0.43 percent of assets after a rebate (the average rebate is 0.37 percent of assets); and an average fund fee for the default fund of 0.16 percent of assets after rebate. Thus, on average, the total fee is 73 basis points, which, as table 7.1 shows, reduces accumulations over a 40-year career by roughly 14 percent.

Sweden has a Globalisation Council charged with analyzing possible reforms to respond to increasing globalization. Among the reports they have arranged is one on pensions (Diamond 2009).

9.9 United Kingdom

Pension arrangements in the United Kingdom have witnessed much change over the years. Under the 1946 National Insurance Act, flat-rate contributions gave entitlement to a flat-rate benefit. The retirement age was 65 for men, 60 for women. For a full pension a man needed 44 years of contributions; a woman, 40. There was no statutory indexation of benefits, which instead were raised periodically.

The 1975 Social Security Act replaced the flat-rate contribution with an earnings-related contribution, which gave entitlement to the flat-rate basic state pension and to the new State Earnings-Related Pension System (SERPS). The contribution conditions remained unchanged, with the important exception that a pension credit was introduced for care activities. Participation in the basic state pension was compulsory. Workers also belonged to SERPS unless their employer had opted out, in which case they belonged to their employer's approved occupational pension plan. Under the 1975 act, contributions were indexed in line with wage changes, and pensions during retirement in line with the greater of wage or price changes, a serious design flaw discussed in box 5.3.

Reforms announced in 1986 changed the indexation of benefits during retirement to changes in prices; extended opting out by allowing individuals to choose to have an individual account in place of SERPS or an employer-provided pension; and announced ways in which SERPS would be less generous from 2000 onward. A further reform consisted of a phased increase in women's retirement age to 65. As a consequence, projected public pension spending in the United Kingdom shows the unusual pattern of declining as a percentage of GDP, as shown in figure 1.9, despite significant aging of the population.

By the mid-1990s, however, the U.K. pension system faced major problems. The cumulative effects of price indexation and the known failings of coverage in contributory systems created problems of pensioner poverty. Occupational pensions concealed many of the problems of the public system but provided inadequate coverage of lower earners. Further reform of the public pension was announced, and attempts were made to introduce individual accounts for lower-paid workers. These added to the complexity of the system but had little impact. Problems with occupational pensions aggravated the situation, partly because of adverse stock market conditions after 2000 and perhaps also because of overregulation.

These problems were the background for the U.K. Pensions Commission, the primary recommendations of which are discussed in section 8.2.3. In accepting those strategic recommendations, the government made a further change: beginning in 2010 a full basic state pension will require only 30 years of contributions.

The U.K. experience exemplifies two strategic errors. First, the system was changed too frequently and with too short a time horizon. Since a central purpose of pensions is consumption smoothing over increasingly long lives, stability over long periods is important; changes should be made infrequently, announced long in advance, and phased in gradually. The second problem, excessive complexity, is in part a result of the first. A system that had originally been simple and well understood ended up not only too complex for many in the general public to understand but also complex to the point where many experts had difficulty understanding it.

The United Kingdom has substantial coverage by funded employer pensions. These have seen a strong trend from defined benefit to defined contribution.

9.10 United States

The U.S. Social Security system has been gender-neutral since 1961. Retirement benefits are available to workers with sufficiently low earnings (that is, a retirement test) between age 62 and the age for full benefits, which is in transition from 65 to 67. There is no retirement test after the age for full benefits. Benefit determination is a four-step process. First, the worker's 35 best wage-indexed annual earnings are averaged (including zeros if needed to reach 35 years; wage indexing is done only up to the year that the worker turns 60, after which nominal earnings are used). Then, a three-stage benefit formula is used to calculate a benefit level. With replacement rates of 0.90, 0.32, and 0.15 for successively higher bands of income, the benefit formula is progressive. The third step is an adjustment for the age at which benefits start. The adjustment is roughly actuarially neutral between age 62 and the age for full benefits but is not large enough to be actuarially neutral for all ages after that. There are auxiliary benefits for spouses. The fourth step is the increase in benefit levels in line with prices after a worker reaches age 62, whether benefits have started or not. For a worker starting benefits at age 65 in 2006 with indexed average lifetime earnings of $30,000 (a little below the median), the annual benefit would be $13,812, for a replacement rate of 46 percent (ignoring auxiliary benefits). In 2006 the system's expenditures were 4.2 percent of GDP.

Revenue for both disability and retirement pensions comes from a 12.4 percent payroll tax rate up to a taxable maximum, which is high enough that roughly 94 percent of workers have all their earnings subject to tax each year (but roughly 15 percent of aggregate earnings are not subject to the tax). Revenue also comes from some of the income tax revenue derived from taxing pensions. Currently revenue exceeds expenditure; the excess goes into a trust fund, which holds U.S. Treasury bonds paying market interest rates. At the end of 2007 the trust funds for retirement and disability benefits held just over $2.2 trillion, equal to just below 3.8 times expenditures in 2007.

There is no mandate to participate in any pension except the public pension, but workers contribute to a wide array of employer and individual systems. As in the United Kingdom, there is wide coverage by funded plans, which have seen a steady trend from defined benefit to defined contribution. The Thrift Saving Plan, which supplements Social Security for federal civil servants and is discussed in box 9.4, offers an interesting example of a simple plan with inexpensive administration.

9.11 Conclusion

Although the institutions supporting pension systems are complex, the conclusions we draw from this chapter and the previous one are simple:

- Systems today look very different from 50 years ago. This is no accident. It is as it should be.
- There are many different ways of achieving the various objectives of pension systems. The diversity of (more or less) well-run systems is considerable. This, too, is as it should be.
- A number of countries have badly designed structures, and those with good ones often have some features that would benefit from change.

Chapter 10

Close Focus: Pension Reform in Chile and China

10.1 Pension reform in Chile

Chile's pension reform of 1981 has fascinated commentators and influenced other countries. We therefore discuss it at greater length than the systems of other countries.[1] In 2005 Chile's newly elected president, Michelle Bachelet, appointed an advisory council to consider changes. The council's analysis and recommendations are the basis for reforms enacted in 2008. Section 10.1.1 describes and assesses the funded individual accounts created in 1981 and reformed over the years, including reforms in 2008. Section 10.1.2 discusses the council's reasoning and its central recommendation—the introduction of a universal pension. Section 10.1.3 touches briefly on coverage.

10.1.1 Individual accounts

The system

The root of the post-1981 system, similar to that in Singapore, is mandatory saving. The major change in 1981 was to introduce mandatory individual

1. For fuller discussion, see chapters 12 and 13 of our longer book (Barr and Diamond 2008). See also Diamond and Valdés-Prieto 1994, Edwards and Edwards 2002, and, for fuller discussion of Chile in the broader Latin American context, Gill, Packard, and Yermo 2005, Arenas de Mesa and Mesa-Lago 2006, and Mesa-Lago 2007.

funded accounts for workers employed in the formal sector in place of the previous array of defined-benefit plans. Each worker is required to place 10 percent of covered earnings into an account and to make an additional payment for disability and survivors' insurance plus a commission to the firm that administers the individual account, collects contributions, and manages the pension fund. A retiring worker may take his or her pension as an inflation-indexed annuity purchased from an insurance company but is not obliged to do so. The alternative is to draw down the accumulation through phased withdrawals; constraints on the rate of withdrawal reduce the risk of outliving the money. In this case the funds remain with a pension management firm. Annuities and withdrawals are subject to mandatory protection of family members. There has been a minimum pension guarantee for people with at least 20 years of pension coverage, replaced by the basic pension discussed below.

A worker is allowed to draw his or her pension early, before the pensionable age (65 for men, 60 for women) provided that the accumulation is large enough. There is a dual test—that the accumulation provide a replacement rate of at least 70 percent (50 percent prior to January 2004) and an absolute level greater than 150 percent of the minimum pension (120 percent prior to January 2004). This use of dual options for access to pension benefits is unusual and interesting. The council proposed to lower the minimum required replacement rate for an early pension for workers nearing retirement age, but the proposal did not become law.

To handle the individual accounts, Chile organized a regulated market in which fund management firms (called *administradoras de fondos de pensiones* or AFPs), originally restricted to handling a single mutual fund each, compete to manage funds. Entry into the business was (and remains) open to any firm meeting sufficient capital and managerial criteria. Thus the exact makeup of the portfolios is left to the private market (in contrast with the U.S. Thrift Savings Plan described in box 9.4).

Choice, competition, and costs

Notwithstanding the intentions of policymakers, however, pension provision became highly concentrated, calling into question the plausibility of effective competition even in a medium-sized economy like Chile's. The point is of particular relevance to smaller economies, as in the case of Bolivia, discussed in box 9.1. The limited diversity in available portfolios has a number of causes.

- Each firm is restricted in the number of its offerings: each firm is now allowed to manage up to five fund portfolios, varying in their mix of stocks and bonds.

- The number of participating firms is small. Although entry into the industry is theoretically free, the number of firms has shrunk considerably: in 2006 only six firms were still active in the market, with the top three holding 80 percent of assets. This results in part from the requirement that AFPs have no other business, restricting the ability to share facilities and thus reducing opportunities for new entrants who might take advantage of economies of scope. It is also in part a result of the difficulty of attracting workers, who exhibit considerable inertia, not least for the reasons discussed in box 2.2 and section 7.3.
- The offerings of the firms are similar. This is to some extent the result of regulations that guarantee a relative rate of return. The approach mimics contracts for fund management that are observed in markets that serve large professional purchasers. In such contracts the fund manager's performance is evaluated periodically by comparison with a peer benchmark (in Chile, the average return of all the pension funds in the same class minus a margin) and where underperformance is penalized (in Chile the penalty is paid to the participant's accounts, hence the usual description of this system as a relative return "guarantee").

As noted in our discussion of behavioral economics, we do not consider a limited set of options *per se* to be a problem.

Concern about the number of firms is linked to concern about the level of administrative charges. Although these are at the lower end of the range in Latin America, at 1.76 percent of salary (compared with 10 percent being deposited) (see table 7.2), concern about the level of charges has been recurrent since the start of the individual accounts. In an attempt to address the problem, regulations have been changed numerous times to encourage more competition among existing firms and to make entry easier; concern about costs continues nonetheless. The law requires each AFP to charge all its participants the same percentage contribution rate. The aim of this regulation is progressive redistribution, since charging the fixed costs of handling accounts would give lower rates of return to lower earners. This structure of charges is perceived as appropriate because of the mandate to purchase the AFP service. Since costs are largely a fixed element per account, clients with high, stable incomes are very attractive: "Marketing based on gifts and discounts makes it possible to reach these clients, side-stepping the obligation to bring prices down for all participants" (Chile Presidential Advisory Council 2006, p. 13).

To encourage more price competition and greater entry, the Chilean council proposed an interesting experiment, which is due to start in 2010. It uses a mix of bidding and individual choice, which might result in lower charges while maintaining quality of service. The experiment is to allow pension providers to bid for all new entrants into the labor force over a one-year period. The new entrants would have to stay with the winning bidder for at least 18 months, and the provider would be obliged to offer the same commission to its existing participants (if lower than they were already being charged) and to any others who wish to enroll to benefit from the lower charges. After 18 months the provider would be allowed to increase its commission for all participants, preserving uniformity. After this 18-month period, the current incentives for attracting the most profitable workers away from the initial firm would apply.

It is interesting to conjecture what might happen over time with such a recommendation. New entrants, naturally having small accounts, are not financially attractive in the short run, though the potential for retention may make them attractive over a longer horizon. We hope that detailed data will be gathered to assist evaluation. Although attempts to strengthen competition may exert some downward pressure on charges, we think that high costs are an inherent consequence of a system that seeks to give workers individual choice over their pension provider.

Funding

Moving to a funded system in 1981 meant that each worker's contributions had to go toward his or her own pension; thus the government had to finance the pensions of existing pensioners and the cost of pensions earned under the old system by continuing workers. To finance the transition, Chile set aside an amount equivalent to 5 percent of GDP at the time of the reform. Substantial and systematic fiscal surpluses from 1987 onward made it possible for the government to take over those legacy obligations without going deeply into debt or reducing benefits. Compared with using those surpluses either for lowering taxes or increasing (noninvestment) public spending, this policy resulted in higher national savings, a key ingredient if a pension reform is to increase economic growth. In this respect Chile's experience contrasts sharply with that of most countries, where recommendations for similar reforms have been made in a context of budgetary deficits,[2] which the pension reform made worse, thus contributing to further financing difficulties insofar as the reform resulted in higher interest rates on government debt.

The fiscal costs of pensions in Chile have been high and continuing. Direct government pension spending in 2004 was 5.5 percent of GDP, close

2. For example, Bolivia, Kazakhstan, Latvia, and Romania had budget deficits over 3 percent of GDP at the time they initiated reform; see World Bank 2006*a*, figure 3.2.

to the 1981–2004 average of 5.7 percent, with official projections for 2005–10—nearly 30 years after the reforms were introduced—of 5 percent of GDP. Part of this is the legacy of financing the transition to a funded pension.[3] But there are several other reasons for high spending. One of these is poverty relief: the minimum pension guarantee and the welfare pension together cost slightly less than 1 percent of GDP in 2003, with additional spending on disability pensions for people under age 65. There is further public spending on pensions for the military and the police (about 1.7 percent of GDP in 2003), which were not part of the 1981 reform.

These high fiscal costs are not in themselves a defect, but they serve as a reminder to other countries that pension systems inescapably involve public spending and that the time horizon of transition costs is likely to be long.

Capital markets

Some advocates of the Chilean approach emphasize the very high real rates of return earned on the assets. Several points are worth noting. One is that in the early years the funds were held completely in government bonds and government-backed bank deposits. Thus the high rates of return reflected high interest rates in Chile, not the acumen of fund managers. Second, since the permitted range of portfolios was expanded, studies have found that, once account is taken of legal restrictions on portfolios, the portfolios have been on the risk-return frontier. The council report stated that

> the claim that the pension system has produced real yields of 10% per year does not provide an adequate reflection of the system's performance. More realistic estimates of the actual yield on the worker's contributions, in other words, the return up to the moment of retirement, net of commissions, indicate that this would be between 4.5% and 6.5% per year. (Chile Presidential Advisory Council 2006, p. 15)

The central point is that the return on the portfolio and the return on deposits differ because of administrative charges; thus it is important to calculate returns net of administrative costs. Also relevant is the expectation that future returns are likely to differ from those from a period when the stock and bond markets underwent such big changes.

The value of Chile's stock market relative to GDP has increased notably over the years. Credit for this improvement is shared among the pension reform itself, the reform of regulation of the stock market, and the opening of the capital account to foreign equity investors. However, since the funds handling the individual accounts mostly pursue a buy-and-hold strategy,

3. For an estimate of public spending attributable to the move to funding, see Valdés-Prieto 2005.

this growth in value relative to GDP has not been accompanied by a matching growth in transactions, so that liquidity has not risen in step. The long-term bond market, meanwhile, has grown and is important for financing both government and firms. Indeed, the bond market did not exist in its present form until faced with increased demand from mutual funds and insurance companies, which needed to hold indexed bonds as backing for indexed annuities. Credit for this goes to the pension reform and to successful indexing for inflation. The political pressures to ensure that mandatory savings invested in stock and bond markets were invested well apparently also contributed to the political effort to regulate those markets.

Regulation

Chile is often described as relying on unrestricted markets ("free markets") with little role for government. This is a misreading. The AFPs, the stock and bond markets, and the insurance companies are subject to tight regulation. Indeed, Chile created a new regulatory body just to supervise the AFPs. The Chilean experience illustrates the workings of government and markets in tandem in producing a well-functioning pension system that relies on markets.

10.1.2 The basic pension

The council identified a number of strategic shortcomings of the pension system, particularly its inadequate provision of poverty relief and its impact on women. They proposed a basic pension, alongside the individual accounts, so as to address more fully all the objectives of pension systems.

The system

The individual accounts, intended to provide consumption smoothing, were supported by two sets of institutions that predate the 1981 reforms. First, for low earners who contributed to the pension system for at least 20 years, a subsidy from general revenue brought their pension benefit up to a minimum guaranteed level. Second, there was a means-tested welfare pension for the elderly poor, which was financed by general revenue at about half the minimum pension guarantee. Dissatisfaction with the workings of these two instruments led the council to recommend introduction of a basic pension. Following the council's recommendation, the government established a basic pension (with parallel benefits for disability and survivors) to be payable at age 65 (the same for men and women) and not subject to any contribution conditions. The council's report set as an explicit objective that the basic pension benefit should be above the poverty line. When the new system is fully phased in, the basic pension will replace the minimum pension guarantee and the welfare pension.

The basic pension is withdrawn at higher levels of individual and family income based on a dual test: it is gradually withdrawn as the contributory pension income of the *individual* rises; it is withdrawn also as the total income from all sources of the *household* rises and is withdrawn completely from a household that does not belong to the poorest 40 percent of households (legislated to rise to 60 percent).

Gender

The noncontributory pension is particularly important for women. Importantly for gender equality, husband and wife in a poor family are each entitled to the full basic pension in his or her own right. On the other hand, a woman with little or no pension entitlement of her own but who has a rich husband will not get a basic pension. In addition, the council recommended several other changes addressing gender issues.

As legislated in 2008, women in the poorest 60 percent of the population are eligible upon the birth of a child for a contribution to their individual account equal to one year's minimum wage, the contribution to be financed from general revenue. The provision is intended to preserve pension rights that a woman would otherwise lose when leaving the labor market for maternity reasons.

There is some protection for surviving wives, since men are required to buy annuities that pay 60 percent of their pension to a surviving spouse; women are not required to make the same arrangement for their husbands. The report recommended symmetrical rules for survivor benefits, thus including the husband as beneficiary of a survivor pension on his wife's contributions.

Women's earliest age for access to benefits is less than that for men (60 rather than 65). This affects not only access to retirement benefits but also eligibility for disability benefits and for voluntary tax-favored contributions, which both end at the earliest retirement age. Contingent on the gender-relevant measures having been put into place, the council report recommended that, after a 10-year grace period, women's retirement age for contributory pensions should rise gradually until it equals that of men.

Pension providers are allowed to use gender-specific mortality tables for annuities and programmed withdrawals and hence to pay lower benefits to women for a given accumulation to reflect their greater life expectancy.[4] The rationale for this arrangement is that in poor families it is mainly the man

4. Annuity providers are also allowed to use wealth-specific mortality tables in which lifetime wealth is estimated in terms of the size of the pension accumulation at retirement. This is designed to capture the fact that wealthier people tend to live longer. In the absence of such a measure, actuarial benefits, which redistribute from short-lived to long-lived people, would thereby redistribute from poor to rich.

who participates in covered employment, and therefore unisex tables would put low-income families at a disadvantage.

10.1.3 Coverage

Coverage in Chile, measured as the ratio of contributors in a particular year to the total workforce, was around 64 percent in 1980; that figure has remained at about 60 percent—low, but one of the best in Latin America. The coverage problem is common to middle-income countries. What is noteworthy, however, is that problems of coverage persist despite Chile's solid administration, an outcome that should not be surprising given the discussion of actuarial benefits in section 3.1.2 and of effective consumer choice in box 2.2 and section 7.3. The outcome in Chile offers little support to earlier arguments that a tighter relationship between contributions and benefits would generate a large improvement in compliance. The reform extended the pension mandate to some of the self-employed to expand coverage, phased in over five years.[5] The reform includes subsidy for the contributions of low-income workers under age 35 for the first 24 months of contributions. Presumably the idea is based on the behavioral insight that getting workers started in the system may help overcome noncompliance associated with inertia.[6]

In sum, experience in Chile since 1981 suggests the following conclusions:

- Mandatory funded individual accounts can be part of a good reform, but such a reform is not easy and depends on complementary reforms.
- Private supply plus competition are not on their own sufficient to keep down transactions costs or charges.
- Unless accompanied by a robust system of poverty relief, individual accounts are not a pension system, but only a part of a pension system.

10.2 Pension reform in China

Since 1997, China has moved from an enterprise-based system of defined-benefit pensions based on final salary toward a unified system for urban workers. The new system has three elements: a defined-benefit, PAYG, first-tier pension (the social pool); a mandatory, funded, defined-contribution pension; and voluntary, enterprise-based pensions. This system makes long-run strategic sense, addressing the objectives of pensions, but has not functioned

5. The mandate affects only the "formal" self-employed, defined as having honorarium income reported to the Internal Revenue Service.

6. The United States subsidizes contributions by low- and moderate-income workers to voluntary retirement savings through the so-called saver's credit, an additional tax credit for such contributions.

as intended. There are serious problems of fragmentation, system financial deficits, and administrative difficulties. These are particularly visible with the funded individual accounts. This section describes the pension system in China and sets out proposals for reform developed by a panel on which we both served.[7] We discuss the basic pension in 11.2.1, individual accounts in 11.2.2, and issues of coverage in 11.2.3.

Before the economic reforms, there was near full employment and most benefits were rooted in the enterprise and thus based on a model of formal sector, lifetime urban employment in state-owned enterprises. Given the predominance of agriculture and other rural activity, employment in the state-owned enterprises was only a small fraction of total employment, resulting in a pension system with very low coverage. The strategic incompatibility of this system with a competitive market economy with growing formal employment is clear and led to reform.

Economic growth has been strong and sustained over the past 25 years, and the saving rate is exceptionally high. Around that growth trend, however, is considerable regional variation. China is experiencing rapid aging, as shown in the population pyramid in figure 1.5, both because of rising life expectancy, as in other countries, but also because of China's policy of one child per family. Although the one-child policy has an important bearing on the ratio of the older population to the working-age population, it is less important for the flow of contributions relative to the flow of benefit payments because the pension system still covers such a small fraction of the labor force. However, the system dependency ratio (see glossary) has deteriorated rapidly.

10.2.1 The basic pension

The system

Subject to contribution conditions, all urban workers are eligible. Benefits are different for different cohorts as the system is phased in. Workers who joined the workforce in 1997 or later are entirely in the reformed system. Under this system the basic pension is a PAYG, defined-benefit pension, in principle payable at 20 percent of the local average wage after 15 years of contributions. In practice, the level of benefit can fall short of the target, and coverage, even within the urban sector, is low.

There is considerable discretion in the system, particularly in the way pensions are adjusted as prices and earnings rise, the magnitude and frequency

7. Asher et al. 2005, available at www.oup.com/us/pdf/social_security_study_2005. For fuller discussion, see Barr and Diamond 2008, chapters 14 and 15, and for other assessments and proposals for reform, Drouin and Thompson 2006, Salditt, Whiteford, and Adema 2008, and Williamson 2004.

of such adjustments being a matter for provincial governments. There are mandatory retirement ages for men (at 60) and women (55 for those in white-collar, 50 for those in blue-collar jobs); in what are classified as hardship jobs, the respective retirement ages are 55 and 45. Pensionable age is the same for the basic pension and for pensions from individual accounts. In practice, however, many people are allowed to retire even earlier without any reduction in either element. The panel recommends the end of mandatory retirement and that the age for full benefits from the basic pension should be slowly increased to 65 for men and women; also, that the earliest eligibility age for the basic pension and individual accounts should be the same for men and women.

Since 1998, costs have been shared among workers, employers, and different levels of government. The contributions base is the "standard wage," a narrower definition of income than typical taxable earnings in market economies. Alongside dedicated contributions, central and local governments provide substantial subsidies from general revenue, since not all regions receive sufficient contributions to finance all benefits. And in 2000 the State Council set up the National Social Security Fund to create a strategic reserve. Finally, some of the finance of the basic pension has been through the use of funds meant for the individual accounts.

Despite the objective of unifying the pension system at least at the provincial level, organization remains highly fragmented, largely at the municipal or county level, and in some areas pensions are still enterprise based. At the municipal level, governments have often been unable to enforce contributions.

Pensions in most parts of the country run a deficit, the joint result of high pension spending and limited capacity to collect contributions. Current rules and the anticipated rise in the dependency ratio suggest that deficits are likely to persist. High pension spending has multiple causes, including high replacement rates and a high system dependency rate from early retirement and slow expansion of coverage.

Separately, the methodology of indexation is faulty. The real value of pensions should not vary significantly with the level of inflation. Yet that is exactly what happens in China because pensions are not indexed in a properly weighted way. Currently the increase in benefits is supposed to be somewhere between 40 and 60 percent of nominal wage growth. That makes the real value of benefits erratic. To illustrate, workers can have 5 percent real wage growth either with 5 percent nominal wage growth and zero inflation or with 10 percent wage growth and 5 percent inflation. If nominal benefits increase at half the rate of nominal wage growth, these two circumstances produce very different outcomes: with zero inflation, nominal and real benefits grow by 2.5 percent (half of 5 percent) or half the growth in real wages; with 5 percent inflation, nominal benefits grow by 5 percent (half of 10 percent), which means no growth in real benefits. Thus real benefits do not grow at half the rate of real wages. Higher inflation can make this more severe. With 15 percent wage growth and 10 percent inflation, nominal benefits grow at 7.5 percent—a *decrease* in real benefits of 2.5 percent. Proper indexing avoids this erratic response to inflation.

To address faulty administration and collections, the panel recommended a single national pensions administration, a single system of record keeping and standard software, a single national financial pool, and contribution collection by the tax authorities, with contributions and benefits both defined to match the tax base (as opposed to the current use of a "standard wage").

The basic pension should be adjusted on a pro rata basis for individuals with less than a full career and for those who have worked in different locations over their career. Actuarial adjustments are needed for the age at which benefits start. Indexing of benefits in payment should be based on a proper weighted average of wage and price growth in order to reflect the desired relationship between wage and benefit growth rates without the problems arising from faulty indexing described in boxes 5.2 and 5.3.

Legacy obligations

The basic pension is relevant not only to people working today but also to those who retired under the old system. An important question is how to finance these inherited obligations. The most appropriate measure of net implicit debt in this situation (discussed in section 4.2) considers benefits and contributions together and uses the shutdown method, which reflects the intention to honor past promises by continuing to pay benefits to people who have already retired and to pay benefits accrued to date of current workers when they finally retire.

Countries reforming their pension systems can finance such obligations either from inside the pension system (from future contributions) or from outside or through a mix. Poland and Bolivia used proceeds from the sale of public assets to create a social security trust fund. Chile issued "recognition bonds" to individuals as a way of recognizing the obligations of the old system being dismantled, relying on later general revenue to finance the bonds as they matured. Thus the legacy burden in Chile falls on all taxpayers.

As discussed in section 4.2, a country need not fully fund its legacy obligation from outside the pension system, just as it need not fully pay off its national debt. However, if an ongoing legacy obligation remains within the pension system, future workers receive lower benefits than could be financed by their contributions had the obligation been paid off by someone else. Thus it may be sound policy to pay off part of the legacy obligation.

One option for China is to place some shares in the privatized state-owned enterprises into a trust fund. Since the market for these shares is currently thin, the proposal is not that the trust fund would sell shares to pay benefits or reinvest in other assets; rather it would use the flow of dividend payments as a source of ongoing finance. Any question of selling some of the shares would remain a matter for the future.

As a step in this direction, the government of China decided in 2003 to transfer some of its shares in state-owned enterprises to the National Social Security Fund. Progress as of the 2004 panel report was slow, however, and only a small quantity of shares had been transferred. The panel recommended continuing transfers, both to help financing and in the hope that they would contribute to the quality of corporate governance.

Adding the National Social Security Fund as a shareholder can contribute to improved corporate governance of state-owned enterprises, a key ingredient in economic efficiency and growth.[8] The transfer of shares gives the National Social Security Fund the opportunity to function as a long-term strategic shareholder in these companies with a major interest in protecting shareholder rights, including the right to a reasonable level of dividends. Moreover, the interest of the National Social Security Fund in corporate governance could lend more weight to the entire process of enterprise reform, including better legislation and better regulation, just as in Chile the investment of mandatory individual accounts in the stock market assisted the reform process by contributing to efforts to improve the regulation of the stock market. Given that the State Asset Management Bureau will continue to own substantial shares in state-owned enterprises even after the transfer of some shares to the National Social Security Fund, the ownership roles of the two bodies, with their different perspectives, can complement and reinforce each other.

Other forms of poverty relief

Alongside the pension system is a minimum livelihood guarantee scheme (*di bao*), which started in Shanghai in 1993 and subsequently became a national urban policy, administered by the Ministry of Civil Affairs. The system's main deficiency is coverage. At least half of the potentially eligible population receive no benefit, and the program covers only a small fraction of the aggregate income gap below the *di bao* line. Although in principle the design of the system should result in nobody receiving less than this amount, in practice the impact on poverty is small.

8. See the symposium on corporate governance in the *Oxford Review of Economics Policy*, vol. 21, Summer 2005. For a skeptical view of the robustness of corporate governance in China, see Hutton 2007.

10.2.2 Individual accounts

The system

Since 1998, urban workers in the state and nonstate sectors are expected to contribute also to a system of funded, defined-contribution individual accounts. Each worker's benefit from his or her individual account is a monthly pension of 1/120th of the account's accumulation at retirement; that is, pensions are based on the assumption that average life expectancy at retirement age is 10 years, and interest is ignored. This method of calculating the monthly benefit is technically incorrect. An actuarially accurate benefit would yield roughly half as much per month.[9] Workers allowed to retire early receive a pension from their individual account without actuarial reduction.

A move from PAYG toward funding incurs inescapable up-front cash flow costs because it is necessary simultaneously to finance the PAYG pensions of the current retired generations and to pay contributions into the funded individual accounts of current workers. In China the deficits just described meant that it was not possible to meet these cash flow costs, resulting in "empty individual accounts" as local governments often used the contributions of workers to their individual accounts to finance deficits in the social pool, replenishing the account with IOUs, which are, in effect, government bonds.

Further problems are that the accounts lack a suitable institutional structure for holding private assets, and there is in any case an inadequate supply of suitable private-sector assets and inadequate regulation of capital markets. Thus, where individual accounts are funded, their main holdings are low-interest government bonds and bank deposits. There are also problems of corrupt misuse of pension funds, exemplified by a major scandal in Shanghai in 2006.[10] Corruption, which is a serious problem in China, also aggravates the problem of incomplete compliance with contribution conditions.

The panel concluded that individual accounts funded with an asset portfolio did not constitute the best policy for China at present. The analysis in

9. This calculation assumes an annual interest rate (adjusted for inflation) of 3 percent, annual growth of benefits in force of 1.5 percent, and a retirement of certain duration of 25 years.

10. In August 2006 investigators discovered that about one-third of the Shanghai Social Security Fund had been invested in speculative real estate projects, and suspicions were that officials had personally benefited. The city's Communist Party chief (who was also a member of the Party's 24-member Politburo) was jailed for corruption, as was the head of China's National Bureau of Statistics. See "Beijing Probes Shanghai Pension Scandal," *Financial Times*, August 27, 2006; "Chinese Real Estate Executive Detained in Shanghai Pension Fund Case," *International Herald Tribune*, November 7, 2006; and Salditt, Whiteford, and Adema 2008.

earlier chapters suggests that funding is desirable if it leads to one or more of the following: increased national saving in a country with a shortage of savings, improved allocation of saving to productive investment, and desired intergenerational redistribution. In addition, funding needs to be administratively feasible. None of these appear to apply in China today, as savings are high, the capital market does not do a good job of allocating savings to investment, future cohorts of covered workers are likely to be much better off than current ones, and the administrative structure does not seem feasible. These conclusions apply to China today but not necessarily to China in the future. It is therefore important that today's individual accounts be designed to allow a smooth transition to funding if and when policymakers regard that as desirable. The panel recommends the notional defined-contribution approach, which offers the potential of such a smooth transition. An alternative approach, based explicitly on additional government debt, also can prepare for future funding.

Funding individual accounts with newly issued government bonds

If the government wishes to retain the principle of mandatory, fully funded individual accounts, one approach would be to place into workers' accounts newly issued government bonds paying a market interest rate. Any bonds transferred should be indexed for inflation. If annuitization is to be done by private insurance companies, consideration should be given to making indexed bonds available to insurance companies as backing for indexed annuities and possibly to the public. Another approach would be to include allocation of government-owned foreign bonds to the accounts, including the interest actually earned on these bonds. This approach differs from the current practice of placing IOUs in "empty" accounts in that it would provide explicit assets with a rate of interest that can be determined by the market.

The NDC approach leaves open the option of a move to mandatory funded accounts in the future rather than forcing the decision now. In contrast, the funding-with-bonds approach effectively makes the judgment now that mandatory funding to increase saving will be desirable in China in the future, leaving open only the timing of portfolio diversification or of increased contributions to increase saving.

10.2.3 Coverage

Urban coverage

Coverage is limited, extending to fewer than 20 percent of urban workers. Despite the announced extension of the mandatory system to all urban workers, contributions from employers and workers outside the state sector remain very limited. Thus coverage of the mandatory pension system is patchy in urban areas and does not extend beyond them. A priority for the future should be to extend the system to uncovered urban workers (already decreed but with slow implementation) and to the rural population. Enforcing the extension of coverage will make additional demands on administrative capacity. In addition, a sudden imposition of a high contribution rate on earnings can disrupt young, growing businesses. For both reasons, change should be phased in carefully, perhaps starting with the largest firms. Compliance should be enforced by the income tax authority. Civil servants should be included as well. This change does not require a reduction in the pensions of civil servants, since their participation in the national system should be supplemented by a government-organized pension, just as private firms are encouraged to supplement the mandatory pension.

Voluntary pensions

In principle, pensions can be voluntary at the level of either the firm or the individual. Currently, only the former arrangement exists in China, with no provision for individual plans. Both approaches are likely to develop over time, once there are legal arrangements for individual plans. In a country with a well-developed defined-benefit system, a combination of a government guarantee and a funding requirement may preserve the system while also addressing its worst problems. In a country with few or no existing voluntary pension plans, there seems no reason to go down a route that is known to be difficult to maintain (see box 8.1). The need for sophisticated regulation of funding levels adds to the case against such pensions in China today. Thus all voluntary supplemental pensions that receive tax-favored treatment should be defined-contribution plans.

Rural pensions

The panel report concentrated on urban pensions, which at best would cover one-third of the population. It recognized that a high priority should be old-age security for the remaining two-thirds of the population, whose traditional forms of economic security have eroded over the past decade and who, with the migration of younger workers into urban areas, face an aging problem more severe than that for the average for the country as a whole. Within pensions specifically, one policy direction is to extend existing urban arrangements to embrace the more developed parts of the rural economy. The township and village enterprise sector is one of those parts.

A core question is how to address poverty in the face of fiscal constraints and a shortage of administrative capacity. Administrative problems are particularly intractable. Targeting via an income test is administratively demanding in the West and much more so in a country like China, with a large informal sector in both urban and rural areas and where a large part of the income of the rural population derives from home-produced goods, in particular food. Thus it is difficult to measure income accurately or cost-effectively, reducing the usefulness of income testing as a mechanism for targeting.

Perhaps the simplest approach would be through local discretion plus block grants. An alternative to local discretion is indicator targeting (box 5.1), which awards benefits not on the basis of income, but on other, more easily measurable characteristics that are highly correlated with poverty, notably, in the Chinese context, ill health and sufficiently old age. China might consider the experience of South Africa (box 9.2).

In sum, the 1997 strategy of a pooled element and individual accounts was a sound one, but the decision to implement individual accounts as fully funded was mistaken given economic conditions in China. Retaining the strategy but instead implementing individual accounts as notional accounts is a better strategy for China today.

Chapter 11

Principles and Lessons for Policy

This chapter draws together our main arguments. Section 11.1 discusses principles, section 11.2 considers the resulting lessons for policy, and section 11.3 sets out our main conclusions.

11.1 Principles

11.1.1 Principles of analysis

PENSION SYSTEMS HAVE MULTIPLE OBJECTIVES. The primary objectives of individuals with regard to pensions are consumption smoothing and insurance. Governments may have additional goals, including poverty relief and redistribution. These objectives will be given different weights in different countries and at different times, but policy needs to bear them all in mind, and governments have to consider them alongside other goals of public policy, including economic efficiency and output growth.

ANALYSIS SHOULD CONSIDER THE PENSION SYSTEM AS A WHOLE. Pension design affects the labor market, economic growth, the distribution of risk, and the distribution of income, including by gender. Analysis of those effects needs to consider the entire pension system and in particular whether a change in one part needs to be accompanied by a change in another. Similarly, analysis needs to consider the impact of any change over the short and the long run, including the time path from one steady state to another.

Analysis of distributional effects should consider the progressivity of the system as a whole rather than of each element. Thus benefits from different parts of the pension system should be considered together and, for many purposes, alongside the taxes that finance them. For example, suppose that everyone gets a flat-rate pension financed by a proportional tax; although the tax side, considered alone, is not progressive, the system overall is because lower earners pay less tax than higher earners, while everyone gets the same pension. Indeed, the pension system can be progressive even if the tax system is regressive so long as the progressivity on the benefits side outweighs the regressivity on the tax side.[1]

ANALYSIS NEEDS TO TAKE ACCOUNT OF MAJOR DEVIATIONS FROM FIRST-BEST. Formulating pensions policy within a first-best framework is analytically simple but a bad guide to policy design in a world with limited policy tools and major market imperfections, of which the most important are information and decision-making problems (box 2.1 and box 2.2). Pensions raise issues of choice over a lifetime, and generally pension products are complex. Thus progress in helping consumers to become better informed has been limited, even in developed countries, not least because consumers choosing specific pension products face not only information problems, which can be resolved by offering more information, but also information processing problems, that is, problems too complicated for many of them to resolve even when given the necessary information. As a result, people often fail to make choices that maximize their long-term well-being or that of their families, and they often make no explicit choice at all—a common result where excessive choice or excessive complexity becomes overwhelming. The design of pension systems needs to take account of these problems of information and decision making. For example, contrary to simple theory, restricting choices can at times improve outcomes; it is also critical to design good defaults for people who make no explicit choice.

Alongside the issue of choosing among pension products, consumers also face problems in deciding when to retire. If pension benefits bear an actuarial relationship to a person's expected duration of retirement, the combination of longer lives and retirement at the earliest possible date (a common occurrence) inescapably aggravates elderly poverty. The concern that some people are retiring too early for their own good or that of their families matters for

1. With a flat benefit financed by a proportional tax up to a cap, the system is progressive up to the cap but does not have further progressivity beyond the cap because everyone beyond the cap pays the same tax and gets the same benefit, whatever their earnings.

the choice of an earliest entitlement age and for the design of incentives to work beyond the earliest entitlement age.

On the supply side, insurers also face information problems. An issue of particular concern is the difficulty of predicting cohort life expectancy. In the absence of a government-organized mandate, insurers also face problems of adverse selection in the market for annuities.

In addition to these information problems, analysis needs to take account of other deviations from first-best, notably incomplete markets and taxation.

ANALYSIS OF FUNDING NEEDS TO CONSIDER HOW THE FUNDING IS GENERATED. The design of the pension system can affect future output. One way to increase funding is to increase contribution rates (or reduce benefits) now in order to have lower contribution rates or higher benefits in the future; another is to place assets with the pension authority rather than hold them elsewhere. The first approach can raise national saving, and thus output, and so enhance the capacity to provide benefits in the future. The central point is very simple: to raise national saving, changes to pension arrangements have to lower someone's consumption, either that of workers, if contributions are increased, or that of retirees, if benefits are reduced. The transfer of assets does not have that effect if the assets would have been saved anyway. It does not create additional output but only changes the distribution of the burden of paying for benefits. That does not mean that transferring assets is necessarily a bad idea, since the change in distribution of paying for benefits may be worthwhile, particularly for benefits that are a legacy of an older pension system, but it is important to be clear that the gain is distributional, not one of additional output.

What matters primarily for the ability of government to finance future benefit payments are effects on saving, not the type of asset in a trust fund. We can see this with two examples. If the government raises contribution rates to buy (and then hold) government debt owned by the public, then the government is in a better financial position, even though the assets in the pension trust fund are government bonds. In contrast, if the government issues additional debt to finance a purchase of stocks, then the government is not in a better financial position, even though the assets are private assets.

These principles underpin good policy design. Failure to observe them leads to analytical errors, summarized in box 11.1, which are the mirror image of the points above.

11.1.2 Principles of policy design

Beyond the general design principles of avoiding changes not needed for government objectives (If it ain't broke, don't fix it) and trying to achieve objectives in the simplest way, a number of more specific principles for pension design are noteworthy.

Box 11.1 Analytical errors: The World Bank and other culprits

Discussion of pensions is prone to analytical errors of which the following—by the World Bank but certainly not only the World Bank—are prime examples. These errors are important. They matter not simply for intellectual reasons, but, most particularly, because analytical errors lead to policy errors illustrated by the discussion in section 8.3.

Tunnel vision. Analysis that focuses, often implicitly, on a single objective, such as consumption smoothing, may be flawed because it pays inadequate attention to other objectives, such as poverty relief. Similarly, it is generally mistaken to consider one part of the pension system in isolation, ignoring the effects of other parts. There is no efficiency gain from moving redistribution from one part of the system to another, even if the change leaves one part with no deviation from full actuarial principles.

Improper use of first-best analysis. It is a mistake to focus on the labor market distortions caused by a given set of pension arrangements while ignoring or downplaying the contributions of those arrangements to the various goals of pension systems—contributions that are not available without distortions. A pension system that includes poverty relief will be distorting; minimizing distortions implies minimizing poverty relief—the cure is worse than the disease. The central idea is that any optimal program will necessarily induce distortions because, starting from laissez-faire, distortions create second-order efficiency costs but first-order distributional gains. The argument that an actuarial relationship between contributions and benefits is optimal in terms of labor market effects is generally mistaken. It is right to design pensions so as to avoid larger distortions than are justified by their contribution to goals, but it does not follow that minimizing distortions is the right objective.

Also mistaken is uncritical acceptance of the argument that competition among pension providers necessarily benefits consumers by increasing choice and driving down administrative charges. Although applicable in a wide set of economic circumstances, this line of argument understates the serious information problems and information-processing problems that particularly affect pensions (see boxes 2.1 and 2.2). These problems do not mean that there should be no consumer choice but, rather, that options should be carefully designed, for example, through constrained choice and well-crafted defaults.

Improper use of steady-state analysis. It is mistaken to focus on the design of a reformed pension system in steady state while ignoring or underplaying the steps that are necessary to get to that steady state. This issue becomes especially important when considering whether or not to move from PAYG toward funded pensions. The argument that funding is inherently superior because stock market returns exceed the rate of wage growth is mistaken

(continued)

Box 11.1 (Continued)

for several reasons, not the least of which is because it takes no account of how the move to funding is to be financed.

Incomplete analysis of implicit pension debt. Simple analysis that looks only at future liabilities (that is, future pension payments) while ignoring explicit assets and the implicit asset that is the government's ability to levy taxes is misleading. Too narrow a focus on the cost side also ignores the considerable improvements in people's well-being from increased old-age security. Just as public debt does not need to be fully paid off (what matters is that the debt-to-GDP ratio should not explode), so too do publicly provided pensions not need to be fully funded (the unfunded obligations should not be set to explode relative to the base for contributions). A related error is to treat implicit and explicit debt as equivalent.

Incomplete analysis of the effects of funding. A pensioner's living standard in old age will depend on his or her ability to consume goods and services produced by younger workers. PAYG and funding are both ways of organizing claims on that output. It is therefore mistaken to focus excessively on how pensions are financed while ignoring future national output and its division between workers and pensioners. A common example of this error is to argue that with funding little action is needed to adjust to demographic change. The error in this claim is its failure to recognize that the effects of funding will depend on the answer to a series of questions, many of which are often addressed incompletely or ignored:

- Will funded pensions increase saving?
- Is increased saving the right objective?
- Will funded pensions strengthen the performance of capital markets?
- If so, are mandatory pensions necessary for this purpose?
- Are redistributive effects across generations—which are inevitable—desirable policy?

Ignoring distributional effects. Because pension systems can redistribute across cohorts of different birth years, it is necessary to consider who gains and who loses because of the need to finance pensions at some time, possibly in the future. An egregious error, discussed more fully in box 4.4, is to ignore the fact that any choice between funding and PAYG necessarily makes choices about redistribution across generations. The point is most obvious when establishing a brand new pension system. If policymakers introduce a PAYG system, the early generations of retirees receive larger pensions, but returns to subsequent generations are lower; if they fully fund, later generations benefit from higher returns, but the first generations receive little or no pension. Thus it is mistaken to present the

(continued)

Box 11.1 (Continued)

gain to pensioners in later generations as a Pareto improvement, since it comes at the expense of the first generation. A move toward funding that increases saving redistributes from today's generation to future generations. Irrespective of the merits of the move, it is faulty analysis to ignore those distributional effects.

The error in ignoring distributional effects is profound: it makes an implicit assumption about the distribution of income across generations; leads to mistaken claims for the Pareto superiority (see glossary) of some policies; and ignores the fact that a PAYG element in a pension system generally can be welfare enhancing because of the resulting possibility of intergenerational risk sharing.

PENSIONS SHOULD BE PORTABLE WITHIN A UNIFIED SYSTEM. Mobility is essential to an efficient labor market. Thus, to the extent possible, pensions should be portable as workers move from one geographical area to another, from one public enterprise to another, from the public to the private sector and vice versa, from one private firm to another, and from the uncovered (informal or rural) to the covered sector, and in and out of self-employment,. Such portability is achieved most readily when the system has a uniform structure across the covered population, both across localities and across sectors. This does not rule out differences in benefit levels—indeed, such differences are essential in large countries with wide differences in living standards and living costs—but it does mean that the framework should be national. If a system has separate pension funds in different regions or industrial sectors, the contributions of mobile workers in their former region or sector should count toward their pension in the new. And the question of a nationwide system is acutely relevant to a country as large and diverse as China. A uniform structure does not rule out supplementary pension systems (voluntary at the firm level) in private firms or for government employees.

Uniformity in structure has important political implications as well. A multiplicity of pension systems can give rise to political pressures to transfer resources to those systems that cover workers and retirees who are politically well connected. Uniformity offers some protection against political pressures that run counter to shared social goals.

PENSION DESIGN SHOULD PAY CLOSE ATTENTION TO INCENTIVE STRUCTURES. Pensions have major effects on labor markets and saving. As discussed in box 11.1, it is a mistake to seek to minimize distortions, since the achievement of some of the goals of pensions, notably poverty relief, insurance, and redistribution, inevitably involves distortions. Instead policy should seek to limit adverse incentives, bearing in mind their trade-off with the achievement of the goals of the pension system. That said, it is known that certain types of policy design create adverse incentives that can be avoided; for example, defined-benefit pensions should be based on a person's earnings over an extended period thereby avoiding heavy reliance on a person's wages at the end of his or her career.

Particular attention should be paid to retirement incentives. A national mandatory retirement age is a bad design and should be avoided. It is important to have adequate incentives for people to continue to work past the earliest age at which a pension can be claimed. This can be done by paying pensions while a person continues to work or by increasing benefits for a delayed start to collecting pension.

POLICY DESIGN SHOULD PAY CLOSE ATTENTION TO ADMINISTRATIVE CAPACITY AND COSTS. Different types of pensions make different demands on institutional capacity. For example, mandatory pensions should not rely prematurely on privately marketed assets; consideration of such a system should wait until adequate regulatory structures are in place for the accounts and for annuity providers, for financial markets, and for accounting by firms. Reliance on privately marketed assets for a mandatory system for all workers should be based on demonstrated successful experience, either with voluntary private pensions or with some experimental group, such as civil servants.

Different types of pensions have very different costs, and annual costs can compound to have larger effects than might be realized, as illustrated in table 7.1. Costs are generally highest where workers can choose their provider of investment services or can purchase their individual portfolio directly in the market. Clearly, a major issue for policymakers is how to regulate pensions generally and charges in particular.

Among the advantages claimed for funded individual accounts are that they increase individual choice and that they offer a higher return than PAYG pensions. Given the decision-making problems already discussed, the welfare gains from the first can be questioned. The second claim ignores important issues concerning the distribution of benefits, of costs, and of risks: as discussed in box 4.4, the move to funding inescapably redistributes across cohorts; in addition, the claim ignores the fact that funded individual accounts generally have higher administrative costs, which largely are a fixed cost per account; charges, if they parallel costs, thus bear most heavily on small accounts.

Sweden has sought to address these issues through a clearinghouse model whereby the administration and maintenance of individual accounts are centralized. Like Sweden, the U.S. Thrift Savings Plan (discussed in box 9.4) has centralized administration; it also limits the choices available to workers, further lowering costs. In both countries the delivery of funds to private firms for investment is done in aggregate by the government, not separately worker by worker.

THE SYSTEM SHOULD HAVE THE CAPACITY TO ADAPT AND EVOLVE. Any pension system will need adjusting over time. As incomes rise, reforms proceed, and institutional capacity grows, the system should adapt accordingly and should therefore be designed with an eye to the future as well as the present. The system should have some degree of automatic response to economic and demographic outcomes, particularly wage growth, inflation, and changes in life expectancy.

11.2 Lessons for policy

This section summarizes the lessons from economic theory for pension design generally, for finance and funding, and for political and administrative implementation.

11.2.1 Pension design

Lessons from economic theory

Many countries have pension systems with three parts: a basic pension, mandatory individual accounts, and voluntary pensions. Each part, if well designed, helps the others fulfill their social goals. Other countries, such as the United States, address concerns about redistribution and consumption smoothing by integrating both into a single public pension. And other countries, such as Sweden, address redistribution primarily through income support for poor elderly people with little redistribution (apart from the guarantee pension) within the pension system itself. Any of these approaches can be used to incorporate a good design that addresses the system's multiple goals.

A BASIC PUBLIC PENSION IS A VITAL COMPLEMENT TO INDIVIDUAL ACCOUNTS. By themselves, individual accounts do not adequately provide poverty relief, income redistribution, or insurance against adverse labor market outcomes. Policy must address the fact that many people are poor; individual accounts alone would leave them below the poverty line even after contributing to the system throughout a lengthy career. And in many countries policymakers have redistributive ambitions broader than poverty relief. Thus there is unambiguous support on technical grounds, largely independent of ideology, for a mix of a basic pension and individual accounts or for some other integrated mechanism that addresses the various objectives. The relative size and specific design of each element will depend on the weights that policymakers give to these different objectives.

Since pension systems are designed mainly for workers who have worked for most of their adult lives, some other mechanism is needed to address poverty among people who do not have a long record of covered employment or self-employment. Poverty protection for these people can be provided within the pension system (for example, through a noncontributory universal pension) or through a separate mechanism (for example, through income-tested social assistance) or both.

INDIVIDUAL ACCOUNTS ARE ONE WAY TO FACILITATE CONSUMPTION SMOOTHING. In a country in which most people are poor, an earnings-related element of the pension is relatively unimportant. But in countries where earnings are high or, as in China and the European former communist countries, where earnings are rising rapidly and the distribution of those earnings is widening, a separate element of consumption smoothing becomes an increasingly important complement to the basic pension. The design—whether fully funded, notional, or related to earnings in some other way—will depend on both the country's preferences and its fiscal and institutional capacity.

VOLUNTARY ACCOUNTS ARE ESSENTIAL TO INCREASING INDIVIDUAL CHOICE. People have different needs, tastes, life expectancies, and careers: some are more risk averse than others, some care more than others about their standard of living in old age, some are more eager than others to retire early. Thus different people should be saving for retirement at different rates, and the optimum timing of that saving during a person's career varies. Some people have children early in life, some later, so the cost of raising children is borne at different times in their lives. Similarly, the pattern of housing costs, particularly purchase prices, varies both within and across countries. Yet national pension systems are limited in the degree of complexity they can usefully (and politically successfully) incorporate. Voluntary supplementary pensions offer a mechanism for accommodating these different preferences, though sound regulation is needed to make sure that they serve their social purposes. The size of the mandatory system and the tax treatment of voluntary pensions are both important for the extent of their use.

DIFFERENT SYSTEMS SHARE RISKS DIFFERENTLY. In a pure system of individual accounts organized in the private sector and based on private financial assets, the risk of unsatisfactory outcomes is imposed on the individual worker (an exception is the longevity risk, if benefits are taken in the form of an annuity). The allocation of risk in the pure case can be altered by government guarantees or government bailouts. In a pure, privately organized, defined-benefit arrangement, the risk is borne by the employer and thus ultimately by the employer's current and future workers as well as shareholders, and by their customers if the costs of a deficit fall partly on prices; hence the risk is shared more broadly. This allocation, too, is altered if an employer fails to pay promised benefits and can be altered by government bailouts. In a pure PAYG defined-benefit system financed out of social insurance contributions, risks are shared across contributors, that is, across the current working generation and, if benefits are adjusted, across beneficiaries. The allocation in the pure PAYG case can be altered by variations in partial funding or by borrowing, which transfers risks across different generations through adjustments of contributions or benefits. Finally, in a system financed out of general revenues as well as, or in place of, payroll taxes, the risks are shared by all taxpayers and hence across generations (since debt financing, partially in place of current taxes, results in higher future taxes or lower government spending). A central question for policymakers, one with both efficiency and equity implications, is how widely risks should be shared.

DIFFERENT SYSTEMS HAVE DIFFERENT EFFECTS BY GENDER. Pension systems, like other institutions, create incentives that affect decisions about paid work, care activities, and leisure. Analysis therefore needs to reflect diversity in social values, individual preferences, and economic situations within a country and across countries. Survivor pensions may be very important for alleviating poverty. As with the broader aspects of pensions, there is no single unambiguous best design, but some designs are unambiguously bad.

The lessons above can be encapsulated in a single message:

THERE IS NO SINGLE BEST PENSION SYSTEM DESIGN FOR ALL COUNTRIES. Sound principles of pension design take account of the multiple objectives and market capacities and imperfections mentioned earlier and of incentives for work and saving. Proper application of those principles can and does lead to widely different systems; that is entirely as it should be: as discussed in box 2.3, countries differ in weights on their objectives, behavioral parameters, fiscal positions, and implementation capabilities. Designs that do not conform with sensible principles or the capacity of a country to implement the design will not work well.

The following questions for policymakers illustrate the multiplicity of options.

Questions for policymakers

HOW CAN THE ELDERLY BE PROTECTED FROM POVERTY? Countries vary in the resources they devote to relieving poverty among the elderly, and in the ways they combine different instruments in doing so.

All developed and many developing countries have a means-tested guaranteed minimum income for the elderly, but its level relative to the country's average income varies considerably.

Some countries have noncontributory pensions for the entire elderly population. New Zealand and the Netherlands, for example, provide income in the form of a tax-financed, flat-rate pension available to everyone beyond a given age.[2] In Australia and South Africa a uniform pension is awarded subject to an affluence test (so that it screens out the best off), and Chile introduced such a program in 2008.

In addition, mandatory contributory pension systems address poverty by requiring covered workers to contribute resources when working, after which they receive benefits in retirement. This reduces poverty insofar as they might not otherwise have provided as much for themselves.

Some countries, but not others, incorporate redistribution in their contributory pension systems, further reducing poverty. For example, the systems in Argentina and China include a basic pension that pays a flat rate per year of contributions along with a proportional earnings-related system. Mexico provides a tax-financed, flat-rate annual contribution to funded individual accounts. Chile has had a guaranteed minimum pension for workers with at least 20 years of coverage. The U.S. Social Security system has a progressive benefit formula that provides a higher replacement rate for those with lower lifetime earnings histories. In other countries pension credits for those caring for children raise the benefits of some workers with shorter earnings histories; rules affecting spouses after divorce can do the same.

Many of the elderly poor are widows. Survivor benefits are a key element in reducing poverty among widows. In addition, policies that encourage women to have a career and so receive a larger pension also serve to address poverty.

A good system, one that alleviates poverty while accomplishing other objectives, can be constructed with different mixes of these general approaches. It is our view that countries with different mixes of objectives and different economic and demographic circumstances ought to rely on different approaches in varying degrees. The appropriate extent of reliance on noncontributory pensions depends largely on the level of labor force participation of women and the degree of coverage of the pension system. All systems that involve

2. The benefit level does not vary with past earnings but does vary with length of time in residence.

redistribution and provide insurance distort the labor market. Good systems do not distort more than is needed to achieve these goals, and they recognize the cost of distortions when balancing goals. Systems with means testing also distort saving decisions. But different systems distribute the distorted incentives differently, making the choice of design dependent on observed behavioral parameters and the distribution of earnings.

WHAT TYPES OF DESIGN ASSIST CONSUMPTION SMOOTHING? The design of the mandatory contributory element of the pension system ranges widely, from fully defined-benefit to fully defined-contribution, with some countries having one of each. Any of these arrangements can be structured to function well. France, Germany, Italy, and Sweden have linear benefit formulas in which, within limits, benefits are an almost constant proportion of earnings. Other countries have progressive, earnings-related structures, either within a single system, as in the United States, or through a combination of a flat-rate element and a linear element, as in Argentina and China. Whatever the approach, benefits should depend on all or a large part of a worker's earnings history.

WHAT BALANCE BETWEEN MANDATORY AND VOLUNTARY CONTRIBUTIONS? This question has at least two elements.

How high should the mandatory contribution be? Different countries have different rates of mandatory contributions and accumulated funding with corresponding differences in replacement rates. Countries differ also in the maximum level of earnings subject to contributions. Another variation is to exempt workers with low earnings from contributions or to give such workers an income tax credit that at least partly offsets their contributions.

Compulsory earnings-related pensions play two key roles. The first is to limit the consequences of people making bad choices about saving and annuitization (box 2.2). This concern extends to those well above the usual poverty line but not to those who are very well off. The second role, if a country has a means-tested minimum income guarantee, is to reduce the distortions to saving caused by means testing.

Mandates have uniform rules, which for some workers are not efficient given that the sensible level and timing of saving and the appropriate age of retirement vary from worker to worker. Voluntary arrangements can be flexible but allow greater room for poor choices, and typically they have administrative costs that are higher than those of well-run mandatory arrangements. Thus a mix of mandatory and voluntary is often a good solution, and different proportions can be appropriate in different settings.

How strongly should voluntary pensions and individual retirement saving be encouraged? The importance of voluntary pensions also varies widely across countries, depending on prevailing attitudes and the size of the mandatory system. The choice has significant distributional implications if voluntary contributions, generally made by the better off, receive tax advantages. The magnitude and design of tax provisions can be chosen so as to improve the workings of the voluntary system and to limit adverse distributional effects. Voluntary pensions need to be funded and carefully regulated. Systems can be voluntary for the individual or can be provided voluntarily by firms; in the latter case, participation by the firm's workers may be mandatory or not. Some countries, for example Australia and the Netherlands, have systems that grew from voluntary beginnings but have over time become de facto or de jure compulsory.

All private retirement savings plans (and mandatory private individual accounts) rely on financial markets. Good regulation of those markets is thus a key component of good pension policy. Countries with poorly functioning markets for individual savings need to improve their regulation and enhance the development of simple savings instruments with low administrative costs. Additionally, countries need macroeconomic stability as a precondition for the financial markets and the pension system to work well.

HOW SHOULD PENSIONS BE ADJUSTED AT AND AFTER RETIREMENT? This question has several elements.

Should receipt of a pension be conditioned on stopping work? Well-designed systems can include a retirement test (stopping work as a condition for receiving a pension) or not or have different rules for workers at different ages. If a system does have a retirement test, the answer to the next question is especially important.

How much should benefits increase with a delayed start? The international evidence is clear that retirement decisions are strongly affected by the implicit tax on continued work that arises if benefits do not adequately reflect both a delayed start to receiving benefits and possibly also an extra year of contributions. High implicit taxes should be avoided. There are two straightforward ways of doing so: either benefits should start at a given age, whether or not the person continues to work, or benefits should increase after a delayed start by an amount that does not vary greatly from what is actuarially fair.

How should pensions be adjusted after retirement? A major question is how to protect pensions against inflation. Pensions based on a nominal annuity are vulnerable to inflation and should be avoided. Some countries index benefits to prices, others to wages, and others to a proper weighted average of the two. Any of these approaches may be appropriate. In contrast, weights that do not add to one should be avoided.

HOW SHOULD THE FAMILIES OF WORKERS BE PROTECTED? Pension systems often include a life insurance element to cover young children if a worker dies. Similarly, disability systems are an important part of supporting families when earnings in the family drop sharply. Among the elderly, living standards may fall precipitously following the death of one member of a couple, especially if it is the higher earner. It is important that protection of a surviving spouse, through joint-life annuities, pooled contributions, or both, be sufficient to avoid too steep a decline in living standards. Similar considerations apply to a divorced spouse.

11.2.2 Finance and funding

The finance and funding of pension systems raise issues that are both complex and controversial. They are also fruitful territory for some of the analytical errors discussed in box 11.1.

UNSUSTAINABLE PENSION PROMISES NEED TO BE ADDRESSED DIRECTLY. A frequently heard, but flawed, argument runs along the lines that PAYG pensions face major fiscal problems; therefore they should be privatized. This is a non sequitur: the "therefore" does not logically follow. Whatever financing problems a pension system may face, privatization does little or nothing to alleviate them; indeed, it may exacerbate them (as it did, for example, in Argentina and as it would as a result of some U.S. proposals). It is important to distinguish between two questions:

- Is the fiscal cost of public pensions a problem?
- Would a move toward funding be beneficial?

These are separate questions requiring separate answers. If a public pension is running a deficit that is regarded as unsustainable, the only solution is to make it sustainable by increasing contributions, reducing benefits, or a mix of the two. In contrast, if there are potential benefits from funding, a move in that direction may be sound policy even when the fiscal costs of a public pension are sustainable.

A MOVE TO FUNDING GENERALLY HAS MAJOR FISCAL COSTS. In a PAYG system the contributions of younger workers pay the pensions of older people. But if a country moves to a funded system, the contributions of younger workers will instead go into their individual accounts, and so the pensions of retired people must come from some other source: higher taxation, or additional government borrowing, or reductions in spending on other government programs. Thus a move toward funding generally imposes an added burden on today's workers, who have to pay not only their own contributions but also some or all of the taxes that finance current pensions.[3]

3. An exception arises to the extent that a country can finance the transition by drawing down an accumulated general budget surplus—the case in Chile. Since these funds were being saved anyway, there is no increase in saving. Similarly, if additional borrowing does not strain the bond market, additional borrowing can be used.

One way to spread (but not eliminate) the fiscal costs of the transition is to phase in funded pensions gradually. A country that wants to introduce individual accounts but cannot absorb the fiscal costs of transition, or one where institutions are not yet strong enough to support mandatory funded accounts, has the option of introducing mandatory notional defined-contribution pensions supplemented by voluntary funded accounts. This approach maintains the structure of individual accounts but avoids the additional fiscal and administrative burdens of funding; it also keeps open the option of phasing in mandatory funded accounts at a later stage. The strategy is applicable to China and potentially to other countries where mandatory funding might be premature or where mandatory funding might have been adopted prematurely.

A MOVE TO FUNDING HAS INTERGENERATIONAL EFFECTS. If funding is to raise output growth in the future, it has to increase saving today. But for saving to increase, consumption by today's workers must decline through higher contributions or consumption by today's retirees must decline through lower benefits or a mix of the two. Thus a move to funding generally imposes a burden on today's generation to the benefit of future generations. Depending on country specifics, this may or may not be sound policy. More generally, introducing a new PAYG system allows the early cohorts to receive larger pensions than if the new system were fully funded. Thus any choice among PAYG, partial funding, and full funding is also and necessarily a choice about the intergenerational distribution of income.

THERE IS NO AUTOMATIC RELATIONSHIP BETWEEN FUNDING AND GROWTH. Funding will raise the rate of economic growth if it increases saving or improves the efficiency with which saving is channeled into investment. But some methods of providing funds may not increase saving; others, such as increased mandatory pension saving, may be offset by declines in other saving; and funding may not be good policy in any case if the saving rate is already high. And the efficient channeling of saving into investment requires formal capital markets that are capable of allocating funds to good investment opportunities more effectively than informal capital markets. Gains in the effectiveness of capital markets are possible but depend on effective administration and on political support for the deployment of that administration in regulating financial markets. Thus the economic case for funding has to be analyzed in terms of each country.

A related point is that funding is not an automatic solution to demographic problems. Rather, its operation is indirect and its helpfulness contingent on whether it has beneficial effects on growth. Without additional resources, longer lives require either later retirement or reduced monthly benefits, however they are financed.

To sum up the previous points:

A MOVE FROM PAYG TOWARD FUNDING IN A MANDATORY SYSTEM MAY OR MAY NOT BE WELFARE IMPROVING. Whether it is welfare improving depends on the design details and the country specifics, but all countries should bear in mind the following conclusions:

- Explicit public debt is not equivalent to implicit pension debt.
- Funding may increase national saving or explicit public debt or some of each.
- Funding may improve the operation of capital markets and may increase economic growth. Either is possible; neither is inevitable.
- Funding that increases national saving generally has major fiscal effects. Thus the analysis needs to take account of the costs of moving from one steady state to another; it is faulty analysis simply to compare steady states before and after. The analysis also needs to take account of differences in risk and differences in the administrative costs of different pension arrangements.
- Funding can be organized in a variety of ways, both with and without funded individual accounts.
- For the reasons set out in box 4.4, any decision that a system should be funded rather than PAYG is necessarily a decision about the intergenerational distribution of both income and risk. Hence, even if funding does increase output, the change cannot be presented as a Pareto improvement.

Questions for policymakers

The following are only the most basic questions.

WHAT METHODS SUPPORT LONG-RUN SUSTAINABILITY? Adjusting pension systems for financial shortfalls is politically difficult. A key first step is good-quality, professional, nonpolitical projections of the financial future of the existing system and of any proposed reforms. For countries that choose not to perform this task, or that lack the resources to do so, provision by an international body would be useful. To assist the political process in decisions about pension reform, such projections need to be not only of good quality but also organized and presented so that they are accepted as such by the public. A second element supporting long-run sustainability is to incorporate some degree of automatic adjustments additional to inflation protection in order to address anticipated growth in life expectancy at retirement age; this can be done in a number of ways. Uncertainty about the speed of increase in life expectancy makes automatic adjustment particularly useful. Fully defined-contribution systems, which by design have no sustainability issues, nonetheless need careful projections to evaluate how well the system is fulfilling its social goals, in particular, providing an adequate replacement rate.

WHAT TOOLS ARE AVAILABLE TO RESTORE SUSTAINABILITY? As discussed in section 8.2.2, sustainability can be restored through a combination of higher revenue and lower expenditure.

Revenue can be increased by raising contribution rates without increasing benefits in step, assuming the rate is not already so high that any increase per worker is more than fully offset by decreased covered employment. Another possibility is to expand coverage or to increase the maximum level of earnings subject to contributions; these increase revenue in the short run but may not strengthen sustainability in the long run because of the induced increase in future pension benefits.

Expenditure can be reduced either by decreasing the average benefit or by decreasing the number of pensioners. Raising the age at which pension benefits can first be paid without any matching increase in benefit to reflect such a delay is one way to achieve this outcome.

Which package is most suitable depends on the country's circumstances: for example, if contributions are already high, a further increase may be undesirable; if the average retirement age is low, there is scope to increase it. Sustainability requires respect both for fiscal constraints and for preserving the ability of the pension to fulfill its social goals. Increased funding—from higher contributions, lower benefits, or transfers from outside the system—can help sustainability if it entails higher national saving and so greater total consumption in the future.

HOW MUCH FUNDING SHOULD THE MANDATORY SYSTEM HAVE? Some countries have no funding: Italy, for example, relies on general revenue to cover shortfalls. Others, like Chile, have full funding of contributory pensions but not of the old minimum guarantee or the new noncontributory basic pension. Some countries fall in between: the United States has a partially funded defined-benefit system, and Sweden combines a partially funded NDC system with a separate, mandatory, fully funded defined-contribution system. For reasons that have emerged throughout this book, different levels of funding are appropriate under different circumstances. Whatever the level of funding, long-term financial sustainability is a critical element in a well-designed system.

WHAT BALANCE BETWEEN PUBLIC AND PRIVATE MANAGEMENT IN A MANDATORY PENSION SYSTEM? The country descriptions in chapter 9 illustrate that management of mandatory systems covers a wide spectrum from fully public (United States) to fully private (but regulated) (the pre-2008 system in Chile).[4] Theoretical analysis argues that diversity across countries is appropriate where it reflects different situations in different countries. However, in at least some aspects of account administration, costs decline with the scale of the operation; for example, it is cheaper to collect pension contributions along with other payroll deductions, such as for income tax. Thus well-designed systems generally include some role for government in providing for or organizing the performance of certain specific administrative tasks.

WHAT ORGANIZATION OF FUNDING IN A MANDATORY PENSION SYSTEM? Alongside questions about account administration are questions about fund management and the types of assets it makes sense for a pension fund to hold. Some countries with defined-benefit systems hold only government debt. Others hold diversified portfolios, both across assets and across countries. These portfolios can be managed by government agencies or by private firms hired to handle investment transactions or even to make investment decisions. Countries with defined-contribution systems range from those that use publicly organized investment management (Singapore) to those that use fully private, but heavily regulated, financial intermediaries (Chile). The political and administrative capacities of government and the quality of politically available private options are important for comparing alternative methods. With adequate political and technical ability, some portfolio diversification is good policy.

When portfolio diversification makes sense, there are different ways to organize portfolio choice. The simplest approach is to have a single, government-organized fund, as a trust fund for a defined-benefit system or a provident fund for a defined-contribution system. In either case, the management could be outsourced. As discussed in chapter 7, individual accounts make much greater demands on institutional capacity.

WHEN DO FUNDED INDIVIDUAL ACCOUNTS MAKE SENSE? A move to funding may or may not be welfare improving, depending on the country's circumstances. A more specific question to ask is when funded individual accounts make sense, either with increased funding or as a substitute for centralized funding. Chile, for example, increased funding through its development of individual accounts, whereas Sweden viewed individual accounts largely

4. For useful institutional description see OECD 2007 and U.S. Social Security Administration 2007*a*. For links to descriptions provided by agencies and organizations see "Social Security in Other Countries" at the U.S. Social Security website, www.ssa.gov/international/links.html/. See also the resources in AARP's Global Aging Program at www.aarp.org/research/international/map/.

as a substitute for centralized funding. The deviations from first-best (box 2.1) and the resulting problems with consumer choice (box 2.2) argue that uncritical reliance on consumer choice and market competition is based on mistaken analysis. The issue of administrative cost also interacts with the implementation capacity necessary for a system to be feasible. The problem of cost is compounded by the fact that the administration of funded individual accounts is largely a fixed cost and thus bears most heavily on systems with small accounts, particularly those in poorer countries. Depending on how costs are allocated to accounts, they may bear more heavily on the smaller accounts of lower earners.

For these reasons, increased funding through individual funded accounts makes sense only in countries where the increase is likely to raise the economic growth rate and improve intergenerational distributional outcomes *and* where the necessary institutional capacity is in place. Where those conditions hold, if policymakers wish to introduce funding through individual accounts, there are good grounds for simplifying the choices facing individual workers and for organizing accounts in a way that keeps administrative costs very low. The Thrift Savings Plan for federal civil servants in the United States (box 9.4) is such an example.

11.2.3 Political and administrative implementation

IMPLEMENTATION MATTERS. Effective reform requires much more than good policy design, but rests on a tripod of abilities: policy design, political implementation, and administrative implementation. The importance of implementation is often underestimated. It requires skills that are just as demanding as policy design, and those skills need to be involved when the policy is designed, not introduced as an afterthought.

Policymakers need to ask a series of questions: What relative weights should be attached to the objectives of consumption smoothing, insurance, poverty relief, and redistribution? How tight are the fiscal constraints? And how binding are institutional capacity constraints? The discussion below sets out some of the main issues.

THE SCALE OF MANDATORY PENSIONS MUST RESPECT FISCAL CAPACITY. In macroeconomic terms, pensions are in part a device for dividing output between workers and retirees; they also influence how output is divided between consumption and investment. Thus spending on pensions must be compatible with a country's financial capacity, notably the ability to finance the consumption of retirees and the investment from which future economic growth derives.

GOVERNMENT IS AN ESSENTIAL PARTICIPANT IN ANY PENSION SYSTEM. All pension systems depend critically on public sector technical capacity. With PAYG systems this includes the ability to collect taxes and contributions, to keep track for many years of the contributions of workers who are mobile and who may change names, and to project future contributions and benefits with reasonable accuracy so that government can adjust the system gradually to changes in financial capacity, thereby avoiding sharp shocks for retirees or workers close to retirement.

It is a fundamental error to suppose that private pensions get government out of the pension business. Given the major market imperfections discussed in box 2.1, purely private arrangements for insurance and consumption smoothing will be either inefficient or nonexistent. Thus government has a major role in pensions in all countries, whatever the specific configuration of arrangements. Government must be able to enforce compliance with contribution conditions, to maintain macroeconomic stability, and to ensure effective regulation and supervision of pension plans and financial markets, including the annuities market. Such regulation is vital to protect individuals in areas too complex for them to protect themselves. More generally, private markets function best when government has put in place good, clear rules and when enforcement is even-handed, honest, prompt, and predictable.

PRIVATE SECTOR CAPACITY IS ESSENTIAL FOR PRIVATE PENSIONS. Alongside government capacity, private pensions also require considerable private sector capacity. Administrative tasks include the ability to collect contributions, to keep individual records over long periods, to inform workers about their accumulations and expected benefits, and to determine and pay benefits. Financial tasks include the ability to manage large investment portfolios.

THE CAPACITY OF CONSUMERS IS IMPORTANT. Participants in pension arrangements need to be educated about what they can expect to have at retirement and about how to think about the choices they can make. This task, difficult enough in developed countries, is even harder in an economy in which most workers have no experience making such financial decisions.

CONTROVERSY IS INESCAPABLE. No pension system anywhere has been able to avoid all controversy. Controversies arise particularly around possible reforms that imply losses for some groups, in light of differences in values or political views about who should bear those losses. Many countries have systems with bad design features, which give rise to adverse labor market incentives and unsustainability and lead in turn to excessive and avoidable uncertainty for workers and financial markets. Controversy also arises in other areas, including the earliest entitlement age, the balance between public and private pensions, the design of the public pension, the rules for gender equity, and the size of any private sector mandate. Effective politics to create and sustain good design are therefore central to any successful reform.

11.3 Conclusions

11.3.1 Policy conclusions

THE MAIN CAUSE OF THE PENSIONS "CRISIS" IS A FAILURE TO ADAPT TO LONG-RUN TRENDS. Pension systems in many countries face the overarching long-term trends discussed in chapter 1: increasing life expectancy, declining fertility, and earlier retirement.[5] The first two, at least, are ongoing (with some sad exceptions in parts of the world on the mortality side). Superimposed on these are two more recent phenomena: the baby boom (widespread, though not universal) and the general increase in the scale of pension systems since World War II in terms of both coverage and benefit levels.

Pension systems with contribution rates, monthly benefits, and retirement ages set for an earlier era are not consistent with the longer retirements implied by increasing life expectancy and earlier average retirement; this is all the more true given the future shrinkage in the workforce implied by declining fertility. Some adjustment is necessary in almost every country. The scale of that adjustment is amplified by the fact of the baby boom and the increasing scale of pension systems, although, as shown by the age pyramids in figure 1.5, the problem would exist even in their absence. The main source of financing problems is that, with the exception of adjustment to price and wage growth, defined-benefit systems have had a static design with no automatic adjustment to long-term trends.

THE MAIN SOLUTIONS TO PROBLEMS OF PAYING FOR PENSIONS. In responding to these trends, any improvement to the finances of a pension system must involve one or more of

- higher contribution rates,
- lower benefits,
- later retirement at the same benefit,
- policies, such as increased saving, designed to increase national output.

That statement remains true whatever the degree of funding. If a public pension is regarded as unsustainable, the problem needs to be addressed directly by one of the methods just listed.

Some people think that later retirement will aggravate unemployment. That is a fallacy because it ignores the reaction of the supply of jobs to the supply of workers.

5. The long-term trend to earlier retirement has attenuated or reversed in a number of countries. But we have not seen a trend in the other direction proportional to continuing increases in life expectancy.

REFORMING PENSIONS. Unsustainable pension systems should be put on a sustainable footing. Many pension systems are badly designed: many have poor coverage; some excessively discourage the labor supply of some prime-age workers; some unduly discourage participation in the pension system; some encourage too-early retirement. Such designs should be changed:

- Pensions should provide poverty relief. The design of poverty relief should recognize that gaps in contributions will occur. Gaps in contributions can be addressed in contributory systems through a variety of mechanisms, including minimum guarantees and credits for caring activities; an alternative is a noncontributory universal pension. These mechanisms can work well along with guaranteed minimum incomes for the elderly.
- Pensions should assist consumption smoothing in ways that take account of deviations from first-best (box 2.1) and problems with choice and competition (box 2.2).
- The rules of pension systems should be gender neutral and chosen with sensitivity as to how they affect men and women differently.

11.3.2 Policy choices and economic development

The discussion in this section is about the implications of fiscal and institutional constraints; it is not about optimal design, but about what limits on policy choices make sense for countries at different levels of development.

We illustrate implementation in terms of three stylized types of country: a low-income developing country, a middle-income developing country, and a developed country. Actual countries may occupy intermediate positions and mixed positions for different parts of the economy. The discussion here uses the conventional terms of first-tier pensions (aimed primarily at poverty relief), second-tier pensions (mandatory, intended to strengthen consumption smoothing), and third-tier pensions (voluntary at the level of the firm or the individual, subject to regulation and perhaps tax favored, to accommodate differences in individual preferences). Although illustrated here in terms of these three separate tools, some countries use only two; in the United States and Mexico, for example, a single system addresses supplemental poverty relief and consumption smoothing. We refer to pension systems in specific countries without intending to imply that those countries are typical of the category.

The examples below are intended only as illustrations; they should *not* be taken as a template. A country's administrative capacity may, for example, have some parts that are typical of middle-income countries and others at a level more commonly found in low-income countries. Similarly, fiscal constraints may call for different systems for different sectors or forms of employment within a single country: for example, a middle-income country may have a formal system for urban areas and a much simpler one (or none) for rural areas. Similarly, a system designed for civil servants will differ sharply from one designed for an entire country. Once there is a national system, civil servants should be part of it, typically with a supplemental pension; large private firms may have a similar arrangement.

All the examples are based on the following assumptions:

- that the parameters of the system, such as benefit levels and the age at which a pension is first awarded, are consistent with fiscal sustainability, and
- that alongside pensions, all countries with the necessary administrative capacity provide some degree of means-tested support for the elderly.

Illustrative pension systems for a low-income country

FIRST TIER. The choice is highly constrained:

- A very poor country may be unable to finance or organize a national system of poverty relief, instead relying on family, charitable organizations, and local government.
- As capacity allows, it becomes possible to use general revenues to offer limited poverty relief through transfers to local governments or through a national system that targets by age.

A country at a low level of development—typically with a large informal sector and substantial household production—will generally not have the capacity to administer an income test. A system of local discretion may be able to do so in an approximate way, based more on local knowledge than on formal assessment of a household's income.

SECOND TIER. A country at this level of development will generally not have the capacity to manage a mandatory earnings-related system, which requires, among other things, enforcing contributions and measuring and recording a person's income over 40 years or more. Such countries should leave such a system as an agendum for the future.

THIRD TIER. Any voluntary saving plans operating in the country should not be tax favored, since fiscal resources are highly constrained and tax advantages are typically regressive. Nevertheless, provision of a simple, reliable opportunity for voluntary savings is important.

Illustrative pension systems for a middle-income country

FIRST TIER. Countries in this category have a choice of

- a noncontributory, tax-financed pension with or without an affluence test (as in Australia, Canada, the Netherlands, New Zealand, South Africa, and, beginning in 2008, Chile); or
- a simple contributory PAYG pension, for example, a flat-rate pension based on years of contributions (such as the basic state pension in the United Kingdom).

SECOND TIER. The choice is between

- a publicly organized, earnings-related, defined-benefit pension, or possibly an NDC pension; or
- a defined-contribution pension as part of a provident fund (as in Malaysia and Singapore) or with sharply limited individual choice.

If there is a contributory first-tier pension, either of these can be separate from or integrated into it. Tax treatment of contributions and benefits should consider the extent to which tax favoring is regressive.

THIRD TIER. Voluntary, defined-contribution pensions at the level of the firm or the individual are possible; regulation is important, and any tax favoring should be designed to avoid excessive regressivity. Regulation of the funding of defined-benefit plans is likely to be too difficult to justify tax favoring such pensions.

Options for pension systems in a developed country

FIRST TIER. Countries should consider either

- a contributory pension aimed at poverty relief (used in many countries), with any of an array of different designs; or
- a noncontributory, tax-financed pension, either with an affluence test (as in Australia, Canada, Chile, and South Africa) or without (as in the Netherlands and New Zealand).

SECOND TIER. The menu includes, separately or in combination (though these vary in the difficulty of use):

- a publicly organized, defined-benefit pension, which may be integrated as a single system with the first-tier contributory pension (as in the United States) or not (as in France and Germany);
- an NDC system (as in Sweden);
- an administratively cheap savings plan with access to or requirement of annuities (like the Thrift Savings Plan for federal employees in the United States);

- mandatory, funded, defined-benefit pensions sponsored by industry (the de facto system in the Netherlands); or
- funded, defined-contribution pensions (as in Chile and Sweden), possibly including an antipoverty element (as in Mexico).

THIRD TIER. Voluntary, defined-contribution pensions can be organized at the level of the firm or the individual; regulation (particularly of the funding of defined benefit plans) is important (and difficult), and any tax favoring should seek to avoid excessive regressivity.

IN SUM. Clearly the range of choices widens as fiscal and administrative capacities grow. The less developed a country, the more narrowly feasibility concerns constrain choices. Specifically, a country should *not*

- set up a system beyond its financial and administrative capability;
- introduce a mandatory, earnings-related pension system until it has a robust capacity to keep records accurately over 40 or more years; or
- introduce individual funded accounts (whether mandatory or as an option in a mandatory system) until it can regulate investment, accumulation, and annuitization.

It is clear that a developed country has a full range of choices. Thus it is not surprising that the systems of richer countries vary greatly: from the United States, with its progressive, earnings-related, partially funded pensions supplemented by voluntary employer and individual pension plans; to Sweden, with its NDC pension system plus mandatory, individual funded accounts; to the Netherlands, with its system of noncontributory, flat-rate pensions augmented by near-mandatory participation in a funded occupational pension plan. But the fact that the range of options is not greatly constrained by issues of feasibility should not be misinterpreted: that a country is capable of implementing an administratively demanding plan does not mean that such a plan is a good idea or that it is necessarily superior to a less administratively demanding system. New Zealand has a simple pension system through choice, not constraint.

The pensions "crisis" is an outcome of adapting too little or too slowly to long-term trends. Pensions are complex and not easy to understand, and pension reform is politically difficult when it disrupts long- and widely held economic expectations. Yet good pension reform is important for people's lives—as workers and as current or future pensioners—and for the economy as a whole. And, despite the many challenges, pension reform can be done well. The principles in this book suggest how.

Glossary

Actuarial benefits. A stream of benefits for which the expected PRESENT DISCOUNTED VALUE equals the annuitant's accumulation at the time the benefits start. For a given accumulation, the size of the periodic benefit (for example, monthly) therefore depends on the person's remaining life expectancy and the rate of return on assets available to the pension provider over the period during which benefits will be paid. A pension system that follows this approach in broad outline, but without precise use of projected life expectancy and market interest rates, is referred to as quasi-actuarial.

Adverse selection. The tendency for INSURANCE to be bought by people who are more likely to collect on the policy. This can occur when the purchasers are better informed than the insurer of their personal risk. For example, individuals with above-average life expectancy are more likely to buy ANNUITIES. This type of buyers' self-selection is adverse to the insurer.

Affluence test. A measure of eligibility for benefits that is designed to screen out only the best off. It thus differs from an INCOME TEST, which screens out all except the poor.

AFPs. *Administradoras de fondos de pensiones*: competitive private pension providers in Chile.

Age dependency ratio. See DEPENDENCY RATIO.

Age for full benefits (also called NORMAL RETIREMENT AGE). The youngest age at which a person is entitled to a full pension. See also EARLIEST ELIGIBILITY AGE.

Annual management fee. The annual administrative charge imposed by a pension fund manager, expressed as a percentage of the account balance being managed. See also CHARGE RATIO, REDUCTION IN YIELD.

Annuity. An arrangement that pays benefits (for example, annual or monthly) as long as a person is alive. A single-life annuity pays an income for the life of one person. A JOINT-LIFE ANNUITY (also called a joint-and-survivor annuity) pays a regular income to two people until both have died. The size of the monthly payment typically depends on whether one or both are still alive and may depend on which of the two is still alive. The payment can be from a DEFINED-BENEFIT system or in a DEFINED-CONTRIBUTION system when an individual exchanges his or her pension accumulation for an annual or monthly benefit or from a purchase using some other lump sum. This allows the individual to insure against the risk of outliving his or her pension savings. With an immediate annuity, payments begin immediately; with a deferred annuity, payments are delayed until some point after the purchase date. Different forms of annuities adjust payments on different bases.

Assets test. See MEANS TEST.

Bonds. Financial securities that constitute a loan from the purchaser (the bondholder) to the seller. Bonds normally specify a date on which the bondholder will be repaid (the redemption or maturity date) and a periodic interest payment stated in dollars (or other currency unit). Contrast with STOCKS.

Broad funding. An increase in the assets of a public pension system that derives from increased contributions or decreased benefits. Such an increase in assets increases national saving unless it is offset by a decline in voluntary or other government saving. Contrast with NARROW FUNDING.

Charge ratio. The percentage decrease in a person's pension accumulation at retirement due to administrative charges. Under plausible assumptions, over a full career, an ANNUAL MANAGEMENT FEE of 1 percent generates a charge ratio of about 20 percent; that is, the accumulation at retirement, and hence the value of any ANNUITY for which it is exchanged, is 20 percent lower than it would be if the annual management fee were zero. See also REDUCTION IN YIELD.

Citizens pension. See NONCONTRIBUTORY UNIVERSAL PENSION.

Compliance. Adherence of a worker or employer to the laws and regulations governing a pension system. A covered worker who is not making contributions that are legally required is noncompliant (that is, is evading contributions); but a person who is not making contributions because he or she is currently not working in a covered job is not noncompliant.

Consumption smoothing. Behavior that allows a household to maintain its desired level of consumption over time despite variations in income. Pensions assist consumption smoothing by allowing individuals to redistribute their resources over their lifetime, that is, by saving in their productive years in order to consume more in retirement. See also REDISTRIBUTION.

Contributory basic pension. A pension paid, often at a flat rate, to a person with a full record of contributions or pro rata to a person with an incomplete contributions record. See also NONCONTRIBUTORY UNIVERSAL PENSION, EARNINGS-RELATED PENSION.

Coverage. As most commonly measured, the proportion of the employed population contributing to the pension system at a given time. This is distinct from the set of people with covered earnings records or individual accounts in that it omits workers who have contributed in the past and acquired at least some rights. See also COMPLIANCE.

Defined-benefit (DB) pension. A pension in which the benefit is determined as a function of the worker's history of pensionable earnings. The formula may be based on the worker's final wage and length of service or on wages over a longer period, for example, the worker's full career. A fully funded, pure defined-benefit plan adjusts funds to meet anticipated obligations, and so the risk of varying rates of return to pension assets falls on the sponsor, that is, the employer or the government. A defined-benefit plan need not be fully funded.

Defined-contribution (DC) pension. A pension in which the benefit is determined by the value of assets accumulated in the worker's name over his or her career. The benefit may take the form of a lump sum, or a series of equal payments, or an ANNUITY but in all cases is determined only by the size of the worker's lifetime pension accumulation. Full matching of funds and obligations is in principle preserved by adjusting obligations to available funds.

Dependency ratio. The term is used in two different ways. The age dependency ratio is the ratio of people beyond some specified age (for example, 65) to people of working age (for example, 16 to 64). The system dependency ratio is the ratio of people receiving pensions to the number of active contributors.

Earliest eligibility age. The youngest age at which the rules of a pension system allow a person to receive any pension. See also AGE FOR FULL BENEFITS.

Earnings-related pension. A pension with benefits that are positively related to the worker's earnings; the relationship may be strictly proportional, as with a NOTIONAL DEFINED-CONTRIBUTION PENSION, or less than strictly proportional, as in the U.S. Social Security system.

Equities. See STOCKS.

Equity. The principle that resources should be distributed or shared among individuals according to some notion of fairness. Equity *may* imply equality but does not have to. See also HORIZONTAL EQUITY, VERTICAL EQUITY.

Final-salary pension. A DEFINED-BENEFIT PENSION that is based on years of service and salary in a worker's final year or final few years.

Finance and funding. We use the term financing to refer to the cash flow used each year to pay benefits; the term funding, to indicate financial assets held by the pension system.

First-best analysis. Analysis based on the assumptions, common in simple economic models, that economic agents are well informed, that there are no INCOMPLETE MARKETS, and that the government uses interventions in the economy that do not cause economic distortions. That is, the government can intervene without having to rely on taxes that vary with earnings or savings. Contrast with SECOND-BEST ANALYSIS.

Formal sector. The part of an economy that lies within the regulatory environment. Workers employed in the formal sector will typically have an employment contract and explicit conditions relating to pay and hours of work and will pay tax on their earnings and contributions to the pension system; similarly, their employers will generally pay relevant company taxes. Contrast with INFORMAL SECTOR.

Funded pension. A pension paid from an accumulated fund built up over a period of years out of participants' contributions and the returns on the assets purchased with those contributions.

Funded individual account. See DEFINED-CONTRIBUTION PENSION.

Horizontal equity. Distribution in accordance with equal treatment of equals, for example, the same taxes for families of the same size with the same taxable income. When taxing families of different sizes, taxes must be suitably adjusted for the greater cost of reaching a given living standard for a larger family. What adjustments are suitable is not obvious, and economists differ. See also EQUITY, VERTICAL EQUITY.

Implicit debt. A measure of the unfunded obligations of a pension system.

Implicit tax rate. The rate at which a family receiving a benefit subject to an INCOME TEST loses the benefit as a consequence of extra income. If the benefit is lost dollar for dollar as earnings rise, the implicit tax rate is 100 percent.

Income test. A way of determining benefit eligibility that awards benefits only to individuals or families with low incomes; that is, benefit is withdrawn as income rises. See also AFFLUENCE TEST, MEANS TEST.

Incomplete markets. A market system in which not all goods and services that a person might wish to buy are available at some price. An example is the impossibility of buying INSURANCE against future price inflation in a standardized market.

Index fund (in the United Kingdom sometimes called a tracker fund). An investment fund that holds a portfolio with a return designed to match the return on some category of assets, as measured by a standard price index for those assets. The assets may be either BONDS or STOCKS, for example, the stocks in the Dow Jones Industrial Average in the United States or the FTSE-100 in the United Kingdom. When the index is based on a very large number of bonds or stocks, the fund may hold a subset chosen to have a high statistical probability of matching the index.

Indicator targeting (also called PROXY TARGETING). A mechanism for targeting benefits to poor people that identifies them not by their income, but by some other indicator, ideally one that is highly correlated with poverty, that the individual cannot control, and that is easily observable.

Individual account. See DEFINED-CONTRIBUTION PENSION.

Informal sector. The part of an economy characterized by small-scale, largely unregulated and unregistered activity. A worker in the informal sector will generally be self-employed or working without an employment contract and will generally not declare income or pay taxes or pension contributions. Contrast with FORMAL SECTOR.

Insurance. The term is used in two different ways. Insurance can be an arrangement (such as a government program) that offers individuals protection against risk or a contract to make payments under certain defined future circumstances, the latter normally organized in the private sector. The former defines insurance in terms of its objective; the latter, as a mechanism that provides payments under the circumstances insured against. An idealized market has actuarial insurance.

Joint-life annuity (also called joint-and-survivor annuity). An annuity that pays a regular monthly income to two people until both have died. The size of the monthly payment depends on whether one or both are still alive and may depend on which of the two is still alive. Contrast with SINGLE-LIFE ANNUITY.

Legacy costs (also called legacy debt). The obligation of an unfunded pension system to pay the future benefits of RETIREES and the entitlements earned to date by workers who have not yet retired. In a partially funded system, the legacy cost is the obligation less the value of assets in the fund. In either case it is a future cost resulting from the previous working of the pension system.

Life-cycle fund. An investment fund in which, as the account holder grows older, the assets in the account are gradually and automatically shifted from mainly stocks to mainly bonds.

Means test. A measure of benefit eligibility that includes individuals whose income and wealth from all sources are both (or in combination) below a given amount. The term thus embraces both an INCOME TEST and a wealth test (the latter also called an ASSETS TEST). See also AFFLUENCE TEST.

Moral hazard. A situation in which a person with INSURANCE can affect the insurer's liability without its knowledge, for example, by taking less care to avoid an accident covered by the insurance than the person would without insurance.

Multipillar pension system. A pension system with several components designed to serve multiple objectives. As originally defined by the World Bank, the system comprises three pillars: a publicly managed PAYG system; a system of mandatory, privately funded plans, usually DEFINED-CONTRIBUTION plans; and a system of voluntary, privately funded plans. The meaning of the term has evolved to include systems with multiple parts. The categorization in this book talks about "parts" or "tiers" rather than "pillars" to make it clear that there are many ways of organizing the system as a whole.

Narrow funding. An increase in the assets of a national pension system brought about by the government transferring assets—newly created government BONDS or shares in state enterprises—into the system (typically, into worker's individual accounts). This transfer creates funded accounts and affects the distribution of LEGACY COSTS but has little effect on national saving. See also BROAD FUNDING.

NDC. See NOTIONAL DEFINED-CONTRIBUTION PENSION.

Noncontributory universal pension. A public pension paid at a flat rate, usually on the basis of a record of residence rather than on the basis of contributions, and sometimes restricted to citizens (hence sometimes referred to as a CITIZENS PENSION). Such a pension may or may not be subject to an AFFLUENCE TEST. Contrast with CONTRIBUTORY BASIC PENSION.

Normal retirement age. See AGE FOR FULL BENEFITS.

Notional defined-contribution (NDC) pension. A pension financed through SOCIAL INSURANCE contributions where benefits bear a quasi-actuarial relationship to lifetime pension contributions.

Old-age dependency ratio. See DEPENDENCY RATIO.

Pareto efficiency (also called allocative efficiency). A situation in which resources are allocated in such a way that no reallocation can make any individual better off without making at least one other individual worse off. A policy that makes someone better off and nobody worse off is referred to as Pareto improving.

Pay-as-you-go (PAYG) pension. A pension paid (usually by the government) out of current tax revenues rather than out of an accumulated fund. A pension system may also have some assets and so be partially funded.

PDV. See PRESENT DISCOUNTED VALUE.

Pensioner. A person receiving pension benefits whether or not he or she has stopped working. Contrast with RETIREE.

Present discounted value. The capital value today of a stream of income received over some future period calculated on the basis of a specified discount rate.

Provident fund. A publicly organized, mandatory DEFINED-CONTRIBUTION PENSION plan in which workers have no choice of portfolio but, rather, hold shares in a single, centrally held portfolio.

Proxy targeting. See INDICATOR TARGETING.

Redistribution. The transfer of resources from one person or group to another. Pensions can bring about redistribution either within a generation (for example, from richer to poorer pensioners) or across generations (for example, from current workers to pensioners). Redistribution makes it possible to subsidize the CONSUMPTION SMOOTHING of lower-earning workers.

Reduction in yield. A measure of all charges that reduce the net return an individual realizes on his or her pension accumulation. For example, if the rate of return before charges is 5 percent but the individual receives a return of 3 percent after charges, the reduction in yield is 2 percent. See also ANNUAL MANAGEMENT FEE, CHARGE RATIO.

Replacement rate. The ratio of pension benefits (for example, monthly) to monthly earnings (after taxes and transfers) during work. The term can be defined in different ways. Defined as the average person's pension benefit as a percentage of the average wage, the replacement rate is a measure of the living standards of the elderly relative to those of the working population. Defined as an individual's pensioner's benefit as a percentage of his or her previous wage, the replacement rate is a measure of the effectiveness of CONSUMPTION SMOOTHING. In this book the term is used with the latter meaning unless otherwise stated. Sometimes replacement rates are reported gross of taxes and transfers rather than net. A survivor replacement rate is the ratio of the benefit going to a widow or widower compared with what was received by the couple when both were alive.

Retiree. A person who has stopped work whether or not he or she is receiving pension benefits. Contrast with PENSIONER.

Retirement. The term is used in two different ways. It sometimes refers to the end of work and sometimes to the start of pension benefits. These are two separate events, which can happen at two separate times.

Second-best analysis. Analysis that seeks the optimal policy when government must rely on distorting taxes to alter the income distribution or to respond to economic distortions and other departures from the simple theoretical model, such as imperfect information, INCOMPLETE MARKETS, and existing taxation. Contrast with FIRST-BEST ANALYSIS.

Shares. See STOCKS.

Single-life annuity. An ANNUITY that pays an income (for example, per year or per month) during the life of one person. Contrast with JOINT-LIFE ANNUITY.

Social insurance. A set of arrangements, modeled on private insurance, under which individuals receive public benefits in respect of (for example) unemployment or RETIREMENT, often without any test of means or need, on the basis of previous (usually compulsory) contributions.

Social pension. See NONCONTRIBUTORY UNIVERSAL PENSION.

Social security. This term is ambiguous because it is used with different meanings in different countries. In the United States it refers to public retirement and disability benefits; in the United Kingdom, to all publicly provided cash benefits; and in the European Union, to all publicly provided cash benefits plus health care benefits. Where the term is used in this book, it refers to retirement pensions only.

Stocks (also called EQUITIES or SHARES). Financial securities that represent ownership of a fraction of a corporation. A corporation sells stock as a means of financing its investment and may pay a dividend, usually annually, to stockholders. If the corporation flourishes, the value of its stock rises, resulting in a capital gain to stockholders. If it goes bankrupt, the value of its stock is based on whatever value remains in the corporation after its creditors have been paid. Thus stocks represent a title to ownership, in contrast with BONDS, which are a form of loan.

System dependency ratio. See DEPENDENCY RATIO.

Taper of benefit. See IMPLICIT TAX RATE.

Thrift Savings Plan (TSP). A retirement savings plan for U.S. federal employees established in 1986 as part of the Federal Employees' Retirement System Act and administered by the Federal Retirement Thrift Investment Board. The TSP is a tax-deferred DEFINED-CONTRIBUTION PENSION plan with three main characteristics: choice by participants restricted to a small number of clearly differentiated investment funds; centralized administration; and fund management on a wholesale basis. See box 9.4.

Tracker fund. See INDEX FUND.

Trust fund. An accumulation of financial assets intended to cover at least part of a pension plan's future liabilities. In a system that is mainly PAYG, the trust fund will hold only a few months worth of outflows as a buffer against temporary shortfalls, but trust funds can have a much greater degree of funding and even be fully funded, that is, containing resources sufficient to pay all liabilities generated to date.

TSP. See THRIFT SAVINGS PLAN.

Unfunded pension. See PAY-AS-YOU-GO (PAYG) PENSION.

Vertical equity. Distribution in accordance with the principle that the better off in a society are able to bear a disproportionate share of the burden of providing for government expenditures and for transfers to the needy and thus a basis for redistribution of income, consumption, or wealth from richer to poorer people. See also EQUITY, HORIZONTAL EQUITY.

Voluntary pension. The term is used in two different ways. A voluntary pension may be that which an individual worker chooses to provide for himself or herself, such as (in the United States) an Individual Retirement Account. Alternatively, it can be a plan that an employer chooses to introduce for its employees (without a government mandate), participation in which may be either voluntary or compulsory on the part of the workers.

Withdrawal rate. See IMPLICIT TAX RATE.

References

Arenas de Mesa, Alberto, and Carmelo Mesa-Lago. 2006. The structural pension reform in Chile: Effects, comparisons with other Latin American reforms, and lessons. *Oxford Review of Economic Policy* 22 (Spring): 149–67.

Arza, Camila. 2006. Distributional impacts on pension policy in Argentina: Winners and losers within and across generations. *International Social Security Review* 59 (3): 79–102.

Asher, Mukul, Nicholas Barr, Peter Diamond, Edwin Lim, and James Mirrlees. 2005. *Social security reform in China: Issues and options*. Policy Study of the China Economic Research and Advisory Programme (Jan.); www.oup.com/us/pdf/social_security_study_2005 (in Chinese, www.oup.com/us/pdf/china_social_security_study).

Atkinson, A. B. 1999. *The economic consequences of rolling back the welfare state*. Cambridge, Mass.: MIT Press.

Augusztinovics, M., R. I. Gál, Á Matits, L. Máté, A. Simonovits, and J. Stahl. 2002. The Hungarian pension system before and after the 1998 reform. In *Pension reform in Central and Eastern Europe*, vols. 1–2, ed. Elaine Fultz. Geneva: International Labour Organization.

Banks, James, and Peter Diamond. 2009. The tax base. In *Dimensions of tax design: The Mirrlees review*, ed. J. Mirrlees, S. Adam, T. Besley, R. Blundell, S. Bond, R. Chote, M. Gammie, P. Johnson, G. Myles, and J. Poterba. Oxford: Oxford University Press for Institute for Fiscal Studies.

Barr, Nicholas. 2000. Reforming pensions: Myths, truths, and policy choices. Working Paper, no. WP/00/139. Washington: International Monetary Fund; www.imf.org/external/pubs/ft/wp/2000/wp00139.pdf.

——. 2001. *The welfare state as piggy bank: Information, risk, uncertainty, and the role of the state.* London and New York: Oxford University Press; www.oxfordscholarship.com/oso/public/content/economicsfinance/0199246599/toc.html.

——. 2003. *The economics of the welfare state,* 3rd ed. Chinese translation including a new preface. Beijing: China Labour and Social Security Publishing House.

——. 2004. *The economics of the welfare state,* 4th ed. Oxford and Stanford, Calif.: Oxford University Press and Stanford University Press (3rd ed. in Chinese as Barr 2003).

Barr, Nicholas, and Peter Diamond. 2008. *Reforming pensions: Principles and policy choices.* New York and Oxford: Oxford University Press; also see Oxford Scholarship online at www.oxfordscholarship.com//oso/public/index.html.

Barr, Nicholas, and Michal Rutkowski. 2005. Pensions. In *Labor markets and social policy: The accession and beyond,* ed. Nicholas Barr, pp. 135–70. Washington: World Bank.

Bertranou, Fabio M., Rafael Rofman, and Carlos O. Grushka. 2003. From reform to crisis: Argentina's pension system. *International Social Security Review* 56 (2): 103–14.

Beshears, John, James Choi, David Laibson, and Brigitte Madrian. 2008. The importance of default options for retirement saving outcomes: Evidence from the United States. In *Lessons from pension reform in the Americas,* ed. Stephen J. Kay and Tapen Sinha, pp. 59–87. Oxford: Oxford University Press.

Blake, David. 2006. Overregulating your pension out of existence: The long term consequences of British pension policy over the last 30 years. Discussion Paper, no. PI-0616. London: City University, Cass Business School, Pensions Institute. www.pensions-institute.org/workingpapers/wp0616.pdf.

Borowski, Allan. 2005. The revolution that faltered: Two decades of reform of Australia's retirement income system. *International Social Security Review* 58 (4): 45–65.

Börsch-Supan, Axel. 2005. The 2005 pension reform in Finland. Working Paper, no. 2005:1. Helsinki: Finnish Centre for Pensions.

Burns, Justine, Malcolm Keswell, and Murray Leibbrandt. 2005. Social assistance, gender, and the aged in South Africa. *Feminist Economics* 11 (Jul.): 103–15.

Case, Anne, and Angus Deaton. 1998. Large cash transfers to the elderly in South Africa. *Economic Journal* 108 (Sep.): 1330–61.

Chile Presidential Advisory Council. 2006. *El derecho a una vida digna en la vejez: Hacia un contrato social con la previsión en Chile; Resumen ejecutivo* [The right to a dignified old age: Toward a welfare social contract in Chile: Executive summary]. Santiago. www.consejoreformaprevisional.cl/view/informe.asp.

Chlon-Dominczak, Agnieszka. 2002. The Polish pension reform of 1999. In *Pension reform in Central and Eastern Europe,* vol. 1: *Restructuring with privatisation: Case studies of Hungary and Poland,* ed. Elaine Fultz, pp. 95–205. Budapest: International Labour Organization, Central and Eastern European Team.

Chlon-Dominczak, Agnieszka, and Marek Góra. 2006. The NDC system in Poland: Assessment after five years. In *Pension reform: Issues and prospects for non-*

financial defined contribution (NDC) systems, ed. Robert Holzmann and Edward Palmer, pp. 425–49. Washington: World Bank.

Choi, J., D. Laibson, B. Madrian, and A. Metrick. 2001. Defined contribution pensions: Plan rules, participant decisions, and the path of least resistance. NBER Working Paper, no. W8655. Cambridge, Mass.: National Bureau of Economic Research; www.nber.org/papers/w8655.

Coady, David, Margaret Grosh, and John Hoddinot. 2004. *Targeting of transfers in developing countries: Review of lessons and experience*. Washington: World Bank.

Costa, Dora L. 1998. *The evolution of retirement: An American economic history, 1880 to 1990*. Chicago: University of Chicago Press.

Devesa-Carpio, José E., and Carlos Vidal-Meliá. 2002. Reformed pension systems in Latin America. Social Protection Discussion Paper Series, no. 0209 (May). Washington: World Bank.

Diamond, Peter A. 1965. National debt in a neoclassical growth model. *American Economic Review* 55 (5, pt. 1): 1126–50.

——. 2000. Administrative costs and equilibrium charges with individual accounts. In *Administrative aspects of investment-based Social Security reform*, ed. John Shoven, pp. 137–71. Chicago: University of Chicago Press.

——. 2002. *Social Security reform*. Oxford and New York: Oxford University Press.

——. 2003. *Taxation, incomplete markets, and social security*. Cambridge, Mass.: MIT Press.

——. 2004. Social security. *American Economic Review* 94 (Mar.): 1–24.

——. 2006. Système de retraite et vieillissement de la population. *Revue Française d'Economie* 20 (Apr.): 21–49 (Pensions for an Aging Population, http://econ-www.mit.edu/files/695).

——. 2009. Economic Globalisation and Swedish Pensions. Expert Report No. 28 to Sweden's Globalisation Council. Available at http://www.sweden.gov.se/sb/d/9150/a/119904.

Diamond, Peter A., and James A. Mirrlees. 1971*a*. Optimal taxation and public production I: Production efficiency. *American Economic Review* 61 (Mar.): 8–27.

——. 1971*b*. Optimal taxation and public production II: Tax rules. *American Economic Review* 61 (Jun.): 261–78.

Diamond, Peter A., and Peter R. Orszag. 2005*a*. *Saving Social Security: A balanced approach*, rev. ed. Washington: Brookings Institution.

——. 2005*b*. Saving Social Security. *Journal of Economic Perspectives* 19 (Spring): 11–32.

Diamond, Peter A., and Salvador Valdés-Prieto. 1994. Social security reforms. In *The Chilean economy: Policy lessons and challenges*, ed. Barry Bosworth, Rudiger Dornbusch, and Raúl Labán, pp. 257–328. Washington: Brookings Institution.

Drouin, Anne, and Lawrence H. Thompson, with Aidi Hu, Mike Whitelaw, and Hiroshi Yamabana. 2006. Perspectives on the social security system of China. ESS Paper, no. 25. Geneva: International Labour Organization.

Dublin, Louis I., Alfred J. Lotka, and Mortimer Spiegelman. [1936] 1949. *Length of life—A study of the life table*. New York: Ronald Press.

Dutta, Jayasri, Sandeep Kapur, and J. Michael Orszag. 2000. A portfolio approach to the optimal funding of pensions. *Economic Letters* 69: 201–6.

Economic Policy Committee of the European Union. 2006. The impact of ageing on public expenditure: Projections for the EU25 Member States on pensions, health care, long-term care, education, and unemployment transfers (2004–2050). Special Report, no. 1/2006. Brussels: European Commission Directorate-General for Economic and Financial Affairs.

Edwards, Sebastian, and Alejandra Cox Edwards. 2002. Social security privatization reform and labor markets: The case of Chile. NBER Working Paper, no. 8924. Cambridge, Mass.: National Bureau of Economic Research; www.nber.org/papers/w8924.

Escobar, Federico, and Osvaldo Nina. 2004. Pension reform in Bolivia: A review of approach and experience. Development Research Working Paper, no. 04/2004. La Paz: Institute for Advanced Development Studies.

Feldstein, Martin S. 1996. The missing piece in policy analysis: Social Security reform. *American Economic Review* 86 (May): 1–14.

——. 2005. Structural reform of Social Security. *Journal of Economic Perspectives* 19 (Spring): 33–55.

Garibaldi, Pietro, Claudia Olivetti, Barbara Petrongolo, Christopher Pissarides, and Etienne Wasmer. 2005. Women in the labour force: How well is Europe doing? In *Women at work: An economic perspective,* ed. Tito Boeri, Daniela Del Boca, and Christopher Pissarides, pp. 7–11. Report for the Fondazione Rodolfo DeBenedetti. Oxford: Oxford University Press.

Geanakoplos, John, Olivia S. Mitchell, and Stephen P. Zeldes. 1999. Social Security money's worth. In *Prospects for Social Security reform,* ed. Olivia S. Mitchell, Robert J. Myers, and Howard Young, pp. 79–151. Philadelphia: University of Pennsylvania Press.

Gill, Indermit, Truman Packard, and Juan Yermo. 2005. *Keeping the promise of social security in Latin America.* Stanford, Calif.: Stanford University Press for the World Bank.

Golinowska, Stanislawa, Katarzyna Pietka, and Maciej Zukowski. 2003. *Study on the social protection systems of the 13 applicant countries: Poland country study.* Brussels: European Commission.

Góra, Marek, and Michal Rutkowski. 1998. The quest for pension reform: Poland's security through diversity. Social Protection Discussion Paper, no. 9815. Washington: World Bank.

Gruber, Jonathan, and David A. Wise, eds. 1999. *Social security and retirement around the world.* Chicago: University of Chicago Press.

——. 2004. *Social security programs and retirement around the world: Micro-estimation.* Chicago: University of Chicago Press.

Hills, John. 2006. A new pension settlement for the twenty-first century? The UK Pensions Commission's analysis and proposals. *Oxford Review of Economic Policy* 22 (Spring): 113–32.

Holzmann, Robert, and Richard Hinz. 2005. *Old age income support in the 21st century: An international perspective on pension systems and reform.* Washington: World Bank.

Hutton, Will. 2007. *The writing on the wall: China and the West in the 21st century.* London: Little Brown.

James, Estelle. 1998. New models for old-age security: Experiments, evidence, and unanswered questions. *World Bank Research Observer* 13 (Aug.): 271–301.

Jefferson, Therese, and Alison Preston. 2005. Australia's "other" gender wage gap: Baby boomers and compulsory superannuation accounts. *Feminist Economics* 11 (Jul.): 79–101.

Kakwani, Nanak, and Kalanidhi Subbarao. 2007. Poverty among the elderly in Sub-Saharan Africa and the role of social pensions. *Journal of Development Studies* 43 (Aug.): 987–1008; www.informaworld.com/smpp/content?content=10.1080/00220380701466476.

Leach, Jennifer. 1998. Bolivia's Bonosol. Presented at the Transfers and Social Assistance for the Poor in the LAC Regional Workshop, Washington, February 24–25; wbln0018.worldbank.org/network/prem/premdoclib.nsf/58292ab451257bb9852566b4006ea0c8/fb45d2fe76c4e27b852567130004bca2?OpenDocument.

Loewenstein, George, and Peter A. Ubel. 2008. Hedonic adaptation and the role of decision and experience utility in public policy. *Journal of Public Economics* 92 (8–9): 1795–1810.

Lund, Frances. 2002. "Crowding in" care, security, and micro-enterprise formation: Revisiting the role of the state in poverty reduction and in development. *Journal of International Development* 14: 681–94.

Madrian, B., and D. Shea. 2001. The power of suggestion: Inertia in 401(k) participation and savings behavior. *Quarterly Journal of Economics* 116 (4): 1149–87.

Martinez, Sebastian. 2004. Pensions, poverty, and household investments in Bolivia. Berkeley: University of California; emlab.berkeley.edu/users/webfac/bardhan/e271_f04/martinez.pdf.

Matits, Agnes. 2004. Practical experience with the second pillar of the Hungarian mandatory pension system. Paper delivered at an International Labour Organization pension conference, Budapest, December 9–10.

Mesa-Lago, Carmelo. 2007. *Reassembling social security: A survey of pensions and health care reforms in Latin America.* New York and Oxford: Oxford University Press.

Mitchell, Brian R. 1998*a*. *International historical statistics: Africa, Asia, and Oceania, 1750–1993*, 3rd ed. New York: Stockton.

——. 1998*b*. *International historical statistics: The Americas, 1750–1993*, 4th ed. New York: Stockton.

——. 1998*c*. *International historical statistics: Europe, 1750–1993.* New York: Stockton.

Müller, Katharina. 1999. *The political economy of pension reform in Central-Eastern Europe.* Cheltenham, U.K., and Northampton, Mass.: Edward Elgar.

Muturi, Slawomir, Marcin Zdral, Marcin Zajkowski, and Agnieszka Chlon-Dominczak. 2000. Transformation of social security institution (ZUS) under the Polish pension system reform. Warsaw: ZUS.

Orbán, Gábor, and Dániel Palotai. 2005. The sustainability of the Hungarian pension system: A reassessment. Occasional Paper, no. 40. Budapest: Magyar Nemzeti Bank.

Organization for Economic Cooperation and Development (OECD). 2004. *Reforming public pensions: Sharing the experiences of transition and OECD countries. Transition Economies,* vol. 2004, no. 1. Paris: OECD; titania.sourceoecd .org/vl=6782642/cl=20/nw=1/rpsv/~6686/v2004n1/s1/p1l.

——. 2007. *Pensions at a glance: Public policies across OECD countries.* Paris: OECD.

Orszag, Peter. 1999. Individual accounts and Social Security: Does Social Security really provide a lower rate of return? Washington: Center on Budget and Policy Priorities; www.cbpp.org/3–11–99socsec.pdf.

Orszag, Peter R., and Joseph E. Stiglitz. 2001. Rethinking pension reform: 10 myths about social security systems. In *New ideas about old age security: Toward sustainable pension systems in the 21st century,* ed. Robert Holzmann and Joseph E. Stiglitz, with Louise Fox, Estelle James, and Peter R. Orszag, pp. 17–62. Washington: World Bank.

Pestieau, Pierre. 2006. *The welfare state in the European Union.* Oxford: Oxford University Press.

Pestieau, Pierre, and Uri M. Possen. 2000. Investing Social Security in the equity market: Does it make a difference? *National Tax Journal* 53 (1): 41–57.

Queisser, Monika, and Edward Whitehouse. 2006. Comparing the pension promises of 30 OECD countries. *International Social Security Review* 59 (3): 49–77.

Rofman, Rafael. 2007. Pension reform and the development of pension systems: An evaluation of World Bank assistance. Background paper, Peru Country Study, Independent Evaluation Group. Washington: World Bank.

Rofman, Rafael, and Leonardo Lucchetti. 2006. Pension systems in Latin America: Concepts and measurements of coverage. Social Protection Discussion Paper Series, no. 0616 (Nov.). Washington: World Bank.

Salditt, Felix, Peter Whiteford, and Willem Adema. 2008. Pension reform in China. *International Social Security Review* 61 (3): 47–71.

Shanley, Mary Lyndon. 1986. Suffrage, protective labor legislation, and married women's property laws in England. *Signs* 12 (Autumn): 62–77.

Sigg, Roland. 2005. Extending working life: Policy challenges and responses. In *Toward newfound confidence,* ed. Richard Levinsky and Roddy McKinnon, pp. 25–140. Geneva: International Social Security Association.

South Africa National Treasury. 2007. Social security and retirement reform. Second Discussion Paper (Feb.). Pretoria: National Treasury.

Tapia, Waldo, and Juan Yermo. 2007. Implications of behavioural economics for mandatory individual account pension systems. OECD Working Paper on Insurance and Private Pensions, no. 11. Paris: OECD; www.oecd.org/dataoecd/5/22/39368306.pdf.

Thaler, R. H., and S. Benartzi. 2004. Save more tomorrow: Using behavioral economics to increase employee saving. *Journal of Political Economy* 112 (1, pt. 2): 164–87.

Thaler, Richard H., and Cass R. Sunstein. 2008. *Nudge: Improving decisions about health, wealth, and happiness.* New Haven, Conn.: Yale University Press.

Thompson, Lawrence H. 2006. US retirement income system. *Oxford Review of Economic Policy* 22 (Spring): 95–112.

Turner, John. 2007. Social security pensionable ages in OECD countries: 1949–2035. *International Social Security Review* 60 (1): 81–99.

U.K. Department for Work and Pensions. 2006. *Security in retirement: Towards a new pensions system*. Cm 6841. London: The Stationery Office.

U.K. Pensions Commission. 2004*a*. *Pensions: Challenges and choices; The first report of the Pensions Commission*. London: The Stationery Office. www.webarchive.org.uk/pan/16806/20070802/www.pensionscommission.org.uk/publications/2004/annrep/index.html.

——. 2004*b*. *Pensions: Challenges and choices; The first report of the Pensions Commission, Appendices*. London: The Stationery Office; www.webarchive.org.uk/pan/16806/20070802/www.pensionscommission.org.uk/publications/2004/annrep/appendices-all.pdf.

——. 2005. *A new pension settlement for the twenty-first century: Second report of the Pensions Commission*. London: The Stationery Office; www.webarchive.org.uk/pan/16806/20070802/www.pensionscommission.org.uk/publications/2005/annrep/annrep-index.html.

U.S. Social Security Administration. 2007*a*. *The 2007 annual report of the Board of Trustees of the Federal Old-Age and Survivors Insurance and Federal Disability Insurance Trust Funds*. Washington: SSA.

——. 2007*b*. *Social security programs throughout the world*. Washington: SSA; www.ssa.gov/policy/docs/progdesc/ssptw/index.html.

Valdés-Prieto, Salvador. 2005. Para aumentar la competencia entre las AFP [How to increase competition among pension fund managers]. *Estudios Públicos* 98 (Autumn): 87–142.

——. 2007*a*. Pension reform and the development of pension systems: An evaluation of World Bank assistance. Background paper, Bolivia Country Study, Independent Evaluation Group. Washington: World Bank.

——. 2007*b*. Pension reform and the development of pension systems: An evaluation of World Bank assistance. Background paper, Regional Summary: Latin America and the Caribbean, Independent Evaluation Group. Washington: World Bank.

von Gersdorff, Hermann. 1997. The Bolivian pension reform: Innovative solutions to common problems. Policy Research Working Paper, no. 1832. Washington: World Bank, Financial Sector Development Department.

Whiteford, Peter, and Edward Whitehouse. 2006. Pension challenges and pension reform in OECD countries. *Oxford Review of Economic Policy* 22 (Spring): 78–94.

Williamson, John B. 2004. Assessing the pension reform potential of a notional defined contribution pillar. *International Social Security Review* 57 (1): 47–64.

Willmore, Larry. 2004. Universal pensions in low income countries. Discussion Paper, no. IPD-01–05 (Oct.). New York: Initiative for Policy Dialogue, Pensions and Social Insurance Section, Columbia University.

——. 2006. *Non-contributory pensions: Bolivia and Antigua in an international context*. Santiago: CEPAL, Special Studies Unit.

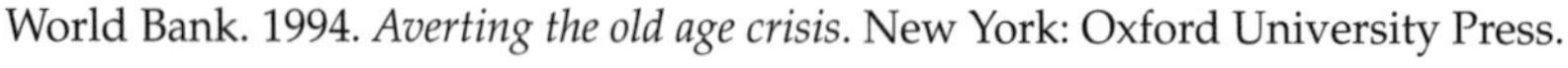

World Bank. 1994. *Averting the old age crisis*. New York: Oxford University Press.

——. 2004. *World development indicators*. Washington: World Bank.

——. 2005. Hungary: Pension—Competition and performance in the Hungarian second pillar. Financial Sector Assessment Program Update (Dec.). Washington: World Bank and International Monetary Fund.

——. 2006*a*. *Pension reform and the development of pension systems: An evaluation of World Bank assistance*. Washington: Independent Evaluation Group, World Bank; lnweb18.worldbank.org:80/oed/oeddoclib.nsf/DocUNIDViewForJavaSearch/43B436DFBB2723D085257108005F6309/$file/pensions_evaluation.pdf.

——. 2006*b*. Pension reform: How to strengthen World Bank assistance. *IEG Reach*, Feb. 2; lnweb18.worldbank.org:80/oed/oeddoclib.nsf/DocUNIDViewForJavaSearch/86FAFFBFBA032ED085257108005EDE9E/$file/pensions_evaluation_reach.pdf.

Index

Contents of *Reforming Pensions*

PART II POLICY CHOICES

PART III CONCLUSION